How God
Leads & Guides!

Twenty Ways God Speaks!

Dr. Michael H. Yeager

Copyright © 2015 Dr. Michael H Yeager

All rights reserved.

ISBN-13: 9781508929864

ISBN-10: 1508929866

DEDICATION

We dedicate this book to those who are longing to be led by the spirit of God in every area of their life. Those who have grasped the revelation that we were made for God's pleasure and purposes. *Romans 8:14 For as many as are led by the Spirit of God, they are the sons of God.*

Please Read This Introduction

It is imperative that every one of us as believers in Christ become sensitive and obedient to the voice of God. It is not sufficient just to know how God leads and guides his people. The truths in this book, which are all based on biblical principles, will radically transform your life, if you put them in to practice.

David had an understanding and revelation of being led by the spirit of God. Psalms 23 and 29 gives to us wonderful spiritual insight into the life of David, who had a heart after God. He was consistently inquiring of the Lord in every matter. Whenever he did not seek the face of the Lord about what he should do, is when the enemy was able to bring terrible defeat and misery into his life. It is my hope and prayer that the spirit of God would use this book in helping you to know the voice of God, and to walk in the perfect will of the Father.

Psalm 23 - A Psalm of David.
1 The Lord is my shepherd; I shall not want.
2 He maketh me to lie down in green pastures:
he leadeth me beside the still waters.
3 He restoreth my soul:he leadeth me in the paths
of righteousness for his name's sake.
4 Yea, though I walk through the valley of the shadow of death,
I will fear no evil: for thou art with me;
thy rod and thy staff they comfort me.
5 Thou preparest a table before me in the presence of mine enemies:
thou anointest my head with oil; my cup runneth over.
6 Surely goodness and mercy shall follow me all the days of my life:
and I will dwell in the house of the Lord forever.

Psalm 29 - A Psalm of David.
1 Give unto the LORD, O ye mighty,
give unto the LORD glory and strength.
2 Give unto the LORD the glory due unto his name;
worship the LORD in the beauty of holiness.
3 The <u>voice</u> of the LORD is upon the waters:
the God of glory thundereth: the LORD is upon many waters.
4 The <u>voice</u> of the LORD is powerful;
the <u>voice</u> of the LORD is full of majesty.
5 The <u>voice</u> of the LORD breaketh the cedars;
yea, the LORD breaketh the cedars of Lebanon.
6 He maketh them also to skip like a calf;
Lebanon and Sirion like a young unicorn.
7 The <u>voice</u> of the LORD divideth the flames of fire.
8 The <u>voice</u> of the LORD shaketh the wilderness;
the LORD shaketh the wilderness of Kadesh.
9 The <u>voice</u> of the LORD maketh the hinds to calve,
and discovereth the forests:
and in his temple doth every one speak of his glory.
10 The LORD sitteth upon the flood;
yea, the LORD sitteth King for ever.
11 The LORD will give strength unto his people;
the LORD will bless his people with peace.

CONTENTS

ACKNOWLEDGMENTS

To our heavenly Father and His wonderful love.

*To our Lord, Savior and Master —Jesus Christ, Who saved us and set us free because of His great love for us.

*To the Holy Spirit, The Comforter, Who leads, guides and brings us into the realm of absolute truth and life.

*To all of those who had a part in helping us get this book ready for the publishers.

*To our precious children, Michael, Daniel, Steven, Stephanie, Catherine Yu, who is our precious daughter-in-law, and Naomi, who is now with the Lord!

Dr. Michael H. Yeager

CHAPTER ONE

#1 Jesus

I believe that every human being hears the voice of God, they simply do not respond to him. They hardened their hearts to the voice of God, because the carnal flesh wars against the spirit, and the spirit against the flesh. When man committed sin in the garden the seed of lust entered in to the flesh and heart of man, the DNA of satan. Before man committed sin he responded instantly to the voice of God, but Adam and his wife partook of the forbidden fruit, and now instead of running to God at the sound of his voice, they found themselves running from him. They became slaves to the dictates of the desires and lust of the sin in their flesh.

Genesis 3:8 And they heard the voice of the Lord God walking in the garden in the cool of the day: and Adam and his wife hid themselves from the presence of the Lord God amongst the trees of the garden.

There is the voice of the spirit and the voice of the flesh, and you have to know which voice it is that is speaking to you. Granted sometimes it gets a little bit difficult and challenging to determine which voice is speaking to us. The very first thing we need to do is to build a solid foundation by which we can determine if what we're hearing is the voice of God's spirit or the voice of our flesh. In this first chapter I would like to share with you the two main ways that God speaks to His people. You need to read this first chapter over and over, unto you truly understand these two major ways that God leads and guides us. It may seem like these two ways are exactly the same, but believe me when I say: that they are not.

For this particular chapter I will be using **Hebrews chapter 1**, and the gospel of **John chapter 1**. These two chapters will help build an amazing foundation for hearing the voice of God, and with spiritual discernment, for every situation. If you will embrace what is revealed in these two chapters, your understanding will be greatly enlightened. Let us now take a look at Hebrews chapter 1.

Hebrews 1:1 God, who at sundry times and in divers manners spake in time past unto the fathers by the prophets, 2 hath in these last days spoken unto us by his Son, whom he hath appointed heir of all things, by whom also he made the worlds; 3 who being the brightness of his glory, and the express image of his person, and upholding all things by the word of his power, when he had by himself purged our sins, sat down on the right hand of the Majesty on high;

In Hebrews 1 it is revealed that God had spoken to the fathers by the prophets, but has now spoken to us by his son Jesus Christ. According to *Ephesians chapter 2:20 the kingdom of God is built upon the apostles and prophets, Jesus Christ himself being the chief cornerstone.* Please notice that in times past God spoke specifically by the prophets to the father's, now we have a more sure word of prophecy, a deeper revelation, a more precise understanding of the perfect will of our heavenly Father. Why? Because he's going to speak to us in a very clear and dramatic way. If we will believe the words, the life, and the example of Jesus, it will radically transform our lives forever. Remember all the words that had been spoken up to the coming of Christ were to prepare us for the coming of Christ. The life of Jesus is the perfect will of God manifested in the flesh. This is the mystery which had been hidden before the foundation of the world. Notice Hebrews 1: in verse 2 *hath in these last days spoken unto us by his Son!* The foundation of my understanding of the voice of God, the will of God, the purposes of God, the plan of God, the mission of God, the mysteries of God cannot be discovered in any greater revelation than the person of Jesus Christ! **There is no greater revelation of God's perfect divine will or voice then that we discover in Jesus Christ.** I cannot emphasize this enough!

John 1:14 And the Word was made flesh, and dwelt among us, (and we beheld his glory, the glory as of the only begotten of the Father,) full of grace and truth.

If you do not understand that God is speaking to you very precisely through his son Jesus Christ, you will end up being mixed up, confused, and led astray. Learning to hear the voice of God very precisely is only found in Jesus Christ, whom he has appointed heir of all things, by whom also he made the worlds. Notice Hebrews chapter 1 Verse 3 boldly declares that Jesus Christ is the brightness of the Father's glory, the manifestation of the Fathers presence, and the express image of His personality. He is like a mirror reflecting the perfect image of the heavenly Father to all of humanity. Jesus declared:

John 14:9 Jesus saith unto him, have I been so long time with you, and yet hast thou not known me, Philip? He that hath seen me hath seen the Father; and how sayest thou then, Shew us the Father? 10 Believest thou not that I am in the Father, and the Father in me? The words that I speak unto you I speak not of myself: but the Father that dwelleth in me, he doeth the works.

Jesus Christ is the absolute perfect will of the Father revealed to you and me. The deepest revelation of the Father is only discovered in Jesus Christ! Paul the apostle commands us to have the mind of Christ.

Philippians 2:5 Let this mind be in you, which was also in Christ Jesus: 6 who, being in the form of God, thought it not robbery to be equal with God: 7 but made himself of no reputation, and took upon him the form of a servant, and was made in the likeness of men: 8 and being found in fashion as a man, he humbled himself, and became obedient unto death, even the death of the cross. 9 Wherefore God also hath highly exalted him, and given him a name which is above every name: 10 that at the name of Jesus every knee should bow, of things in heaven, and things in earth, and things under the earth; 11 and that every tongue should confess that Jesus Christ is Lord, to the glory of God the Father.

When we look at Jesus and hear His words, it is the Father we are looking at! The apostle John boldly declares this in John 1.

John 1:1 In the beginning was the Word, and the Word was with God, and the Word was God. 2 The same was in the beginning with God. 3 All things were made by him; and without him was not anything made that was made.

All things were made by the word. What word is it talking about in these scriptures? Is it talking about the written word or Christ the word? It is obvious that it is talking about the person Christ Jesus, Emmanuel God with us!

John 1:14 And the Word was made flesh, and dwelt among us, (and we beheld his glory, the glory as of the only begotten of the Father,) full of grace and truth.

The reality is that we have to know the person of Christ discovered in the four Gospels for us to rightly discern the word of God. What do I mean by this statement? When I gave my heart to Jesus Christ on February 18, 1975, at about 3 PM in the afternoon, all I had available was a little military green Bible. At the moment Christ came into my heart I picked up that little Bible, and began to devour it. Matthew, Mark, Luke, and John, the 4 Gospels of Jesus Christ became my favorite books. I just could not get enough of the wonderful reality of Jesus. As I read these 4 Gospels I walked with Christ every step of the way. From his birth, through his childhood, his baptism by John when he was 30 years old. When he was baptized by the Holy Ghost, and he was led of the Spirit into the wilderness, tempted of the enemy overcoming by boldly declaring "It is written."

I spent my first three years as a believer eating and drinking nothing but Jesus from the four Gospels. Yes, I did read the epistles, and they were wonderful, but nothing captured and captivated my heart as much as the life, the words and the ministry of Jesus Christ. I wept as I read of his sufferings, his crucifixion and his death. I wept when I saw that the Heavenly Father had to turn his face away from his own Son, because of his love for us. I shouted at the triumphant conquest and victory that Jesus had over every satanic power.

Jesus Christ is the perfect reflection of the Heavenly Father. There is no more perfect revelation of the will of the Father than Jesus Christ. Actually I am extremely happy that I was not influenced by the modern day church for the first three years of my salvation. When I eventually came to the lower 48, after living and ministering in Alaska, I was shocked and surprised at what most Christians believed. I did not realize that there was such a large variety of different interpretation of the Scriptures in the churches. Many of God's people are extremely confused. Many ministers declare insane false doctrines that are so contrary to what I discovered in Christ, it is hard for me to believe that they even believe what they're teaching. To truly know the voice of God, all you have to do is look at Jesus Christ: His words, deeds, actions and reactions; His lifestyle and his attitude, mannerism, wonderful character, and the fruit of his life. I can truly say that since I have been born again I have only had one person who I truly want to be like: His name is Jesus Christ.

If the body of Christ would simply go back to the 4 Gospels, and walk with Jesus every step of the way, from his birth to his resurrection, to his ascension, much of their confusion would be gone. I believe the reason why so many believers are being deceived by false doctrines and philosophies in America today is because they really do not know or understand Jesus Christ.

Hebrews 13:8, "Jesus Christ the same yesterday, and today, and forever."

In the old covenant God says **"I am the Lord and I change not"**. Without truly seeing the Father through the words ministry, and the life of Jesus Christ you can easily be led astray by crafty men misusing Scriptures. You have to see Jesus to understand not just the Old Testament but also the epistles of the New Testament. Jesus is the voice of God, the absolute perfect will of the Father.

I have actually heard ministers use the Bible to contradict the teachings of Jesus Christ. The reason why false doctrines have been able to take root in the church is because people have not really looked and listened to Jesus in the four Gospels. If in your mind and heart you will exalt Christ, and his teaching above all else, will be very difficult for the enemy to lead you astray with false teachings and doctrines. Here is an example when it comes to the will of God pertaining to divine healing.

Why God heals me Every Time. 1975

While reading my Bible as a brand new believer, (1975) I discovered that Jesus Christ went about healing **ALL** who were sick and oppressed of the devil. I began to search the Scriptures on this particular subject, and as I studied I discovered many Scriptures that support this:

Surely he hath borne our griefs, and carried our sorrows: yet we did esteem him stricken, smitten of God, and afflicted. But he was wounded for our transgressions, he was bruised for our iniquities: the chastisement of our peace was upon him; and with his stripes we are healed (Isaiah 53:4-5).

Who his own self bare our sins in his own body on the tree, that we, being dead to sins, should live unto righteousness: by whose stripes ye were healed.1 Peter 2:24

When the even was come, they brought unto him many that were possessed with devils: and he cast out the spirits with his word, and healed all that were sick: That it might be fulfilled which was spoken by Esaias the prophet, saying, Himself took our infirmities, and bare our sicknesses. Matthew 8:16-17

As I read and meditated upon these Scriptures, something wonderful happened within my heart. Great, overwhelming sorrow took a hold of me as I saw the pain and the agony that Jesus went through for my healing. In my heart and in my mind I saw that Jesus had taken my sicknesses and my diseases. I then experienced a great love for the son of God, and recognize the price he paid for my healing. And then it happened! It was like an open vision in which I saw my precious **Lord and Savior** tied to the whipping post. I saw the Roman soldiers striking the back of Jesus with the cat of nine tails. In this vision I saw the flesh and the blood of my precious Savior sprinkling everything within a 10 foot radius, with each terrible strike of the soldiers whip causing his blood to splatter. As I saw this open vision, I wept because I knew it was for me this was done. To this day, even as I retell this story great love and sorrow fills my heart, yet I have great joy because I know that by the **stripes of Jesus I am healed**.

In this moment of this vision something exploded within my heart, an amazing faith possessed me with the knowledge that I no longer have to be sick. In the name of Jesus for over 40 years I have refused to allow what my precious Lord went through to be for nothing. I have refused to allow sickness and disease to dwell in my body, which is the temple of the Holy Ghost.

Jesus has taken my sicknesses and my diseases. No if, ans, or butts, no matter what it looks like or how I feel, I know within my heart Jesus Christ has set me free from sicknesses and diseases. At the moment of this revelation great anger, yes great anger, rose up in my heart against the enemy of my Lord. The demonic world has no right to afflict me or any other believer, because Jesus took our sicknesses and bore our diseases.

Now I had been born with terrible physical infirmities, but now I found myself speaking out loud with authority to my ears, commanding them to be open and to be normal in the name of Jesus Christ of Nazareth. Then I spoke to my lungs, and commanded them to be healed in the name of Jesus Christ of Nazareth. Next I commanded my sinuses to be delivered, so I could smell normal scents in the name of Jesus Christ of Nazareth.

The minute I spoke the Word of God to my physical man, my ears popped completely open. Up to this moment I had a significant hearing loss, but now as I was listening to Christian music playing softly (at least I thought it was) the music became so loud that I had to turn it down. My lungs were clear, and I haven't experienced any lung congestion since in 40 years. I used to be so allergic to dust that my mother had to work extra hard to keep our house dust-free. I would literally end up in an oxygen tent in the hospital. From that moment to now dust, allergies, mold, or any such thing have never come back to torment me or cause me problems. Instantly my sense of smell returned! I had broken my nose about four times due to fights, accidents, and rough activities. I could barely smell anything.

Suddenly, I could smell a terrible odor. I tried to find out where it was coming from and then I looked at my feet and wondered if it could be them. I put my foot on a night stand and bent over toward it. I took a big sniff and nearly fell over. Man, did my feet stink! I went straight over to the bathroom and washed them in the sink.

For over 40 years I have aggressively, violently, persistently, taken a hold of my healing. I refuse to let the devil rob me of what Jesus so painfully purchased. It is mine, and the devil cannot have it. The thought has never even enter my mind to go see a doctor when physical sickness attack my body, for I already have a doctor , his name is Jesus Christ of Nazareth . He is the great physician, and he has already healed me with his stripes. Yes there has been times when the manifestation of my healing seemed like it would never come, there has been many times when it looked like in the natural I was going to die, but I know, that I know, that I know by the stripes of Jesus I am healed. Jesus Christ is the final authority in my life when it comes to the divine will of the Father. His life, and his word is the absolute voice of God pertaining to every situation. Without this revelation and foundation the enemy will be able to easily lead you astray, and destroy you.

The very 1st thing we must do is to let go of all our traditions, philosophies, doctrines, and experiences that contradict what is revealed to us through Jesus Christ. We must go back to Matthew, Mark, Luke and John rediscovering who Jesus Christ really is. Whatever Jesus said and did is what we agree with wholeheartedly. Any voice or teaching that contradicts Christ, and his redemptive work I immediately reject.

John 10:3 To him the porter openeth; and the sheep hear his voice: and he calleth his own sheep by name, and leadeth them out.

John 10:27 My sheep hear my voice, and I know them, and they follow me:

John 10:4 And when he putteth forth his own sheep, he goeth before them, and the sheep follow him: for they know his voice.

Rev 3:20 Behold, I stand at the door, and knock: if any man hear my voice, and open the door, I will come in to him, and will sup with him, and he with me.

Prov 8:20 I lead in the way of righteousness, in the midst of the paths of judgment:[21] That I may cause those that love me to inherit substance; and I will fill their treasures.

Isaiah 42:16 And I will bring the blind by a way that they knew not; I will lead them in paths that they have not known: I will make darkness light before them, and crooked things straight. These things will I do unto them, and not forsake them.

Jesus Stepped into My Body

I was standing in my office in the midst of prayer one day looking towards the east, which was nothing but my office wall. To my shock and amazement, Jesus Christ stepped right through the wall and into my office! This happened so fast that it frightened me. I was only about four feet away from this wall. When Jesus stepped into my room, He did not say a word to me, but just kept walking right toward me.

The next thing I knew, Jesus walked right into my body. It was one of the strangest experiences I have ever had. My body did not resist in the least. It was as if my body was made for Him to dwell in. It was almost like when someone comes home to their house, opens the door, and simply steps in. When Jesus stepped into me, His face would've been looking out of the back of my head. I know this is hard to believe, but I literally felt Him turn around inside of me. His arms and hands went into my arms and hands. His legs and feet went into my legs and feet. The moment Jesus was in His proper position, I instantly grew a hundred feet tall! I was gigantic in size. My head and half of my body were outside of the building I was in and I was looking down upon everything. My whole being was filled with amazing power, authority, and knowledge. All the problems and difficulties of this world were to be laughed at compared to the One who was within me. All of creation itself could not compare to Him!

As fast as it had begun, it was over. The next thing I knew, I was back to normal size. Then the Spirit of the Lord spoke something to me that would change the course of my life forever. He said to me, Go tell my children who they are! They know not who they are! The reason why so many Christians walk around defeated is because they've never had a quickening of the Spirit, which brings revelation of who Christ really is. They do not realize that the same Jesus Christ who overcame principalities and powers, rulers of darkness, and spiritual wickedness in high places now lives in us. The very one who brought all things into existence now lives in us? Christ in us the hope of glory!

Colossians 1:27 To whom God would make known what is the riches of the glory of this mystery among the Gentiles; which is Christ in you, the hope of glory: Whom we preach, warning every man, and teaching every man in all wisdom; that we may present every man perfect in Christ Jesus: Where unto I also labour, striving according to his working, which worketh in me mightily.

#2 Word

The Written Word, the Bible equals the audible voice of God. This is the voice of God, and it must become more real to you than anything else in this world. Believers tell me all the time that God does not speak to them, but they are sadly mistaken. He speaks to us through the holy book called the Bible.

2 Timothy 3:16 All scripture is given by inspiration of God, and is profitable for doctrine, for reproof, for correction, for instruction in righteousness:

The **2nd way** that God speaks to us is through the written word. Remember that Christ, His Life and His words are the 1st major way and foundation that we must build upon for hearing the voice of God! Only when this truth is established in my heart, can I go to all of the written word, the epistles, and the Old Testament with understanding. What must take priority over all Scripture is what Jesus said and did. After this reality then I can go to the epistles of Paul, Peter, Philip, James, the book of Jude, and all of the WORD with divine and clear understanding. For example some people are still teaching and promoting physical circumcision, holy days, feast days, Sabbath days, new Moon days because they do not know that Jesus Christ is the embodiment of all of these **Levitical** laws.

Colossians 2:16 Let no man therefore judge you in meat, or in drink, or in respect of an holyday, or of the new moon, or of the sabbath days: 17 which are a shadow of things to come; but the body is of Christ.

Many of the Old Testament miracles were types and shadows of Jesus Christ. The Passover Lamb, manna from heaven, water from the rock, the snake on the brazen pole. Jesus Christ is the will and the voice of God speaking loud and clear to the human race. Now with this reality the pure Word of God can work mightily within our lives.

Hebrews 4:12 For the word of God is quick, and powerful, and sharper than any two edged sword, piercing even to the dividing asunder of soul and spirit, and of the joints and marrow, and is a discerner of the thoughts and intents of the heart.

1 Peter 2:2 as newborn babes, desire the sincere milk of the word, that ye may grow thereby:

1 Peter 1:23 being born again, not of corruptible seed, but of incorruptible, by the word of God, which liveth and abideth forever.

The very 1st voice that will build an unmovable foundation in our hearts is the life of Jesus, the works of Jesus, the words of Jesus, the attitude of Jesus and the conduct of Jesus! David declared that he hid the word of God in his heart in order that he would not sin against God. The apostle Paul shared this amazing revelation in Romans chapter 12.

Romans 12:2 And be not conformed to this world: but be ye transformed by the renewing of your mind, that ye may prove what is that good, and acceptable, and perfect, will of God.

Remember that Jesus in John 17 is no longer speaking to his disciples, but is speaking directly to his heavenly Father. He reveals some amazing realities and spiritual insights into how we are to become one with Him, the heavenly Father, and the Holy Ghost.

John 17:17 Sanctify them through thy truth: thy word is truth.

John 17:19 And for their sakes I sanctify myself, that they also might be sanctified through the truth.

In Ephesians the apostle Paul tells us that husbands are to love their wives as Christ also loved the church. That Christ gave him self for the church in order that he might sanctify and cleanse it with the washing of the water of the word. That he might present to him self a glorious church, without spot or wrinkle or any such thing. Let me challenge you with a bold statement: Christ is the audible, visible manifested voice of the Father sent to the earth in human flesh! All of the other Scriptures from Genesis to Revelation simply verify who Jesus is,what he accomplished, what Jesus taught, and did!

2 Timothy 3:16 All scripture is given by inspiration of God, and is profitable for doctrine, for reproof, for correction, for instruction in righteousness: 17 that the man of God may be perfect, throughly furnished unto all good works.

We have to a look at the word through the person of Jesus Christ. We will never really understand the word of God, or the will of God without looking at it through our Lord Jesus Christ. Many Ministers are wrongly emphasizing on finances, materialism and many other subjects because they really do not know Jesus Christ, or what is important to him and his Father! Ministers are constantly emphasizing the anointing, when they should be emphasizing the reality of Jesus Christ. Many are not even preaching and teaching about Jesus in the pulpit today the way they should because they're not looking at the word of God through Christ. He is the way, the truth and the light. No man comes to the Father but by Jesus Christ. There is no other name under heaven given among men whereby we must be saved. I understand the Father through Jesus Christ. I understand the Bible through Jesus Christ. Because of Jesus Christ, the word of God is more real to me than my natural physical circumstances. Let me share with you one of the amazing experiences that I have had because of this revelation I have in Christ and his eternal word.

HEALED of a Broken Back

In the winter of 1977, I was working at the Belleville Feed and Grain Mill. My job was to pick up the corn, wheat, and oats from the farmers, and bring it to the mill. There it would be mixed and combined with other products for the farmers livestock. One cold, snowy day, the owner of the feed mill told me to deliver a load of cattle feed to an Amish farm. It was an extremely bad winter that year, with lots of snow. I was driving an International 1600 Lodestar. I backed up as far as I could to this Amish man's barn without getting stuck.

The Amish never had their lanes plowed in those days, and they most likely still do not. I was approximately seventy five feet away from his barn, which meant that I had to carry the bags at least seventy five feet. I think there were about eighty bags of feed, with each bag weighing approximately one hundred pounds. During those years I only weighed about 130 pounds. I would carry one bag on each of my shoulders, stumbling and pushing my way through the heavy, deep snow to get up the steep incline into the barn. Then I would stack the bags in a dry location. As usual, nobody came out to help me. Many a time when delivering things to the farms, the Amish would watch me work without lending a helping hand. About the third trip, something frightening happened to me carrying two one-hundred-pound bags upon my shoulders. I felt the bones in my back snap. Something drastic just happened. I fell to the ground at that very moment almost completely crippled. I could barely move.

I had been spending a lot of my time meditating in the Word of God. Every morning, I would get up about 5:00 a.m. to study. I had one of those little bread baskets with memorization scriptures in it. I believe you can still buy them to this day at a Christian bookstore. Every morning I would memorize from three to five of them. It would not take me very long, so all day long I would be meditating on these verses. So what I do next will determine my future. Okay I hear the voice of my body, I hear the voice of my mind, I hear the voice of my emotions, and they all say to me: you are in big trouble! I choose to listen to the voice of my Jesus. He says this to me: by my stripes you our healed now! The voice of Jesus is more real to me then my body. So this is how I responded.

The very minute I fell down, immediately I cried out to Jesus, asking him to forgive me for my pride, and for being so stupid in carrying two hundred pounds on my small frame. After I asked Jesus to forgive me, I commanded my back to be healed in the name of Jesus Christ of Nazareth. Since I believed I was healed, I knew that I had to act now upon my faith. Please understand that I was full of tremendous pain, but I had declared that I was healed by the stripes of Jesus. The Word of God came out of my mouth as I tried to get up and then fell back down.

Even though the pain was more intense than I can express, I kept getting back up, then I would fall back down again. I fell down more times than I can remember. After some time I was able to take a couple steps, then I would fall again. This entire time I was saying, "In the name of Jesus, in the name of Jesus, in the name of Jesus." I finally was able to get to the truck. I said to myself if I believe I'm healed then I will unload this truck in the name of Jesus. Of course, I did not have a cell phone in order to call for help and the Amish did not own any phones on their property. Now, even if they would have had a phone, I would not have called for help. I had already called upon my help, and His name was Jesus Christ. I knew in my heart that by the stripes of Jesus I was healed. I then pulled a feed bag off of the back of the truck, with it falling on top of me. I would drag it a couple feet, and then fall down.

Tears were running down my face as I spoke the Word of God over and over. By the time I was done with all of the bags, the sun had already gone down. I painstakingly pulled myself up into that big old 1600 Lodestar. It took everything within me to shift gears, pushing in the clutch, and driving it. I finally got back to the feed mill late in the evening. Everybody had left for home a long time ago with the building being locked up. I struggled out of the Lodestar and stumbled and staggered over to my Ford pickup. I got into my pickup, and made it back to the converted chicken house. I went back to my cold, unheated, plywood floor room. It took everything in me to get my clothes off. It was a very rough and long night.

The next morning when I woke up, I was so stiff that I could not bend in the least. I was like a board. Of course, I was not going to miss work, because by the stripes of Jesus I was healed. In order to get out of bed, I had to literally roll off the bed, hitting the floor. Once I had hit the floor, it took everything for me to push myself back up into a sitting position. The tears were rolling down my face as I put my clothes and shoes on, which in itself was a miracle. I did get to work on time, though every step was excruciatingly painful. Remember, I was only twenty-one at the time, but I knew what faith was and what it wasn't. I knew that I was healed no matter how it looked, that by the stripes of Jesus Christ I was healed.

When I got to work I did not tell my boss that I had been seriously hurt the day before. I walked into the office trying to keep the pain off of my face. For some reason he did not ask me what time I made it back to work. I did not tell him to change the time clock for me in order to be paid for all of the hours I was out on the job. They had me checked out at the normal quitting time. (The love of money is what causes a lot of people not to get healed.) My boss gave me an order for feed that needed to be delivered to a local farmer. If you have ever been to a feed and grain mill, you know that there is a large shoot where the feed comes out. After it has been mixed, you have to take your feed bag, and hold it up until it's filled. It creates tremendous strain on your arms and your back, even if you're healthy. As I was filling the bag, it almost felt like I was going to pass out, because I was in tremendous pain.

Now, I'm simply saying, "In the name of Jesus, in the name of Jesus, in the name of Jesus" under my breath. The second bag was even more difficult than the first bag, but I kept on saying, "In the name of Jesus." I began on the third bag and as I was speaking Jesus' name, the power of God hit my back and I was completely and totally healed from the top of my head, to the tip of my toes. I was healed as I went on my way. My place of employment never did know what had happened to me.

Matthew 11:12 And from the days of John the Baptist until now the kingdom of heaven suffereth violence, and the violent take it by force.

I have discovered the will of God through Jesus Christ and his Word. I am not letting go of Gods will no matter what anyone says or teaches. I Know the Voice of God, it is Jesus Christ, and I know Gods second major way He speaks to us, which is by Divine Scriptures.

Matthew 24:35 Heaven and earth shall pass away, but my words shall not pass away.

Proverbs 6:22 When thou goest, it shall lead thee; when thou sleepest, it shall keep thee; and when thou awakest, it shall talk with thee.

Luke 16:17 And it is easier for heaven and earth to pass, than one tittle of the law to fail.

Now here a the danger, you can have convictions about what you believe to be the will and the voice of God, when it is not really his will or voice at all. Because you have embrace these convictions as the will of God you will now have to live under these convictions, because anything that is not of faith is sin.

1 Timothy 4:3-5 forbidding to marry, and commanding to abstain from meats, which God hath created to be received with thanksgiving of them which believe and know the truth. 4 For every creature of God is good, and nothing to be refused, if it be received with thanksgiving: 5 for it is sanctified by the word of God and prayer.

There are many Christians who are weak in the faith. Who is weak in the faith? People who take to themselves convictions (voices) that really do not make a difference in the light of eternity.

They get caught up in all kind of crusades dealing with meats, holy days, Sabbath days, clothing, jewelry, when it's really all about the character, the nature, the divine attributes and personality of God.

Romans 14:1-3 Him that is weak in the faith receive ye, but not to doubtful disputations. 2 For one believeth that he may eat all things: another, who is weak, eateth herbs. 3 Let not him that eateth despise him that eateth not; and let not him which eateth not judge him that eateth: for God hath received him. To verse :5 One man esteemeth one day above another: another esteemeth every day alike. Let every man be fully persuaded in his own mind. 6 He that regardeth the day, regardeth it unto the Lord; and he that regardeth not the day, to the Lord he doth not regard it.

Romans 12:12 I beseech you therefore, brethren, by the mercies of God, that ye present your bodies a living sacrifice, holy, acceptable unto God, which is your reasonable service. 2 And be not conformed to this world: but be ye transformed by the renewing of your mind, that ye may prove what is that good, acceptable, perfect, will of God.

The Scriptures declare that if two be not agreed together, they cannot walk together. Faith is when you come into complete and total agreement with God, his Word, and his will. Paul said by the spirit of God, be not conformed to this world, but be ye transformed, (metamorphosis) changed by the renewing of all your mind.

Before your mind is transformed, renewed by the Word, you are like a caterpillar. The number of legs, and feet, that a caterpillar has varies. There is one type of caterpillar that has 16 legs, and 16 feet, with which they use to hold on to anything, and everything they can get their little feet around. When that caterpillar becomes a Butterfly, everything changes. Including the number of feet they have, and even the purpose of their feet. All Butterflies end up with SIX legs and feet. In some species such as the monarch, the front pair of legs remains tucked up under the body most of the time. Their legs become long and slender. Something amazing happens to their feet also. Within their feet are taste buds. That means that whatsoever their feet touch they taste. It prevents them from eating anything that is not good for them. This could be equivalent to discerning what voices are of God. When as caterpillars they were willing to eat anything their little feet took a hold of, now they become very picky and select with what they eat.

You see the Butterfly which came from the caterpillar now lives in a completely different world. It is no longer bound by earthly things. It no longer has feet that cling to the Earth! It is free to fly above all the worries, fears, anxieties, enemies, and circumstances of life. It literally can see into the future, where it is going. It has overcome the law of gravitation, by a superior law. It is called the law of aerodynamics. We as believers, as we renew our minds, leave behind the law of sin and death, entering into a new world called: **The Law of the Spirit of Life in Christ Jesus!** Now we need to be very picky at what we eat mentally, because whatever we place in our minds and in our hearts, will determine what we are meditating upon. The Scripture says: as a man thinketh, so is he! To hear the voice of God correctly, you need to renew your mind. You and I cannot hear the voice of God any clearer than that of the renewing of our minds. Everything that is contradictory to the word, the will, and the divine nature of Jesus Christ must be dealt with. As we bring every thought captive to the obedience of Christ, our ability to hear God will cause us to soar like an eagle. Listen to what James the brother of Jesus said about the renewing of the mind.

James 1:21 Wherefore lay apart all filthiness and superfluity of naughtiness, and receive with meekness the engrafted word, which is able to save your souls.

What if I told you that your usefulness to God equals your level of hearing and obeying the voice of Christ! Of course the obedience that I am referring to is true divine faith. A faith that will take a hold of God (like Jacob wrestling with the Angel) refusing to let go until there is a wonderful transformation in your Heart and in your Mind!

There are so many Scriptures dealing with the renewing of your mind, and the meditation of your heart, that a whole book could easily be written on this subject. I will share with you a number of Scriptures that are important to this particular chapter.

Joshua 1:8 This book of the law shall not depart out of thy mouth; but thou shalt meditate therein day and night, that thou mayest observe to do according to all that is written therein: for then thou shalt make thy way prosperous, and then thou shalt have good success.

Psalm 1:2 But his delight is in the law of the Lord; and in his law doth he meditate day and night.

Psalm 63:6 when I remember thee upon my bed, and meditate on thee in the night watches.

Psalm 119:148 Mine eyes prevent the night watches that I might meditate in thy word.

Psalm 104:34 My meditation of him shall be sweet: I will be glad in the Lord.

Psalm 119:97 O how love I thy law! It is my meditation all the day.

Psalm 119:99 I have more understanding than all my teachers: for thy testimonies are my meditation.

1 Timothy 4:15 Meditate upon these things; give thyself wholly to them; that thy profiting may appear to all.

Psalm 39:3 My heart was hot within me, while I was musing the fire burned: then Spake I with my tongue,2 Samuel 23:2 The Spirit of the Lord Spake by me, and his word was in my tongue.

CHAPTER TWO

#3 Consciences

The **3rd way** that God speaks to every human being is by their conscience. Every human being is born with a conscience that is alive unto God. The definition from the **Webster's dictionary** for the word conscience: **a :** the sense or consciousness of moral goodness or blameworthiness of one's own conduct, intentions, or character, together with a feeling of obligation to do right or be good. **b :** a faculty, power, or principle enjoining good acts. **c :** conformity to what one considers to be correct, right, or morally good : conscientiousness. **d:** sensitive regard for fairness or justice : scruple

Throughout the Bible there are specific scriptures that deal with this very important subject.

John 1:9 That was the true Light, which lighteth every man that cometh into the world.

John 1:4 In him was life; and the life was the light of men.

Genesis 2:7 And the Lord God formed man of the dust of the ground, and breathed into his nostrils the breath of life; and man became a living soul.

Job 32:8 But there is a spirit in man: and the inspiration of the Almighty giveth them understanding.

Proverbs 20:27 The spirit of man is the candle of the Lord, searching all the inward parts of the belly.

Understanding the Tri-unity of Man

The Scriptures reveal that man is a three-part being. The three parts of man are composed of his soul, spirit, and body. There seems to be a lot of misunderstanding over man's three-part composition. Virtually, a book alone could be written on this particular subject. For us to truly comprehend how God leads and guides us we need to understand who and what man is. Really the Scriptures are quite informative and descriptive pertaining to this area. (Many times the indoctrination of men interferes with many biblical truths and revelations.)

When my wife and I attended Bible College, we were taught that we were a spirit, that we have a soul, and that we live in a physical body. If you diligently search the Scriptures I think you will discover that this is not the correct makeup of man's composition.

1st Man is a soul

Over eleven hundred times within the Scriptures the Bible talks about man's soul. We only need to use a small portion of the Scriptures to reveal the truth about this divine mystery. Genesis declared that man became a living soul. The soul of man is also considered his heart, = the thoughts, intents, and purposes, that which decides and determines our eternal destiny.

"And the LORD God formed man of the dust of the ground, and breathed into his nostrils the breath of life; and man became a living soul" (Gen. 2:7).

"And so it is written, The first man Adam was made a living soul; the last Adam was made a quickening spirit" (1 Cor. 15:45).

It is the soul of man that commits sin. It is also the soul of man that dies. The Spirit of the Lord in man did not die as many have been taught. When man committed sin in the garden, he was warned that he would die. It was the soul that God was warning him about. At that moment man sinned the human soul died to being responsiveness, sensitivity, obedient and to loving God. The heart, which is the soul received the corruptible seed of satans DNA, and became a lover of self and the flesh. The controlling and dominating aspect of the human soul came under the influence of corrupted flesh, where at one time it was under the influence of God's Spirit.

"The soul that sinneth, it shall die" (Ezek. 18:20a).

"And you hath he quickened, who were dead in trespasses and sins; Wherein in time past ye walked according to the course of this world, according to the prince of the power of the air, the spirit that now worketh in the children of disobedience: Among whom also we all had our conversation in times past in the lusts of our flesh, fulfilling the desires of the flesh and of the mind; and were by nature the children of wrath, even as others" (Eph. 2:1-3).

It is the soul of man that goes to hell, not the spirit. The unconverted souls of humanity are eternally separated from God and quarantined in hell. It is the soul (the heart) of man that must be converted, born again. It is in the soul that believers experience the new birth. The incorruptible seed of God's divine nature must be implanted into the soil of the soul of man. Our souls must be converted, transformed, renewed, and saved. Jesus came to save our souls.

"Brethren, if any of you do err from the truth, and one convert him; Let him know, that he which converteth the sinner from the error of his way shall save a soul from death, and shall hide a multitude of sins" (James 5:19-20).

"Receiving the end of your faith, even the salvation of your souls" (1 Pet. 1:9).

Please keep in mind that when the Scriptures are speaking about the human soul it is referring to the human heart.

"The heart is deceitful above all things, and desperately wicked:

31

who can know it?"(Jer. 17:9).

"This is an evil among all things that are done under the sun, that there is one event unto all: yea, also the heart of the sons of men is full of evil, and madness is in their heart while they live, and after that they go to the dead" (Eccles. 9:3).

The human soul is one of God's most amazing creations. It bridges the gap of the spiritual and the natural, which literally straddles both dimensions. The human soul was created to house the very essence of God Himself. The Scriptures declare that we are His tabernacle, the dwelling place of God's presence. The demonic world wanted to sit upon God's throne, that's why they endeavor to possess our souls. In order to get a glimpse of the capacity of the human soul we just need to take a look at an amazing example within the Scriptures. When Jesus was casting the devils out of the man from the region of the Gadarenes, the demons declared that they were a legion. In that particular time a full strength of a legion of Roman soldiers was officially made up of 5,200 men. Could it possibly be that this man's soul was inhabited by five thousand devils? Yes, I believe he could have been. This reveals the capacity of the human soul, which was made to be inhabited by God's Spirit.

2nd Man has a spirit

The word spirit is used many times within the Bible. You have to study the context to see what it is referring to. It could be referring to angelic, demonic, the Holy Spirit, or the human spirit. It can also be referring to the attitude or the disposition of a person. A perfect example is when Scripture says that Joshua and Caleb had a different spirit about them.

"But my servant Caleb, because he had another spirit with him, and hath followed me fully, him will I bring into the land where into he went; and his seed shall possess it" (Num. 14:24).

"We having the same spirit of faith, according as it is written, I believed, and therefore have I spoken; we also believe, and

therefore speak" (2 Cor. 4:13).

In the Garden of Eden, God breathed into man the breath of life. When the soul of man died in the garden, he did not lose the Spirit of God. The Spirit of God still resided in his flesh. Actually the Spirit of God is the life of the flesh. It is only when the Spirit leaves man that the flesh will die. The human spirit is similar to electricity in the sense that it provides the active energy the quickening of the human flesh. Of course it is much deeper than this simple statement.

"The burden of the word of the LORD for Israel, saith the LORD, which stretcheth forth the heavens, and layeth the foundation of the earth, and formeth the spirit of man within him" (Zech. 12:1).

"The Spirit of God hath made me, and the breath of the Almighty hath given me life" (Job 33:4).

The spirit within man is the conscience of his heart. It is to be the divine guidance system for his soul given by God. It is the "GPS of man's life." The spirit that God put within man's flesh will and can never die. Men throughout the ages have either yielded or ignored the voice of their Spirits. As I stated there needs to be a whole book written on this particular subject. The description that I am giving here is really an oversimplification of ta deep mystery of the kingdom of God. Man is fearfully and wonderfully made.

"For what man knoweth the things of a man, save the spirit of man which is in him? Even so the things of God knoweth no man, but the Spirit of God" (1 Cor. 2:11).

When a person dies outside of Christ the spirit of man returns to God from whence it came. But his soul goes to hell. The soul (heart) is who you really are. The human spirit is not re-created at the new birth. The spirit of man never died; it was his soul. Our souls need to be born again. Our souls need to be saved.

"Then shall the dust return to the earth as it was: and the spirit shall return unto God who gave it" (Eccles. 12:7).

"If he set his heart upon man, if he gather unto himself his spirit and his breath; All flesh shall perish together, and man shall turn again unto dust" (Job 34:14-15). [This is referring to his body!]

3rd Man inhabits a body

Yes, the human body is an amazing machine. But the simple truth is that it was not created through a process of evilution. It was created by the spirit that God breathed into it. And when you and I die, the human body will turn back to dust from whence it came. At the return of Christ those who are saved will receive a glorified body, but those who are damned will never receive a glorified body, but their souls will be cast into the lake of fire with the devil and his angels for all eternity.

"Thou hidest thy face, they are troubled: thou takest away their breath, they die, and return to their dust" (Ps. 104:29).

"And many of them that sleep in the dust of the earth shall awake, some to everlasting life, and some to shame and everlasting contempt" (Dan. 12: 2).

The conclusion of what we have just briefly studied is that you and I are a soul which is revealed as our hearts. We have a spirit that comes from God Almighty. It is to be the divine guidance system for our souls given by God. It is the "GPS of man's life." We are housed in a physical body. This Spirit is the life source of our flesh.

Christ died to save our souls. When a person dies loving Christ, his soul becomes one with the Spirit of God for eternity. It is like that of the seed of man, entering into the egg of the woman, thereby creating a human life. The new birth and the life of the believer is similar in that a son of God comes forth. We enter into immortal and eternal life. Our corrupted body will put on incorruption, and mortality will put on immortality. Christ is our shepherd and by our conscience he will lead us into paths of righteousness for his name sake.

There was this big explosion back about 30 years ago in the church world because the word of faith people said that Jesus died spiritually. Another part of the body of Christ said Jesus did not die spiritually. The word of faith people basically said that the spirit of Christ went in to hell, and the other group said that Jesus did not go to hell. They were both wrong! When Christ was upon the cross he said: *Father into thy hands commend I my spirit.* Peter said this about Jesus Christ: *thou did not suffer my soul to remain in hell.*

Every human being has a conscience, which is the light of life. What is the conscience? It is the breath of God, the spirit of God, in every human that is speaking to their hearts, trying to instruct them in the ways of righteousness.

1 Corinthians 8:12 But when ye sin so against the brethren, and wound their weak conscience, ye sin against Christ.

1 Timothy 1:19 Holding faith, and a good conscience; which some having put away concerning faith have made shipwreck:

1 Timothy 3:9 Holding the mystery of the faith in a pure conscience.

1 Timothy 4:2 Speaking lies in hypocrisy; having their conscience seared with a hot iron;

1 Peter 3:21 The like figure whereunto even baptism doth also now save us (not the putting away of the filth of the flesh, but the answer of a good conscience toward God,) by the resurrection of Jesus Christ:

John 8:9 And they which heard it , being convicted by their own conscience, went out one by one, beginning at the eldest, even unto the last: and Jesus was left alone, and the woman standing in the midst.

Romans 2:15 Which shew the work of the law written in their hearts, their conscience also bearing witness, and their thoughts the mean while accusing or else excusing one another;)

You and I can harden our hearts, our conscience against the voice of the Spirit and the will of God!

1 Timothy 4:2 speaking lies in hypocrisy; having their conscience seared with a hot iron;

Paul said that when sinners make laws to govern the conduct of society it reveals that there is a God in heaven. You can go into the darkest recesses of the world and discover hidden tribes of people. In every one of these hidden tribes you will discover that they have created laws, rules and regulations. The reason why men automatically create laws is because they have a conscience. Now, it is obvious that animals do not have rules, regulations or laws that bind them together. This truth then boldly proclaims that evilution is a lie. Even if people do not ever hear the preaching of the gospel, God will judge them according to their conscience, and their laws. God will say to them, I gave you your conscience, I was speaking to you through your conscience by my Spirit. I gave you the innocence of childhood, and the candle of my spirit, the light of my presence, but you chose to harden your heart, and go your own way.

Our conscience is the voice of God speaking to us. People knowingly harden their hearts in order to commit the sin which they have chosen to partake of. People are not born as murderers or thieves, liars and evildoers. The conviction is in their heart, given to them through their conscience. Human beings choose to harden their hearts against the spirit of God speaking to them through their conscience.

We must be very careful what convictions we allow to

affect us. A lot of believers permit convictions to come upon them that are not based solidly upon the divine nature of Christ or his word. These are convictions that do not take them into paths of righteousness, true holiness and divine obedience. We are to be the clay and Christ is the Potter. We experience much hurt and pain in our lives because we have not built a solid foundation upon which to hear the voice of God. We harden our hearts, using Scriptures in ways that God never meant for us to use them. Here's one of my own personal examples of thinking and believing. In my heart I was in the will of God, but I was completely wrong in how I was treating my wife.

My Wife's Bags were Packed to Leave Me ! (2000)

My wife and I were going through some major issues in our marriage. We had been married for 21 years up to this point, back in the year 2000. A tragic accident had taken place in 1998 with our little girl Naomi becoming seriously hurt. For 2 1/2 years we both worked day and night keeping her fed, exercised, and taken care of. Then, one night, I put her to bed and she was gone the next morning. She was four and a half years old when she passed on. That same year at Christmas, my mom passed away with whom I was very close. In additional to all of the stress at home, our church was experiencing multiple problems at the same time as well, which served to compound our ongoing marriage problems which we had already been experiencing for a number of years.

One day as I was in prayer in the churches sanctuary, I heard the Lord say to me, **"Leave your wife alone!"** It was not Him suggesting or asking, but demanding. Then he spoke to me, "Her bags are packed, and she is ready to leave you." What I heard from the Lord was so real to me that I began to weep uncontrollably for two reasons: first because I know the voice of God and what I heard was true, and second because I love my wife so much. God had given us to each other. We had been through so much together. I had the privilege of delivering three of our own children. On two of these occasions, the midwife was not there because she had been called away. We had seen God perform so many miracles in our lives and many others. (Read our book:

Living in the Realm of the Miraculous) I did not want to lose my wife. She was my beloved babe, the apple of my eye, the wife of my youth and the mother of my children. She had been my partner through thick and thin. I cried out to God, "Lord, what should I do?" And then he said to me, just love her! That's what your job is: to love her as Christ loves the church and gave himself for her.

And then out of the blue he asked me a very strange question, "Do you wear your wife's bra or girdle"? I said what Lord? Surely he did not say what I thought he just said to me. Once again I heard, "Do you wear your wife's bra or girdle"? I said, **NO LORD**! Then I heard him say to me, "If you do not wear your wife's undergarments then why do you keep trying to use her scriptures?" I said, what do you mean, Lord? And he spoke to my heart saying, **"Ephesians 5:22, 23, and 24 is not yours.** Where it says, wives submit yourselves unto your own husbands……….. Those are not your scriptures, so why do you keep using them? Your Scriptures are **Ephesians 5:25 to 33 Husbands love your wives even as Christ also loved the church and gave Himself for it."**

At that very moment it was like a sledgehammer hit me between the eyes. I clearly saw what I had been trying to do all these years. I had literally put myself in the place of God and was trying to change my wife. My job was not to make her submit to me! My job was to love her even as Christ loves the church! I went back to my house with tears rolling down my face asking my wife to please forgive me, explaining that it was not my job to make her submit and that her submission was completely between her and God. My job is to love her…… end of story!

I just asked her the other day if what I heard the Lord say was correct, did she really have her bags packed, and was she ready to leave me? She replied yes, not only did I have my bags packed but I had called my mom telling her to please be ready to come and pick me up at any moment. I told my mom that I was going to try to stick it out as long as possible, but there was only so much I could handle. Thank God for his mercy, kindness, goodness and love, and that He still speaks today, and tries to turn us away from destruction of our own making. We must maintain a meek and teachable, humble spirit. We must be quick to repent and turn away from our evil deeds.

Psalm 25:9 The meek will he guide in judgment: and the meek will he teach his way.

Job 17:9 The righteous also shall hold on his way, and he that hath clean hands shall be stronger and stronger.

Now Moses was very meek above all the men which were upon the face of the earth. Why was Moses so meek? He meekly stood before the fire of the Lord, he stood before the word of the Lord, and he stood before God himself. I actually believe that Moses was meek before he ever saw the burning bush on the side of the mountain, otherwise God would never have showed him the burning Bush. Moses turned aside to see this strange sight. When you have a meek heart you will turn aside, you will not keep going in the direction you have been going. You will begin to listen to your conscience, and respond to the convictions of the Holy Ghost. Christ declared that he was meek when he said:

Matthew 11:29 Take my yoke upon you, and learn of me; for I am meek and lowly in heart: and ye shall find rest unto your souls.

We need to submit to God, resist the devil, and he will flee from us. Every time you disobey your conscience you are hardening your heart. Jesus said that they have ears, but they hear not, eyes, but they see not. He could have simply said: they choose not to hear, and they choose not to listen. When we harden our hearts we are headed for death and destruction. Right now we need to boldly proclaim in the name of Jesus: I will no longer harden my heart to the voice of God or my conscience. The devil gets people to lie about you, to gossip about you, to attack you, inorder to get you to harden your heart through bitterness. He is hoping that you will become extremely offended, bitter and hateful towards people and then towards God.

Hebrews 12:15 looking diligently lest any man fail of the grace of

God; lest any root of bitterness springing up trouble you, and thereby many be defiled;

Jesus was absolutely innocent and blameless, that's why he was called the lamb without spot or blemish. Jesus had a conscience that was clear before God and man. The Scripture says that Christ was like a **tender root** growing out of the dry ground. His conscience and his heart was tender and sensitive to the voice of his Father. In order to commit sin we must harden our hearts to the voice of our conscience. The more that we do this, the less we will hear, comprehend, or respond to the voice of God. Christ said that the prince of this world was going to come in order to destroy him, but that the enemy would find no sin in his heart. The enemy of our soul wants to get us to be bitter, to be resentful, to be angry, to get you to harden your heart, to not keep a tender conscience, but to become hardhearted. To be meek is to be teachable, sensitive, and responsive to your conscience.

My son Daniel was dying from rabies, and it was my fault!

When my son Daniel was 16 years old in 2000, he brought home a baby raccoon. He wanted to keep this raccoon as a pet. Immediately, people began to inform me that this was illegal. I further learned that in order to have a raccoon in Pennsylvania, one had to purchase one from someone who was licensed by the state to sell them. The reason for this was because of the high rate of rabies carried among them. But stubbornness rose up in my heart against what they were telling me, and I hardened my heart and did not listen to my conscience.

You see, I had a raccoon when I was a child. Her mother had been killed on the highway and left behind a litter of her little ones. I had taken one of the little ones and bottle-fed it, naming her Candy. I have a lot of fond memories of this raccoon, so when my son wanted this raccoon, against better judgment, the warnings of my conscience and against the law of the land, I said okay. I did not realize that baby raccoon's could have the rabies virus lying dormant in them for three months before it would manifest. I knew in my heart that I was wrong to give him permission to keep this raccoon. But, like so many when we are out of the will of God, we justify ourselves. We are completely blind and ignorant of the price that we will have to pay because of our rebellion and disobedience.

Daniel named his little raccoon Rascal. And he was a rascal because he was constantly getting into everything. A number of months went by and one night my son Daniel told me that he had a frightening dream. I should have known right then and there that we needed to get rid of this raccoon. He said in his dream, Rascal grew up and became big like a bear and then attacked and devoured him. Some time went by and my son Daniel began to get sick, running a high fever. One morning, he came down telling me that something was majorly wrong with Rascal. He said that he was wobbling all over the place and was bumping into stuff. Immediately, the alarm bells went off. I asked him where his raccoon was. He informed me that Rascal was in his bedroom. Immediately I went upstairs to his room, opening his bedroom door. And their Rascal was acting extremely strange. He was bumping into everything and had spittle coming from his mouth.

Immediately, my heart was filled with great dread. I had grown up around wildlife and farm animals. I had run into animals with rabies before. No ifs, an, or buts, this raccoon had rabies. I immediately went to Danny asking him if the raccoon had bitten him or if he had gotten any of Rascal's saliva in his wounds? He showed me his hands where he had cuts on them, informing me that he had been letting rascal lick these wounds. He had even allowed rascal to lick his mouth.

Daniel did not look well and was running a high grade fever. He also informed me that he felt dizzy. I knew in my heart that we were in terrible trouble. I immediately called up the local forest ranger. They put me on the line with one of their personnel that had a lot of expertise in this area. When I informed him of what was going on, he asked me if I was aware of the fact that it was illegal to take in a wild raccoon. I told him I did know but that I had chosen to ignore the law.

He said that he would come immediately over to our house to examine this raccoon and if necessary to take it with him. I had placed Rascal in a cage making sure that I did not touch him. When the forest ranger arrived, I had the cage sitting in the driveway. He examined the raccoon without touching it. You could tell that he was quite concerned about the condition of this raccoon. He looked at me with deep regret informing me that in his opinion with 30 years wildlife service experience, this raccoon definitely had rabies. He asked me if there was anyone who had been in contact with this raccoon with any symptoms of sickness. I informed him that for the last couple days my son Daniel had not feeling well. As a matter of fact, he was quite sick. When I told him the symptoms that Daniel was experiencing, it was quite obvious the ranger was shaken and quite upset.

He told me that anybody who had been in contact with this raccoon would have to receive shots. He went on to explain that from the description of what my son Daniel was going through and considering the length of his illness, it was too late for him! He literally told me that he felt from his experience that there was no hope for my son. He fully believed that my son would die from rabies. He loaded the raccoon up in the back of his truck, leaving me standing in my driveway weeping. He said that he would get back to me as soon as they had the test results and that I should get ready for state officials to descend upon myself, my family and our church.

I cannot express to you the hopelessness and despair that had struck my heart at that moment. Just earlier in the spring, our little girl Naomi had passed on to be with the Lord at 4 ½ years old. And now my second son Daniel was dying from rabies. Both of these situations could have been prevented.

Immediately, I gathered together my wife, my first son Michael, my third son Steven, and my daughter Stephanie. We all gathered around Daniel's bed and began to cry out to God. We wept, cried, and prayed crying out to God. I was repenting and asking God for mercy. Daniel, as he was lying on the bed running a high fever and almost delirious, informed me that he was barely able to hang on to consciousness. He knew in his heart, he said, that he was dying!

After everyone disbursed from his bed with great overwhelming sorrow, I went into our family room where we had a wood stove. I opened up the wood stove which still had a lot of cold ashes from the winter. Handful after handful of ashes I scooped out of the stove, pouring it over my head and saturating my body, with tears of repentance and sorrow running down my face. And then I lay in the ashes. The ashes got into my eyes, mouth and nose and into my lungs, making me quite sick. But I did not care, all that mattered was that God would have mercy on us and spare my son and all our loved ones from the rabies virus. As I lay on the floor in the ashes, crying out to God with all I had within me, one could hear the house was filled with weeping, crying and praying family members.

All night long I wept and prayed, asking God to please have mercy on my stupidity. To remove the rabies virus not only from my son but from everyone else that had been in contact with this raccoon. I also asked God to remove the virus from Rascal as a sign that he had heard my prayers. I continued in this state of great agony for over 16 hours praying until early in the morning, when suddenly the light of heaven shined upon my soul. Great peace that passes understanding overwhelmed me. I got up with victory in my heart and soul.

I went upstairs to check on my son Daniel. When I walked into his bedroom, the presence of God was tangible. The fever had broken and he was resting peacefully. Our whole house was filled with the tangible presence of God. From that minute forward, he was completely healed. A couple of days later, I was contacted by the state informing me that, to their amazement, they could find nothing wrong with the raccoon. God had supernaturally removed the rabies virus not only from my son and those in contact with Rascal, but from the raccoon itself. Thank God that the Lord's mercy endures forever!

Books Written by Doc Yeager:

"Living in the Realm of the Miraculous #1"
"I need God Cause I'm Stupid"
"The Miracles of Smith Wigglesworth"
"How Faith Comes 28 WAYS"
"Horrors of Hell, Splendors of Heaven"
"The Coming Great Awakening"
"Sinners In The Hands of an Angry GOD, (modernized)"
"Brain Parasite Epidemic"
"My JOURNEY To HELL" - illustrated for teenagers
"Divine Revelation Of Jesus Christ"
"My Daily Meditations"
"Holy Bible of JESUS CHRIST"
"War In The Heavenlies - (Chronicles of Micah)"
"Living in the Realm of the Miraculous #2"
"My Legal Rights To Witness"
"Why We (MUST) Gather!- 30 Biblical Reasons"
My Incredible, Supernatural, Divine Experiences!
"How GOD Leads & Guides!- 20 Ways"

Phone: 1-800-555-4575

www,docyeager.com

#4 Still Small Voice

In 1st Kings19 Elijah had just called fire down from heaven, which he had done because he had heard the voice of God telling him to do so. God told him to do it, and so he did it out of obedience. None of the prophets of old ever decided to do something on their own, they always heard from heaven first, and they simply obeyed.

2 Peter 1:21 For the prophecy came not in old time by the will of man: but holy men of God spake as they were moved by the Holy Ghost.

They never spoke until the Holy Ghost moved upon them to speak. They were our example in order that we should walk in their footsteps. We need to hear from heaven, that's why we should never say, I am going to do this, or I'm going to do that. We need to say if the Lord is willing, we shall live and do this or that. We need to really become sensitive to God, and strive not to grieve the Holy Spirit, whereby we are sealed unto the day of redemption. We can easily grieve him by not obeying what God is telling us to do.

Elijah heard that Jezebel was going to have him killed. Notice that one minute Elijah's in the spirit, and the next he is in the flesh, running for his life. It's amazing how many times we get ourselves into trouble because we hearkened to the voice of a person that was out of the will of God. Then there are times when God speaks to us through the voice of a person, speaking by the spirit of God. Now at the same time that same person could end up giving us wrong direction in another situation, so we really need to know the voice of the Father. Sarah told Abraham to go in on to Hagar for she could give them a child. Of course that was not God, but when Sarah told Abraham to kick Ishmael out of their house,

God said she's heard from me, do it! This is why you can't have one man telling you what to do. You and I need to have ears that hear from heaven. You and I need to pay the price to hear from heaven in every situation. So many people would rather have somebody tell them what to do instead of hearing from heaven for themselves. They think that it will relieve them from their responsibilities, or the ultimate end results.

Jezebel is going to kill Elijah, so he begins to run for his life operating in fear. He ends up days later in the wilderness where he falls down and begins to talk to God. He tells the Lord to kill him. If he truly wanted to die, he simply could've stayed where he was, and Jezebel would've done the job for him. I am so glad that God does not always answer our prayers.

1 Kings 19:4 But he himself went a day's journey into the wilderness, and came and sat down under a juniper tree: and he requested for himself that he might die; and said, It is enough; now, O Lord, take away my life; for I am not better than my fathers.

As he laid sleeping under a juniper tree behold an angel of the Lord appeared and touched him, waking him up, in order to feed him.

1 Kings 19:6 And he looked, and, behold, there was a cake baken on the coals, and a cruse of water at his head. And he did eat and drink, and laid him down again. 7 And the angel of the Lord came again the second time, and touched him, and said, Arise and eat; because the journey is too great for thee. 8 And he arose, and did eat and drink, and went in the strength of that meat forty days and forty nights unto Horeb the mount of God.

Why was he going to this particular mountain? I believe he had to get there to hear the voice of God. Sometimes we have to be at a certain place, at a certain time in order to hear what God wants to say to us. Many times God has spoken to me when I was at a particular gospel meeting. The directions of my life have been radically altered as I have been at certain places, and at certain times. I have discovered personally 20 different ways that God speaks to his people. I have experienced God speaking to me in every one of these 20 ways that I am sharing with you in this book. The very **1st way** that the voice of God will speak to us is by and through his son Jesus Christ. The **2nd major way** that God speaks to us is by the word, quickened to us by the Holy Ghost. The **3rd major way** that God speaks to us is by our conscience. Our conscience will be affected by what we embrace as truth. It is imperative that we bring our conscience into line with the word of God, and the divine personality of Jesus Christ.

The **4th major way** that God speaks to us is by a **still small voice**. As we read this particular account in the life of Elijah, it becomes obvious that he had to learn to discern what the voice of God was, and what it was not. This story truly is an amazing i set of scriptures that we can learn much from.

1 Kings 19:9 And he came thither unto a cave, and lodged there; and, behold, the word of the Lord came to him, and he said unto him, What doest thou here, Elijah? 10 And he said, I have been very jealous for the Lord God of hosts: for the children of Israel have forsaken thy covenant, thrown down thine altars, and slain thy prophets with the sword; and I, even I only, am left; and they seek my life, to take it away. 11 And he said, Go forth, and stand upon the mount before the Lord. And, behold, the Lord passed by, and a great and strong wind rent the mountains, and brake in pieces the rocks before the Lord; but the Lord was not in the wind: and after the wind an earthquake; but the Lord was not in the earthquake: 12 and after the earthquake a fire; but the Lord was not in the fire: and after the fire a still small voice. 13 And it was so, when Elijah heard it, that he wrapped his face in his mantle, and went out, and stood in the entering in of the cave. And, behold, there came a voice unto him, and said, What does thou here, Elijah? 14 And he said, I have been very jealous for the Lord God of hosts: because the children of Israel have forsaken thy covenant, thrown down thine altars, and slain thy prophets with the sword; and I, even I only, am left; and they seek my life, to take it away. 15 And the Lord said unto him, Go, return on thy way to the wilderness of Damascus: and when thou comest, anoint Hazael to be king over Syria: 16 and Jehu the son of Nimshi shalt thou anoint to be king over Israel: and Elisha the son of Shaphat of Abel-meholah shalt thou anoint to be prophet in thy room. 17 And it shall come to pass, that him that escapeth the sword of Hazael shall Jehu slay: and him that escapeth from the sword of Jehu shall Elisha slay. 18 Yet I have left me seven thousand in Israel, all the knees which have not bowed unto Baal, and every mouth which hath not kissed him.

You and I need to know the voice of God. This will come through obedience, first by being doers of the word. If we do not do that which we know to be the known will of the Father, then why would the Lord speak to us in a still small voice?

1 Timothy 4:7 But refuse profane and old wives' fables, and exercise thyself rather unto godliness.

When I was a child they always told me that practice makes perfect. This is also true with hearing the voice of God. We must exercise and practice ourselves onto godliness. That means we must be doers of the word, and not hearers only. As I simply do that which I know to be the will of God, I will begin to hear the still small voice of the Father. When I was first born again, I decided from my heart to do whatever the word said. For instance the Scripture tells us to lift holy hands without doubting. The Scripture says we are to dance before the Lord. The Scripture says that in everything we should give thanks, for this is the will of God in Christ Jesus concerning you. Paul said by the spirit of God that we are to pray without ceasing. This means we are to continually be in communication with the Father, Son and Holy Ghost. As I acted upon these simple truths, the voice of God began to become very real to me. As a result my life, and those I love have been rescued from certain death and destruction many timesn. Here is one of my experiences that took place in 2008.

When the Dell Lake Damn Broke

If I had not heard the **still small voice** of God, my family and I would have been swept away when the dam broke at Dell Lake in Wisconsin! On June 8, 2008 my family and I were in Wisconsin at Dell Lake ministering in special meetings for an Indian tribe called the Ho-Chunk Nation. We were there by their invitation. They had provided the facility, and all the advertisements. Their reservation was located about five miles away from the lake where we were camping. We had been having some wonderful services. It was the second night of these meetings. At the end of the service, out of the blue, I heard the still small voice of God say: pack up your camper and leave tonight!

It had been a long day and my flesh sure did not want to leave, but I know the still small voice of God. I told the sponsors of the meetings that I was sorry but we had to go back to Pennsylvania, tonight. I could tell they were extremely disappointed. They tried to convince me to stay because God was moving in such a wonderful way, but I know the voice of God.

My family members were also disappointed. They asked me why we were leaving. They reminded me that I have never cancelled or shortened my commitments. I told them I understood this. But we had to leave tonight. I did not know why, but I had heard the still small voice of the Lord in my heart telling me we must pack up and leave tonight.

We arrived back at the Dell Lake camp grounds. It was beginning to rain extremely hard. My family asked if we could simply wait until the next morning because it was late, dark and raining heavily. I said no, we had to go now! I backed my truck up to the fifth wheel trailer. I saw the spirit of God come upon my second son Daniel in a mighty way. It had to be God because he does not like to get wet or even work really hard. I mean he began to work very fast and efficiently. My boys and I connected up the fifth wheel camper; we picked up all our camping equipment and withdrew the extended sides of the trailer.

Everybody was wet and tired as we loaded into the crew

cab Toyota pickup truck. Then, we were on our way. I noticed, as I drove past the Dell Lake dam that water was rushing by like a little river on both sides of the road. Some parts of the road were already flooded. We drove through the night. There were times we had to crawl because the rain was coming down so hard with fog and strong winds. All the way through Wisconsin, Illinois, Indiana, and Ohio the rain came. The weather was extremely violent as we saw eighteen wheeler turned over. Lots of car accidents. Trees and debris were blowing everywhere, yet God was protecting us.

The next day when we finally arrived back in Pennsylvania, we discovered some shocking news. There had been hundreds of twisters and tornadoes right behind us which caused a huge amount of devastation in Wisconsin, Illinois, and Ohio. But that wasn't the only news. The dam at Dell Lake, Wisconsin had completely and totally collapsed. Dell Lake is the largest man-made lake in Wisconsin, and this had never happened before in all of its history. The whole lake rushed out over the town. We would have been washed away in the storm. There is video footage of this disaster on the Internet. Thank God I had heard the still small voice of the Lord. Because I had obeyed His voice, my life and the life of my family was spared.

We need to practice godliness as we experience the school of hard knocks, learning to hear and obey the voice of God. This will be a hit and miss proposition. As you begin to experience God's voice, you will begin to learn what it sounds like. Elijah knew the voice of God was not in these manifestation, the **great and strong wind, the earthquake or the fire***!* I did not say God was not the author of these manifestation, but that God's voice was not in these manifestation. Yes God is mighty and yet many times He is like a gentle dove.

Luke 3:22 and the Holy Ghost descended in a bodily shape like a dove upon him, and a voice came from heaven, which said, Thou art my beloved Son; in thee I am well pleased.

Acts 2:2 And suddenly there came a sound from heaven as of a

rushing mighty wind, and it filled all the house where they were sitting.

After these manifestations came a still small voice. Many times I have heard this still small voice speaking to me, giving me much-needed guidance. It seems to float up out of my belly gently like a helium balloon, simply coming up out of my innermost being. This **still small voice** always agrees with Jesus, always agrees with the word, it always agrees with my conscience. I hear the Father many times when I'm praying in the morning or through the day by this still small voice. I actually have heard the voice of the Father tell me many times what to preach, where to go, what to say. I love to hear the voice of God for He has saved me and my family over and over through the years from dangerous situations. Jesus said: my sheep hear my voice.

Now God speaks to his people all the time, but we are simply listening to the wrong voices. There are so many other voices that are constantly demanding our attention. Modern technology is bombarding our mind, our ears and our eyes with distracting information. I am speaking about the news, movies, books, magazines, radio and the Internet. This bombardment of information, entertainment and vanity have a tendency of getting into our heads and heart, which causes us to become deaf to the voice of God.

Now Elijah heard the still small voice of God, and he wrapped his face in a Mantle. He went out of the cave to communicate with the Lord. The Scripture says there came a voice unto him, and said what does now here Elijah? I believe what he heard from this point forward was the audible voice of God. I have literally heard the audible voice of God numerous times in my life. Every time I heard the audible voice of God it with me to the marrow of my bones to such an extent at times that it has driven me to my knees. He has rescued me by his audible voice, but that's another way that God speak to us. I will speak about this to some extent in another chapter.

Elijah informs God that he has been very jealous for Him

and His purposes. At this point the Lord reveals to Elijah exactly what he is to do. Some may question why are there certain people that God gives such specific directions to, while others seem to walk around in utter confusion in knowing what God wants? I do not think it is just because Elijah was a prophet, but because Elijah was obedient to the written word of God first. If we do not obey this simple written word first, then why would he ever revealed to us more precise directions?

Now what if the Lord doesn't tell you specifically what should you? Just simply do what the word, the Bible tells you to do. Unless God specifically gives me instructions I do what Jesus and the word of God tells me to do. For instance the Scripture tells us to pray, worship, to praise the Lord, to have a thankful heart, to gather together with other believers, to forgive. This list could go on, and on, and on. Simply begin to do what the word of God says and you will begin to experience the voice of God speaking to you in many different ways.

Isaiah 30: 21 and thine ears shall hear a word behind thee, saying, this is the way, walk ye in it, when ye turn to the right hand, and when ye turn to the left.

It is very important that we do not allow our imaginations to run wild with us. I have met many people to the years who declared up-and-down that it was God speaking to them, and no matter what you said you cannot convince them otherwise. In the old covenant the way you perceived whether or not a man was of God was by his fruits, and whether or not the prophetic word he spoke came to pass. That standard is still true today, for the God said I am the Lord and I change not.

Deuteronomy 18:22 when a prophet speaketh in the name of the Lord, if the thing follow not, nor come to pass, that is the thing which the Lord hath not spoken, but the prophet hath spoken it presumptuously: thou shalt not be afraid of him.

If at times we miss the will of God, we must be very quick

to repent otherwise a deceiving spirit will be able to wreak havoc in our lives. I have a simple illustration of this happening in my life at one time, and I believe this story will help you.

I was deceived by the devil

This is a very important story I have to tell. It may not seem important at first but as you read this story, you'll discover that it is. In the spring of 1984, I was really hungry for God, wanting to draw closer to Him. In order to do this, I felt it was necessary for me to get alone with the Lord. So, I asked my wife if she would mind if I rented a room for a week at a rundown motel right down the road from our house; probably about a mile away. She said that would be fine with her and besides, she could visit me anytime that she wanted. With my wife's blessing, I packed up a little suitcase of clothes, got in my car and drove down to the motel to rent a room. After making arrangements, I moved in. In the room I had, there a large TV which I did not want to watch, so I unplugged it and turned the screen towards the wall. Then I sat down with my bible, lexicons, concordances and notepads and began to study and pray. During the coming week, I had determined that I was going to do nothing but pray, seek God's face, fast and deny my flesh.

My motive in this would seem to be right but there was something a little distorted in this quest. You see, I really wanted to hear the voice of God, very precisely and explicitly. Now, you might ask what's wrong with that. At the time I did not realize it, but my motives were all wrong. I was motivated by pride. If the great Dr. Michael Yeager could be used by God using the gifts of knowledge and wisdom, then people would be absolutely stunned with amazement; astounded and dumbfounded as to how God was using me.

You see, I had heard of and read about men that were so precise with their words of knowledge and wisdom that people would sit in complete and utter wonder at their abilities to know their problems and situations. I really, really wanted what they had; all for the glory of God or so I told myself. But in all reality, my endeavor was all about me, me, and me. This is such an easy trap to fall into: to truly believe that our goals are for the glory of God when, in all reality, it is for self.

During my 40 years of ministry plus, I have seen person after person fall into this very trap which had been set for me by the enemy of my soul. Many really and truly believe that they are hearing the voice of God when, in fact, they are listening to familiar spirits. The doorway by which the enemy is coming in is through our hearts filled with pride. I cannot tell you how many times that I have heard people say, "God told me" when it was no more God then there are green, polka-dotted men and black and white striped women living on the moon. I have heard people say, God told me to leave my husband, God told me to leave my wife, God told me to leave my job, God told me that I am Elijah .... etc. etc. etc. This is how all false religions and doctrines begin, by having a spirit of pride wanting to be special or more important than anyone else. It all goes back to the very root of sin, which is me-ism, I, I, I inflated to the utmost degree.

Okay readers, back to the story which I was sharing. So here I was, locked up in this motel room, thinking that I was sincerely seeking the face of God, when actually I was fully motivated by pride. I was doing everything right. I was praying, fasting, reading my bible, memorizing scriptures and getting all pumped up. I absolutely knew the voice of God from almost a decade of walking with Him, but pride had crept in unaware and began to cloud my judgment. What I am sharing with you is extremely important because many well-known men of God have gone astray even, ending up believing that they were Elijah or some other famous prophet.

They heard a voice telling them something that was going to puff up their egos, their self-worth. A lot of the affirmation people are giving and preaching today is simply nothing more than the pumping up of the flesh, which ultimately leads to destruction and death. Our identity does not come from who we are or what we accomplish but who Jesus is in us. "In Christ" realities! It actually frightens me to ponder upon how much pride still dwells in my heart and in the hearts of other ministers, because we can only take people where we are living. If I am egotistical, prideful, self-loving, self-serving and self-centered then that is the only place where I can lead people.

So there I was, about the third day into this endeavor, when early in the afternoon I hear a voice in my mind telling me, "There is a pencil behind the desk." In my mind I saw an image of a long, standard, yellow school pencil with an orange eraser at the top. Oh how my heart got ever so excited thinking that God was going to begin to show me even simple little things. Wow, would people ever be impressed once I came out of this motel room being able to tell them what was even in their pockets. Now, in order for me to get behind this desk, I was going to have to move this very large television from off of it. The first thing that I did was move the chair out of the way, then I grabbed hold of this large, monstrosity of a television set; huffing and puffing, I moved it over to the bed, setting it down onto the mattress. The desk was rather large so I walked to the side of it and grabbed it the best that I could, picking it up on one end and dragging it slowly away from the wall far enough to where I could get behind it. Then, I very excitedly got down on my hands and knees and began to look for this yellow pencil with an orange eraser.

But something was wrong. There was no pencil there. Surely it had to be there because I know the voice of God; I heard it. It was there. It had to be. I kept looking and looking for a very long time. High and low I kept on looking for this pencil that I knew God had showed me was there. I literally had become obsessed with finding this very special pencil because this was the foundation upon which I was going to begin to have a worldwide ministry. All of my success was built upon the fact that I must find that pencil.

All I can say is, thank God that I never did find that pencil! Now, why in the world would I say this? Because if I would have found that pencil, it would not have been the Spirit of God speaking to me but a familiar spirit speaking to and deceiving me. After this incident, I cried out to the Lord asking Him why I could not find that pencil that He showed to me. That's when the

Lord began to speak to me very strongly, revealing to me my haughty and prideful heart. He opened up my understanding to see that many men and women have been completely hornswoggled, deceived, even hoodwinked by the devil through the spirit of pride.

You must always examine your heart in light of scriptures, contrasting it to the nature of Jesus Himself in order to make sure that you are not operating in the wrong spirit. I could share story after story of many women and men I have known whose hearts were filled with pride, arrogance and haughtiness. When this happens, they become extremely argumentative, self-centered and self-loving. They cannot and will not receive correction, even when it's from the Word of God because their hearts have become so hardened through the deceitfulness of the love of self. More times than I can or want to share, I have met people who were listening to the wrong spirits and voices. You could never convince them otherwise. Some of those people had simply become delusional in their own minds, constantly telling people what God has said, yet they displayed little evidence of godliness in their own lives. Such individuals as these will constantly justify the decisions which they have made even though they may be totally and completely contrary to the divine nature of Jesus, the life of Christ or the Word of God. Others have had even more dangerous encounters with such deceiving spirits to the point of hearing voices, having visions and dreaming dreams. Such experiences are of the devil. Appealing to one's vanity and aiming to deceive, he can appear as an angel of light with revelation knowledge that is completely contrary to the Word of God. Every word, deed, thought and action shall one day be judged by God's Word, which is flawless. That is why we must constantly judge our thoughts and our conduct according to God's standard so that we may be blameless and pure on That Day.

I am so glad that I had this ridiculous experience with the pencil because God constantly brings it back to my mind to double check my motives and to make sure that the voice I am listening to is of the Lord. And still, even though I had this experience, I hate to admit that much of my Christianity has been me listening to the wrong voices. How in the world can I say this?

Because I look at what I have poured my life into, the results that it has produced and the fruit that has come from it. I am convinced that most people who say that they know Christ are listening to the wrong voices because the fruit that is being produced is not bringing glory to God. If you really want to hear the still small voice of God, then you need to take the time that is necessary to meditate upon the Scriptures. As you meditate upon the written word, the Holy Spirit will be able to speak to you much clearer.

A Woman fell at my feet weeping!

Through the years I have operated in the word of knowledge. The gift of the word of knowledge is when the Holy Spirit quickens to your heart information of which you have no natural knowledge. The Scriptures declare that we should desire spiritual gifts in order that we can see people set free. In the book of Galatians it declares that the person who ministers to us through the spirit does it by faith. All the gifts of the spirit operate by faith in Christ Jesus. One of the major ways that faith comes is by the written word of God. Faith is when the word of God becomes more real to you than the natural world you live in. The particular Scripture that I decided to meditate on is discovered in first Corinthians chapter 14:

I Corinthians 14:24-25, But if all prophesy , and there come in one that believeth not, or one unlearned, he is convinced of all, he is judged of all: And thus are the secrets of his heart made manifest; and so falling down on his face he will worship God, and report that God is in you of a truth."

I took this particular Scripture and memorized it. Not only did I memorize it, but I meditated on it day and night. I kept speaking it to myself over and over very slowly and passionately. I did this until this Scripture was burning in my heart. It became more real to me than what was around me. This is a major key to the increasing of faith. It is very similar to the development and the building of physical muscles, and so it is with faith. Immediately I began to operate in a more precise word of knowledge.

Here's one illustration. At a midweek service as I was ministering, a lady walked into the back of our church. She was a first-time visitor, who I had never met before. This particular lady looked to be in her 50s. I was just finishing my message when the spirit of God quickened my heart to call her forward. When she came forward to the front of the church, I heard the still small voice of God! I simply repeated what I heard, and out of my mouth came these words, "You have one son, and two daughters. Your one Daughter is married to a man who is physically abusing her. You are in tremendous fear for her life." I began to speak to her in great detail about what was happening in her life and her family.

What is amazing is that when I operate in this realm, I remember very little of what I speak. As I continued to prophesy she began to weep and cry almost uncontrollably, as she literally threw herself to the floor. God brought about an amazing deliverance. She began to proclaim that everything I said was true. And that it was God speaking through me to her in a very precise way. I stood there in amazement as I witnessed first Corinthians 14 being fulfilled in exactly the way that it proclaimed it would, "And thus are the secrets of his heart made manifest; and so falling down on his face he will worship God, and report that God is in you of a truth."

God is not a respecter people, if we would give ourselves to the word of God, meditating upon it day and night, it will surely come to pass! I could write a book on just this particular way that God speaks. This is one of the major ways that I hear the voice of God in my life on a daily basis. It is the will of God for every one of his people to hear his still small voice. As you meditate upon these biblical truths, confessing and agreeing with them, the voice of God will become very clear and precise.

Genesis 3:8 And they heard the voice of the Lord God walking in the garden in the cool of the day: and Adam and his wife hid themselves from the presence of the Lord God amongst the trees of the garden.

CHAPTER THREE

#5 Perceptions

In simple words we can say that Christianity is Christ. Christianity is walking with Christ every day of your life, with every step you take, listening and obeying his voice. I like to explain it this way, God said it was not good for his man - Adam to be alone, so he put the man to sleep. Then he took one of the ribs of Adam and he created a woman. Now, when Adam saw the woman he said: *she is bone of my bone, and flesh my flesh, we shall be one!* God's plan was for that woman to be at the side of Adam at all times. We do not know exactly what happened in the garden, but it seems to me somehow they got separated. The serpent was able to speak to the woman when she was all alone. When we get separated from God, we will get into deep and terrible trouble. We can be easily led astray and deceived in this separation. The woman in the garden is a typology of the bride and the body of Christ in the New Testament. We need to be connected and in communication with the Father at all times.

As we look at the life of Christ the very first words we hear him speak was when he was 12 years old. This Scripture has had a powerful impact on my life for over 40 years. When Mary and Joseph could not find Jesus, they began to search for him high and low. When they finally discovered Jesus in the temple speaking to the priest, they asked him: why have you done this to us, he answered them with an amazing statement.

Luke 2:49 And he said unto them, How is it that ye sought me? wist ye not that I must be about my Father's business?

There is the possibility of being connected to the Father not just spiritually, but mentally, emotionally and physically, 24 hours a day. In the book of Romans it says *if the same spirit that raised*

Christ from the dead dwells you, he will quicken your mortal body. In the old covenant Moses walked with God, and at the age of 120 years old his eyes were not dim, nor was his strength abated. Now, that is the old covenant, so that means there's a possibility of us walking even closer to God then the saints did back then. We are teaching on being led by the spirit of God in every step we take. **For as many as are led by the spirit of God, they are the sons of God.** The Greek word in this Scripture for sons is the Greek word (**huios**) which by definition means mature sons. When we accept Christ, and are born again, we are not instantaneously mature. There must be a desire within us to grow up. This truth is revealed to us in first Corinthians 13.

1 Corinthians 13:11 When I was a child, I spake as a child, I understood as a child, I thought as a child: but when I became a man, I put away childish things. 12 For now we see through a glass, darkly; but then face to face: now I know in part; but then shall I know even as also I am known.

When you begin to walk with God, you begin to hear the voice of God, but it is an ever maturing walk. In this walk you will discover at least 20 ways in which God will speak to you. In order to hear the voice of God though you must want to hear His Voice. You have got to want to be in his will. Your flesh of course will rebel against the will of the Father. You will never be able to be led by the spirit if you do not first crucify your flesh.

Galatians 5: 16 This I say then, Walk in the Spirit, and ye shall not fulfil the lust of the flesh. 17 For the flesh lusteth against the Spirit, and the Spirit against the flesh: and these are contrary the one to the other: so that ye cannot do the things that ye would.

The Scriptures declare that there is a way which seems right unto a man, but the end thereof is death. There is the way of the flesh, the natural, the carnal mind. Then there is the way of the spirit, the quickening of the Holy Ghost. If we walk in the spirit, are led by the spirit, we will not fulfill the lust of the flesh. We overcome the flesh by the spirit of Christ that lives within us. How do we do that? *Submit yourself to God resist the devil and he will flee from you.*

It is extremely important for us to hear from God. The **fifth way** in which God will lead and guide us is by what the Bible calls to **perceive**. If you look up the word perceive in the Scriptures you will discover that it is used over 60 times. If you study this word in Hebrew and Greek, you will discover that it means: to know, to understand, to see. Jesus Christ himself in many situations perceived the thoughts, the intentions, and the purposes of those that were around him. He knew their hearts!

Matthew 16:8 Which when Jesus perceived, he said unto them, O ye of little faith, why reason ye among yourselves, because ye have brought no bread?

Matthew 22:18 But Jesus perceived their wickedness, and said, Why tempt ye me, ye hypocrites?

Mark 2:8 And immediately when Jesus perceived in his spirit that they so reasoned within themselves, he said unto them, Why reason ye these things in your hearts?

Many times by the Holy Ghost I have **perceived** situations in people's lives that I could have never known by the natural. When I use the word perceive, I'm not pertaining to hearing the voice of God with words. It's simply something that I know, that I know, that I know by the Holy Spirit. You could literally say that it is a divine impression in my heart. A holy influence, a holy feeling, or sensation given to you by God. I am not talking about assumptions or presumptions.

If there is pride, bitterness or judgmental attitudes in your hearts you will be easily led astray with impressions, feelings, sensations which are simply demonic assumptions or presumptions. I have met people through the years that dogmatically declared that what they had heard about somebody was of God. When the truth was revealed, it was discovered that it was not God at all, but it was from their own critical fault finding and judgmental attitudes. It is so vitally important that we keep our hearts right with the Lord at all times. That we are motivated and lead with compassion (love in action) for God and others. I could give you hundreds of examples when I have perceived by the Holy Ghost about certain situations. Time will not permit this though, so let me simply give you one illustration.

Prodigal Son Coming Home

One day I was in downtown Gettysburg, taking care of some business. As I was walking across the square, I looked over to the other side of the square and immediately the Spirit caused me to look at a tall African-American man. The minute I put my eyes upon him, I **perceived** by the Spirit that God wanted me to go speak to this particular man. I'm not saying that I was guessing, or I was thinking, or I was assuming. I just knew that I needed to go talk to him right now. At that moment I did not have any idea what I was going to say to him. I just knew, that I knew, that I knew I was to go speak to him.

That's how the Spirit of God leads, and guides, one baby step at a time. As you obey this divine perception, God will take care of the rest. As I walked up to him, the word of the Lord came to me. He was standing there minding his own business, so I stepped right in front of him. When I had his attention, I looked up into his face. This particular man was over 6 feet tall, and I'm only 5'8" and so my head was cranked back pretty far. I looked him in the eyes and I told him that he was a backslidden preacher, that he was a Jonah. I told him that the Lord had revealed to me that God was calling him to come back to the work of the Lord in order to fulfill his calling. That God was not yet done with him. When I spoke these words to him his countenance completely changed. I could see complete shock fill his eyes. Immediately tears began to cascade down his cheeks. He began to audibly cry out loud, throwing his hands up into the air towards heaven. Yes, right there in downtown Gettysburg at the square.

This was the first and last time I have ever seen this man. As I left him, he was standing there on the square of Gettysburg with his hands lifted high towards heaven. He was weeping and praising the Lord. This all began by simply having a deep perception, impression of the spirit of the Lord that I was to go and speak to this particular man. This is one way how God leads and guides. One baby step after another.

The **fifth way** that we are teaching on how God speaks to us is by **perceiving** something in your heart. It is not coming from your head, or guessing, assuming, or being suspicious. By the spirit of the Lord you just know, that you know, that you know. This actually is also how all your prayers are answered. When faith is active in your heart you will simply know, that you know, that it is done.

Mark 11:23 For verily I say unto you, That whosoever shall say unto this mountain, Be thou removed, and be thou cast into the sea; and shall not doubt in his heart, but shall believe that those things which he saith shall come to pass; he shall have whatsoever he saith. 24 Therefore I say unto you, What things soever ye desire, when ye pray, believe that ye receive them, and ye shall have them.

You will discover that as you **perceived** by the spirit of God some event or truth, that the gift of faith will also be in operation with this **perception**. On many occasions when I **perceived** something by the Holy Ghost, the faith was also there to see it performed. Here is one example of this happening as I was preaching in a tent at the Huntington fair.

An Unbelieving Man Healed

One day as I was preaching in a tent, a man who looked to be in his mid-thirties was hobbling by really slow on a pair of crutches. He was not even looking in the direction of our tent, but was looking straight ahead, minding his own business. As I looked at him, I **perceived** by the Spirit of God that the Lord would heal him right now if he would come up for prayer. At the same time the gift of faith rose up inside of me. When God quickens my heart in this way I do not even think what I'm about to do. I simply act upon this quickening and the witness in my heart. When I use the word **perceive**, I am talking about knowing that I know what God wants to do. It is not coming from my head, but up out of my heart.

In this particular situation I found myself calling out to this particular man who was walking by very slowly on his crutches. I kept calling out to him over the loudspeaker system. Everybody could hear me within a hundred feet, if not further. Probably the whole Huntington Fair could hear me as I called out to him! (Actually the fire department was really upset with us because we were disturbing their bingo games.) When I first called out to this man he completely ignored me. Over and over I challenged him to come into the tent so God could heal him. He finally looked my way but kept hobbling along. I called out to him again, encouraging him to come and be healed of his problem.

After repeatedly calling him, he finally responded, and came hobbling into the tent. When he came to the front, I asked him if he had faith to believe that God would heal him. He looked at me as if I had lost my mind. He probably was thinking, you're the one who kept calling me up here. I don't even know what this is all about. Everybody was staring at me, so I had to come! He did not respond to my question. I told him that I was going to pray for him now and God would heal him! I perceived this by the spirit of God, and by the gift of faith that was operating in me at that time. I asked him again if he believed that God would heal him when I prayed. Once again he did not respond. I laid my hands on him and commanded him to be healed In the name of Jesus Christ of Nazareth.

After I was done praying, I told him to put down his crutches and to start walking without them. He stood there staring at me. Everybody else was also staring at me. This was okay because the gift of faith was at work in my heart. I reached forward and took away his crutches. I threw them on the ground and spun him around. When I'm in this realm I'm not thinking, I'm simply acting. Then I pushed him on the back with my hands. He stumbled forward with his legs jerking unsteadily, but then he began to walk normally toward the back of the tent. He was picking his legs high up in the air, and high stepping it. When he got to the edge of the tent he spun back toward me. Tears were now streaming from his eyes and down his cheeks. He came back toward me walking perfectly normal with no limp whatsoever!

I gave him the microphone, and asked him to tell us what had just happened to him. He kept saying, "You don't understand" over and over. Once again, I encouraged him to tell us his story. I had him face the people in that tent and those outside of it who had been watching. He told us that last winter he had been walking on a very icy sidewalk and he lost his footing. Slipping and sliding, he fell forward onto the concrete and ice. He fell down so hard on his right kneecap that he knew that he had done something terrible to it. He could not move his knee whatsoever, and it was extremely painful. He went to the doctor's office and they did x-rays. The x-rays revealed that his kneecap had literally been shattered and destroyed. In just two more days he was scheduled to have a major operation to replace his kneecap.

I encouraged him to go back to his doctor and get x-rays again. Sure enough, a couple days later he came back to the tent filled with great joy and giving a wonderful testimony. He had gone to his doctor. He said when he walked into the doctor's office they could tell that he was walking normal. The doctor asked him what had happened. He told them about the encounter he had with Jesus at our tent meeting. They did an x-ray his kneecap and discovered he had a brand-new kneecap! God had completely healed him. How did God do this? First there had to be a man who was so yielded and surrendered to the spirit of God that the Lord could speak to him. That once God spoke to him, he would respond in obedience no matter how it looked, or what people thought. This is how almost every miracle happens. Hearing the voice of God and obeying what the Lord is speaking.

Now there are well-known men that teach us that we should pray only one time, for those things which we desire. That actually is a biblical principle IF the conditions are met. One of the main conditions is that you **must believe** that when you pray, you have **received**. When do you receive? The minute you pray and believed you received. If as a believer you prayed and you did not believe that you received, then you need to keep praying until you believe that you receive. If when you prayed, you did believe that you received, but somehow the enemy has been able to get you to stop believing that you have received, then you need to pray again. Faith is knowing that when you prayed, God has heard your prayers. Now, because he has heard your prayers, you have received the petitions you have asked of him, because you know you are in his will.

Mark 11:24 Therefore I say unto you, What things soever ye desire, when ye pray, believe that ye receive them, and ye shall have them. 25 And when ye stand praying, forgive, if ye have ought against any: that your Father also which is in heaven may forgive you your trespasses.

1 John 5:14 And this is the confidence that we have in him, that, if we ask any thing according to his will, he heareth us: 15 and if we know that he hear us, whatsoever we ask, we know that we have the petitions that we desired of him.

We need to go back and meditate upon the truth of what God's word says, dealing with what we are asking for. Faith becomes alive as the word takes upon flesh and blood within our hearts. God has so many wonderful blessings for us, if we can simply believe that we receive them by faith.

1 Corinthians 2: 9 But as it is written, Eye hath not seen, nor ear heard, neither have entered into the heart of man, the things which God hath prepared for them that love him. 10 But God hath revealed them unto us by his Spirit: for the Spirit searcheth all things, yea, the deep things of God.

The deep things of God are not revealed to us by our physical eyes, from our head, or our physical ears, but it is given to us by God's Divine Spirit. The spirit is speaking directly to our spirit revealing, showing, opening our eyes to the divine supernatural realm of God's kingdom. Now the carnal mind cannot understand the things of God, for they are spirit, and spiritually discerned. For instance many times I know, that I know, that I know, I am healed.

This is a reality that is in my heart given to me by the spirit of God. Even though my flesh is telling me that I'm not healed, even though the natural says I'm not, I just simply know that I am. You might say that I **perceive** that I am healed. When you get right down to it: Faith is simply when you have heard the voice of God, And now his voice has become more real to you than the situation you have found yourself in.

If you look up the word **perceive** or **perceived** you'll discover that it is used many times in the Bible. Throughout the Scriptures it says they perceived, or he perceived, or she perceived. Here are some examples.

Luke 6:41 (KJV)And why beholdest thou the mote that is in thy brother's eye, but perceivest not the beam that is in thine own eye?

Luke 8:46 (KJV)And Jesus said, Somebody hath touched me: for I perceive that virtue is gone out of me.

John 6:15 (KJV)When Jesus therefore perceived that they would come and take him by force, to make him a king, he departed again into a mountain himself alone.

Pastor Mike how do you know what you **perceived** was really of God? Because **number one**, it will never contradict the known will of God. **Number two**, it will never contradict his divine nature. **Number three**, there will be concrete evidence or you could say absolute proof, that you heard from heaven as you act upon what you **perceived**. The old saying is: the proof is in the eating of the pudding. If you are really hearing from God it will be manifested before everything is said and done. Through the years I have heard some well-known speakers make certain prophetic declarations. I've always watched to see if they came to pass, because that is the proof of whether or not they are really hearing from God. I am sorry to say that I have seen people prophesy about certain men that would become president, and it never happened. That is the evidence that what they proclaimed God told them, was not in fact really of God at all.

Please do not misunderstand me, I personally have missed God at times. When you miss God the first thing you should do is admit it. If you proclaimed something in the public, then you need to repent, and acknowledge it in public that you missed God. If you do not follow this process, then you will be subject to being even more deceived. The **fourth way** in which you can determine if you're hearing from God is your past record of success. What I mean by this is that we should be able to look at your track record? What is the percentage of your fulfillment's in that which you have proclaiming you have heard from God? If you are consistently stating that God has spoken to you about certain situations, but there is no real substantial evidence, then you need to go before the Lord and find out what is going on in your heart. One obvious problem could be that you are not being led, guided, motivated and compelled by God's divine love. If we are not moving in the realm of agape love, we are operating in the wrong kind of spirit.

This particular book is committed to teaching, revealing and sharing the 20 different ways in which God speaks to us. Now, we know that there are many different colors in the natural world. Did you know the total number of colors the human eye can see is about $1000 \times 100 \times 100 = 10,000,000$ (10 million). A computer alone displays about 16.8 million colors to create full color pictures. All of these colors were created by God himself. In our human mind we have limited God to such a small dimension, that it edges on the realm of insanity. We need to understand that God speaks to us in many ways and yet it's the one and same spirit.

1 Corinthians 12:7 But the manifestation of the Spirit is given to every man to profit withal. 8 For to one is given by the Spirit the word of wisdom; to another the word of knowledge by the same Spirit; 9 to another faith by the same Spirit; to another the gifts of healing by the same Spirit;

The gifts of the spirit all operate basically upon the reality of us hearing from heaven. One of the greatest needs in the body of Christ today is for people to hear the voice of God very clearly. We need to hear from heaven! Now, I'm not seeking to hear the voice of God, I am simply seeking God, and at the same time I am believing he will speak to me. Everything I am teaching in this book happens because we are living, moving, functioning and walking by faith.

Galatians 3:5 He therefore that ministereth to you the Spirit, and worketh miracles among you, doeth he it by the works of the law, or by the hearing of faith?

I simply believe I can hear from God. Most of the time my problem is not that I can't hear from God, but my lack of determination to obey his voice. This is one of the major problems in the heart of man. When Adam sinned, he ran from the voice of God. When there is sin in our lives, it will cause us to run away from the voice of God, right into the arms of the devil. All of man's problems are rooted in the fact that we do not want to listen to what God is telling us. The minute we hear the voice of God we need to obey it with all of our heart.

Genesis 3:8 And they heard the voice of the Lord God walking in the garden in the cool of the day: and Adam and his wife hid themselves from the presence of the Lord God amongst the trees of the garden.

Genesis 3:10 And he said, I heard thy voice in the garden, and I was afraid, because I was naked; and I hid myself.

Hearing the voice of God will not help at all you if you are not willing to crucify your flesh. The flesh must be crucified in order to follow our shepherd and our Lord Jesus Christ. When you are truly following God you're not doing your own thing, you're not going your own way, and you no longer belong to yourself. We must become his and his alone. Jesus said that if you are my sheep, you will hear my voice, and follow me. Jesus said: Why do you call me Lord, Lord, and do not what I say? If we pick up the Bible, read it, but we do not do it, we have deceived ourselves.

James 1:22 But be ye doers of the word, and not hearers only, deceiving your own selves.

Now David **perceived** that the Lord had established him king over Israel. The word **perceive** means to realize, to understand, to see, to know. We **perceive** this by the eyes of our heart, the eyes of our understanding.

Ephesians 1: 18 the eyes of your understanding being enlightened; that ye may know what is the hope of his calling, and what the riches of the glory of his inheritance in the saints, 19 and what is the exceeding greatness of his power to us-ward who believe, according to the working of his mighty power.

David did not assume or guess that he was going to be King, he knew or you could say he **perceived** it in his heart. Many times I knew things in my heart before I ever saw the end results. There have been times when I went to pray for people in the hospital and I knew in my heart that they were going to get healed right then and there. I would like to encourage you to study the Scriptures with the word **perceive** or **perceived**. For instance in Nehemiah chapter 6:12 it reveals a situation where Nehemiah **perceived** that the message from a certain man was not of God.

Nehemiah 6:12 And, lo, I perceived that God had not sent him; but that he pronounced this prophecy against me: for Tobiah and Sanballat had hired him.

I cannot tell you the number of times the Lord has protected us from people who came with their own agendas. Through the years I have **perceived** certain realities about people and situations by the spirit of God. By this divine way of God speaking to me, he has kept and preserved my life, my family, the churches I have pastored, and the ministry he has placed me in. This divine way in which God leads is not just for me, but every true and sincere believer. Paul gives us a wonderful illustration of this happening in his life in the book of acts.

Acts 27:10 (KJV) And said unto them, Sirs, I perceive that this voyage will be with hurt and much damage, not only of the lading and ship, but also of our lives.

If you would go to the book of acts and read about this account, you will discover that they did not listen to the warnings of Paul. Now, because they did not listen to the voice of Paul, what he **perceived** by the spirit of God, they lost the ship with all of its cargo. Many believers' lives have been destroyed because they did not listen and obey the voice of God. You will actually hear people say after the fact that they knew in their heart that something was wrong, or what they were about to do was wrong. Yet they refuse to listen to what the Spirit of God was trying to tell them. I am sorry to say that I have experienced this in my own life on numerous occasions. Sometimes our hearts have become so hard because of our own selfish agendas that God just cannot get through to us.

Job 33:14 For God speaketh once, yea twice, yet man perceiveth it not.

When the Scripture says that the person doesn't **perceive**, it means he doesn't grasp it, he cannot hear it, he doesn't see what God is trying to show or tell him. All of us have experienced this problem in our life, not just us but even the disciples of Jesus.

Matthew 16:5 And when his disciples were come to the other side, they had forgotten to take bread. 6 Then Jesus said unto them, Take heed and beware of the leaven of the Pharisees and of the Sadducees. 7 And they reasoned among themselves, saying, It is because we have taken no bread. 8 Which when Jesus perceived, he said unto them, O ye of little faith, why reason ye among yourselves, because ye have brought no bread? 9 Do ye not yet understand, neither remember the five loaves of the five thousand, and how many baskets ye took up? 10 Neither the seven loaves of the four thousand, and how many baskets ye took up? 11 How is it that ye do not understand that I spake it not to you concerning bread, that ye should beware of the leaven of the Pharisees and of the Sadducees?

What is amazing is that the disciples did not **perceive** the miracle of Christ multiplying the fish and the loaves. Having eyes, they saw not, having ears they heard not. There are many examples of this throughout the Scriptures. In Deuteronomy it tells us that they did not **perceive** the miracles that God performed among the Egyptians, neither did they **perceive** the obvious miracles of protection and provision God performed for them in the wilderness.

Deuteronomy 29:3 the great temptations which thine eyes have seen, the signs, and those great miracles: 4 yet the Lord hath not given you an heart to perceive, and eyes to see, and ears to hear, unto this day. 5 And I have led you forty years in the wilderness: your clothes are not waxen old upon you, and thy shoe is not waxen old upon thy foot.

The heart can be so hardened by the deceitfulness of sin, that we do not see that which is absolutely obvious. We must cry out with all of our hearts that God will give us eyes to see, ears to hear, and hearts to receive. It is even as the Scripture declares: the blind leading the blind. Through the years I have seen God touch many people supernaturally. He healed them of incurable diseases. He put back together their broken and wounded hearts and marriages. He saved and rescued thousands of them, yet sad to say most of them went back to the world. I have a sense of urgency in my heart that we are running out of time. That if we are ever going to do anything for God, we must do it now. The signs of the time are everywhere, and yet people do not **perceive** that we are at the end of the ages. I cannot tell you how many times I have met people, and the Lord spoke to me about them, and their situations.

Saw by the Spirit He Was a Pedophile

I have a house where I rent at a very low price to single men. These men are either on assistance, getting out of jail, or even homeless. My whole purpose is to help them get back on their feet, or to help them assimilate back into society. Now to rent from me, there are certain criteria that you have to meet. My house is in a residential area so I never rent to anybody who I would consider a danger to the community. There was an older gentleman who came to me who wanted to rent a room. I **perceived** in my heart that he was a pedophile. I asked him straight out if he was on Megan's list or if he had ever committed a sexual crime! He assured me that he was not on Megan's list; neither had he ever committed a sexual crime. Once again I asked him very bluntly. He very energetically declared that no, he had never committed a sexual crime. I should have gone with that which I had **perceived** by the Spirit of God. Sometimes our natural thinking kicks in, and the enemy blinds us.

Now we also had a house that was close to our church that we would rent rooms to those who seem to be hungry for God. This older gentleman wanted to attend our church and move down to this house to be close to the church. Something in my heart was not enthusiastic about this man moving upon the church's property. In spite of the red flags, I set up an appointment for him to come and look at one of the rooms that we had available. When he arrived at our property my son Daniel was standing there with me. The minute he saw this gentleman, Dan became extremely upset. I told this man to go ahead into the house and I would be with him in a minute.

I asked my son what was wrong. He said, "Dad: I just had a vision of this man!"(This is one way that God speaks to us) I said: "Okay, tell me what you saw." He said, "Dad: this man is a pedophile!" I said, "Dan you've got to be wrong." I told him that I also had **perceived** there was something wrong with him in this area, but I told my son that I had already asked him repeatedly point-blank if he was on Megan's list, or if he had ever messed around with children. He very vocally declared that he had not. Dan told me that he had an open vision, and in this open vision, he saw this man chasing a little girl who was around six years old.

My son Daniel continued to insist that what he saw was of God, and I needed to check it out. I told him: okay, let me go talk to him. I went into the house where this man was looking at one of the rooms. I came right out and said to him, "Harvey I asked you before if you had ever committed a sexual crime, or if you were on Megan's list. You need to tell me the truth right now. I am asking you again: have you ever committed a sexual crime?" He hung his head down, and whispered: I lied, I do have a record of committing

73

a sexual crime.

Because of my sons open vision I asked him: who was it? With his head hung down, he said: my six-year-old niece. Now you might say, Pastor isn't there forgiveness for sexual crimes? Yes there is! But from my experience of almost forty years of pastoring, there is such a strong demonic spirit involved in this act, that unless a person truly repents with all of their heart, and cries out to God for complete deliverance, they never get free. Yes we forgive, but we must also protect our loved ones. May God give us spiritual discernment!

Operating in the Gift of SUSPICION!

First we need to understand that a lot of so-called Christians are operating in the realm of suspicion, assumptions and gossip. If you are constantly filling your mind with TV, secular news, worldly entertainment, and education that is not based upon biblical principles, it will be almost impossible for you to hear correctly from the spirit of God. God says that the theology of this worldly system is an abomination to him.

Luke 16:15 And he said unto them, Ye are they which justify yourselves before men; but God knoweth your hearts: for that which is highly esteemed among men is abomination in the sight of God.

What we are constantly filling our mind and our heart with has an overwhelming effect upon whether or not we can hear clearly from heaven.

Proverbs 23:7 for as he thinketh in his heart, so is he:

There are many today in the modern church who simply do not want to let go of their sins. Jesus said:

Mark 4:12 that seeing they may see, and not perceive; and hearing they may hear, and not understand; lest at any time they should be converted, and their sins should be forgiven them.

It is like hearing talking on the radio but there is so much static that is difficult to understand what they're saying. I run into some so-called Christians who are so dogmatic and accusative about others, yet they themselves are also just as guilty, if not even more guilty than the person that they are accusing and attacking. They are full of pride, full of arrogance, bitterness pours out of them like sewage out of a sewage pipe. People like that are so full of themselves that they are completely blind to their own desperate spiritual need. This is like the Pharisees who caught the woman in adultery. They wanted to kill her in her sins, even though they themselves were full of sin.

Matthew 7:4 Or how wilt thou say to thy brother, Let me pull out the mote out of thine eye; and, behold, a beam is in thine own eye?:5 Thou hypocrite, first cast out the beam out of thine own eye; and then shalt thou see clearly to cast out the mote out of thy brother's eye.

Psalm 25:9 The meek will he guide in judgment: and the meek will he teach his way.

James 4:11 Speak not evil one of another, brethren. He that speaketh evil of his brother, and judgeth his brother, speaketh evil of the law, and judgeth the law: but if thou judge the law, thou art not a doer of the law, but a judge. 12 There is one lawgiver, who is able to save and to destroy: who art thou that judgest another?

God had me Fly 1st class to prevent Death & Destruction!

I was going back to visit relatives in the lower 48, flying out from Anchorage Alaska. When I went to the airline check-in counter, I had no intentions of buying a first-class ticket. To me it was just a waste of money, but as I was standing at the counter this overwhelming unction, a divine perception rose up within my heart to fly home first-class. I perceived, just knew that I knew for some strange reason I was to fly first class. Now a First-class ticket of course is much more expensive than an economy ticket, but thank

God I did have the money. I was not dressed to fly 1st class, seeing that I had just left Dillingham Alaska, with only the clothes on my back, and what I had in a backpack. I had been doing missionary work among the Yupik Indians.

As they were boarding us onto the plane, a 747, they were looking at our ticket stubs. The stewardess began to direct me to those who were flying economy. I informed her that actually I had a first-class ticket. She looked at me like maybe I had lost my mind. I had to double check the ticket, and sure enough it was first-class. Back in those days' people did not dress like hobos with holes in their pants when they flew first-class. People today dress in whatever way they like, and no one thinks anything about it. She grudgingly let me go past her into the 1st class section. One of the stewardesses, whose main job was to cater to the first-class, looked at me as I walked up to her with my ticket extended from my hand. Her look spoke a thousand words, as if to say "What are you doing here you ragamuffin?"

After she looked at my ticket, she directed me to my seat. I had never flown first-class so I really did not know what the seating arrangement would be. Most aisles had four chairs in each row. Two to the left, and two to the right. But where I was directed there was only two chairs, one to the left, where the stewardess sat me down, and one to my right. Now remember this was back in 1976, so first-class is completely different now than it was then. In front of me was nothing but the bulkhead of the plane. I was literally sitting in the nose of this plane. I thought to myself, if this is first-class, it sure is not worth the money I'm paying.

After the plane was completely boarded, I discovered that there was nobody to my right. This particular seat was empty. I remember thinking something is not right, maybe I should not have bought first-class? We were headed to O'Hare airport in Chicago directly from Anchorage Alaska. It was an approximately 6 ½ hour flight. I settled down for a comfortable flight, taking a nap and reading my Bible.

We finally arrived at our final destination, but for some reason the plane was not landing. Actually they had put us into a holding pattern, and we simply kept on flying around.

After what seemed to be a long time, the pilot of the plane came over the loudspeaker, informing us that there had been a technical problem. They had been trying to fix it, but with no success. They informed us that the front landing gear would not lock in place. I remember hearing the landing gear (which was right below me for the front wheel) kept on clunking and making loud noises. They were lifting it and lowering it over and over trying to get it to lock into place. Now imagine this, this is the 1st time I have ever flown first-class, and here I was sitting in the nose of the 747, with the front landing gear not locking in. The pilot informed us that we were going to have to land. There was no other options.

As he was speaking, the Spirit of God spoke to my heart. He said to me in a still small voice: "This is why you are flying 1st class right over the top of the front nose landing gear and wheel! You need to stand upon the word of God, and take authority over this situation, in order to preserve the lives of those on this plane!" I could hardly believe my spiritual ears! I said: "Really Lord?" "Yes." He instructed me to begin to pray that the front landing gear would not collapse, even though it would not be locked in place.

Since that time I have researched this situation and from my research I have discovered that if the front nose landing gear goes out, you are in big trouble, especially on a 747. From all my research it would seem that with the 747 full of people, the pressure on the front nose gear and wheel would be approximately 90,000 pounds, with the weight of the plane and the pressure of our forward motion. Approximately 9% of the whole weight of the plane would be on that wheel. The 747 weighs almost 1 million pounds fully loaded. Now that is some serious weight, and if that nose wheel collapsed, the nose of that 747 would be eating nothing but asphalt, concrete, and ground.

I quietly began to cry out to the Lord for our safe landing. I took authority over the devil and all the demonic powers behind this potential terrible tragedy. I commanded the landing gear to stay in place. There was absolutely no fear in my heart, nothing but peace, knowing now that God had put me there on purpose, not to be destroyed, but to speak his word over this situation.

As we came in for the landing, with all the landing gears extended, the flaps completely down, I could see the fire trucks and the rescue trucks, and ambulances all lined up waiting for the plane to crash. The pilot brought the speed of the 747 to the very edge of its stalling speed, with all the weight we had on board is approximately 160 miles an hour. The back wheels touched down, with the pilot trying to keep the front wheels of the nose off the ground as long as he could. Finally the front landing wheel hit the concrete. You could feel the tension on the plane, and I'm sure there was a lot of people praying.

Thank God the landing gear held! As the plane finally came to a stop, everybody was filled with great joy over our safe landing, never realizing that God had put at least one person in first-class, right over the top of the landing gear in order to stop the enemy from killing or destroy all the precious lives on that plane. Will I ever fly 1st class again? Only if God quickens my heart and tells me that it is necessary!

Matthew 22:18 But Jesus perceived their wickedness, and said, Why tempt ye me, ye hypocrites? [21] They say unto him, Caesar's. Then saith he unto them, Render therefore unto Caesar the things which are Caesar's; and unto God the things that are God's.

Mark 4:12 That seeing they may see, and not perceive; and hearing they may hear, and not understand; lest at any time they should be converted, and their sins should be forgiven them.

1 John 3:16 Here by perceive we the love of God, because he laid down his life for us: and we ought to lay down our lives for the brethren.

#6 Audible

Do you know that even sinners hear the voice of God? First they hear the voice of God by their conscience. Every human is born alive unto the voice of God. Sinners also hear God's voice whenever they hear preaching, or singing about the gospel on radio, TV stations, or when they read tracks, books, or even fliers that people hand out. Many times when unbelievers turn off programs where the Gospels is being preached, they do not realize it, but they are turning their backs on the voice of God. God is speaking to the human race through the Bible, God inspired literature, music, and preaching.

Now the **sixth way** I would like to share with you on how God speaks to us is a little bit more radical. It is literally the **audible** voice of God. The Scriptures declare that God never changes, and that if he ever did it once, he'll do it again.

Malachi 3:6 For I am the Lord, I change not; therefore ye sons of Jacob are not consumed.

In the book of Genesis when the Lord first created man, he would walk and talk with him in the garden. I believe Adam and his wife heard and communicated with God, as he spoke with them in an audible voice, face-to-face.

Genesis 2:16 And the Lord God commanded the man, saying, Of every tree of the garden thou mayest freely eat.

Adam and his wife literally heard the **audible** voice of the Lord as he called out to them. This transpired right after they had partaken of the forbidden fruit, from the tree of the knowledge of good and evil.
Genesis 3:8 And they heard the voice of the Lord God walking in

the garden in the cool of the day: and Adam and his wife hid themselves from the presence of the Lord God amongst the trees of the garden.

Genesis 3:10 And he said, I heard thy voice in the garden, and I was afraid, because I was naked; and I hid myself.

I believe that they heard God with their physical ears. Not only can God speak to us through our physical ears, but he can reveal himself to us physically in the flesh and blood world. Has God ever physically touched you by the Holy Ghost? What I mean by this is has he ever in some way or fashion manifested himself in some physical, mental or emotional way in your life? In over 40 years of ministry I have seen God physically touched many people. He will touch you and me in the physical world because he is a spirit, and he created the physical world! In order to understand how and why God speaks to people audibly we need to take a look at some of the biblical historical examples. One of the amazing examples we can use is revealed to us in the book of acts, when God spoke to Saul on the road to Damascus.

Acts 9:3 And as he journeyed, he came near Damascus: and suddenly there shined round about him a light from heaven: 4 and he fell to the earth, and heard a voice saying unto him, Saul, Saul, why persecutest thou me? 5 And he said, Who art thou, Lord? And the Lord said, I am Jesus whom thou persecutest: it is hard for thee to kick against the pricks.

In Acts 26 Paul not only reveals that God spoke to him audibly, but that he spoke to him in the Hebrew language.

Acts 26:14 And when we were all fallen to the earth, I heard a voice speaking unto me, and saying in the Hebrew tongue, Saul, Saul, why persecutest thou me? it is hard for thee to kick against the pricks.

I have heard the voice of God many times in dreams and visions, but I have also heard the **audible** voice of God on numerous occasions. Please understand that I was not expecting or seeking for God to speak to me in an **audible** voice, in the physical flesh and blood world. If you seek for such an experience, you will open the door to the devil deceiving you. We do not seek these experiences, we seek God.

Gods audible voice said, "You're a Dead Man!"

I was driving into Mount Union, Pennsylvania with my wife to do some grocery shopping. I was driving a 1976 sport Ford Granada with a 302 Engine. The urge came to me to put the pedal to the metal and let it roar. The Lord had already delivered me from speeding years ago, but at that moment it was as if I allowed a devil to take over me. I willingly gave in to this urge as I mashed down the gas pedal, all the way to the metal and began to increase my speed. Yes, I knew better, but I caved and gave into temptation. My wife looked over at me just shaking her head. (Someone else was watching our newborn son Michael so he was not with us.)

I ended up accelerating to over 80 miles per hour. Kathleen was praying out loud that if we had an accident, she would not be hurt because of my stupidity and then she began to pray faster in the spirit. I was coming around the corner on Route 747 right before you enter into Mount Union when I heard the **audible voice of God** say to me, **"You are a Dead Man!"** Instantly the fear of the Lord hit me like a sledgehammer. The voice of God and the fear of God went right to the very marrow of my bones. Instantly I knew that I was in real big trouble.I saw just ahead of me a stop sign to the left and to the right. At that very moment, I slammed on the brakes of my car, instantly slowing down. As I came almost to a complete stop a flash of white flashed past my left to the right. I mean right then and there I saw a totally white, souped-up Dodge charger come speeding through the stop sign from the left.He ran the stop sign without stopping or slowing up in the least. I mean he really had the pedal to the metal.

I'm convinced he must have been going over 80 miles an hour. If I would not have slammed on my brakes exactly when I heard the audible voice of God, his car would have slammed right into my driver's side door. There is no doubt in my mind or my heart that I would have been instantly killed. Thank God he still speaks to us today. Thank God for his long-suffering and mercy never ends.

Now you might ask: why would God have spoken to you **audibly**? I believe it was the only way he could spare my life in this situation. Notice I was not seeking for God to speak to me **audibly**, he simply did this out of his love, and mercy, even though I was completely out of his will.

Saul of Tarsus physically heard the **audible** voice of God speaking to him. What better way is there for God to get your attention? I believe that we are about to see an increase of God's supernatural, divine interventions, revealing himself to a lot more people as we get closer to the end of the ages. Do not think for a moment that God is going to leave this world without revealing himself to humanity? The whole book of Revelation is God speaking to the human race to repent and come back to him.

When Moses went before Pharaoh and he threw down his rod, it became a snake. This rod swallowed up the snakes that Pharaoh's magicians had conjured up. This was God speaking to the nation of Egypt. When the Nile River was turned to blood, or the Red Sea was divided in half, this was God speaking to that generation. I believe that all of these amazing miracles that God did in Egypt, for that generation, is but a glimpse of what he is about to do in our generation. In the book of Revelation it reveals to us that there will be two prophets that God will raise up in order to reveal his power to the human race.

Revelation 11:4 These are the two olive trees, and the two candlesticks standing before the God of the earth. 5 And if any man will hurt them, fire proceedeth out of their mouth, and devoureth their enemies: and if any man will hurt them, he must in this manner be killed. 6 These have power to shut heaven that it rain not in the days of their prophecy: and have power over waters to turn them to blood, and to smite the earth with all plagues, as often as they will.
Many times in the Old Covenant we see where the prophets

literally heard the **audible** voice of God. When God came down upon Mount Sinai and began to speak to the children of Israel, they heard voices and trumpets proceeding from the mountaintop.

Exodus 19:16 And it came to pass on the third day in the morning, that there were thunders and lightnings, and a thick cloud upon the mount, and the voice of the trumpet exceeding loud; so that all the people that was in the camp trembled.....:19 And when the voice of the trumpet sounded long, and waxed louder and louder, Moses spake, and God answered him by a voice.

The voice of God frightened the people to such a degree to where they said Moses: You talk to God for us, we do not want to talk to Him. Many believers have a hard time hearing from God because they have never renewed their minds. They are constantly filling their heads with other voices other than the voice of God's word, or his will. God is talking all the time, but believers cannot hear him because they are listening to their flesh. They are listening to their emotions, they are listening to the circumstances, to the world, to the opinions of people when they should be listening to God! We need to be following Jesus, his word, his will, and his purposes. Paul the apostle said follow me, as I follow Christ.

If the preacher or minister is taking you in the wrong direction, you're going to end up at the wrong location. I'm sorry to say that there are a lot of preachers taking people straight to hell with them! If your minister is not going after Jesus, then you need to stop following him or her. What gets between us and the voice of God is basically only one thing, and it is a five letter word that is spelled F.L.E.S.H! Flesh will always try to get between us and God. Now you can insulate the walls, the ceiling, and the floor of a room so well to where you cannot hear any outside noise. This is to some extent what happened to man after he committed sin. He became so insulated with F.L.E.S.H. that it is almost impossible for the spirit of God to get through to him. God is trying to get through our flesh to reach us with his voice.

Job 33:14 For God speaketh once, yea twice, yet man perceiveth it not.15 In a dream, in a vision of the night,when deep sleep falleth upon men, in slumberings upon the bed;

God had to manifest himself in such an amazing way that Saul of Tarsus would finally hear his voice. Yet he told Saul: it is hard for you to kick against the pricks! It is obvious that God had been dealing with this heart before this visitation, and yet Saul's heart was so hard that he could not perceive that it was God speaking to him. God finally spoke to him in an **audible** voice to wake him up. When Jesus was baptized in the river Jordan by John the Baptist, God spoke in an **audible** voice for all to hear. When he was transfigured before James, John, and Peter, God once again spoke with an **audible** voice.

Matthew 3:16 And Jesus, when he was baptized, went up straightway out of the water: and, lo, the heavens were opened unto him, and he saw the Spirit of God descending like a dove, and lighting upon him: 17 and lo a voice from heaven, saying, This is my beloved Son, in whom I am well pleased.

Matthew 17:4 Then answered Peter, and said unto Jesus, Lord, it is good for us to be here: if thou wilt, let us make here three tabernacles; one for thee, and one for Moses, and one for Elias. 5 While he yet spake, behold, a bright cloud overshadowed them: and behold a voice out of the cloud, which said, This is my beloved Son, in whom I am well pleased; hear ye him. 6 And when the disciples heard it, they fell on their face, and were sore afraid.

Whenever God speaks with an **audible** voice the first thing that will be evident is a great shaking on the inside of the person that hears his voice. This is actually one way in which God fills our hearts with faith. Numerous times when the Lord has spoken to me in an audible voice, the fear of God, and the faith of God exploded on the inside of me. Now some of the people said that what they heard was thunder. Did you know that the Scripture literally says in the book of Job that thunder is the **audible** voice of God? *Job 37:4 After it a voice roareth: he thundereth with the voice of* *his excellency; and he will not stay them when his voice is heard.:5 God thundereth marvellously with his voice; great things doeth he, which we cannot comprehend.*

Job 38:25 Who hath divided a watercourse for the overflowing of waters, or a way for the lightning of thunder;

Job 39:25 He saith among the trumpets, Ha, ha; and he smelleth the battle afar off, the thunder of the captains, and the shouting.

Job 40:9 Hast thou an arm like God? or canst thou thunder with a voice like him?

Peter re-accounts his experience in hearing the voice of God in second Peter where he talks about the excellent voice that came from heaven.

2 Peter 1:17 For he received from God the Father honour and glory, when there came such a voice to him from the excellent glory, This is my beloved Son, in whom I am well pleased.

After this experience Jesus told his disciples that this voice came from heaven not for him, but for them. Everything that God the Father, Jesus Christ, and the Holy Ghost has done is for our spiritual growth and advancement. The Bible says that God will send the heavy snow that men may stop and consider him. God is constantly, consistently reaching out to the human race. There are many examples in the Bible of God speaking to people **audibly**. God spoke **audibly** to Moses out of the burning bush on Mount Sinai. God spoke **audibly** to Nebuchadnezzar when he began to boast and brag about all that he had accomplished. Now, in this particular situation it was God's divine judgment.

Daniel 4:30 The king spake, and said, Is not this great Babylon, that I have built for the house of the kingdom by the might of my power, and for the honour of my majesty? 31 While the word was in the king's mouth, there fell a voice from heaven, saying, O king Nebuchadnezzar, to thee it is spoken; The kingdom is departed from thee. 32 And they shall drive thee from men, and thy dwelling shall be with the beasts of the field: they shall make thee to eat grass as oxen, and seven times shall pass over thee, until thou know that the most High ruleth in the kingdom of men, and giveth it to whomsoever he will. 33 The same hour was the thing fulfilled upon Nebuchadnezzar:

The word of God is filled with examples of the audible voice of the Lord. In Hebrews 12 it tells us that he spoke to the children of Israel by his **audible** voice. Even though God spoke to them audibly they still refuse to obey him. He is about to speak like the roaring of the thunder in the earth once again. I am telling you that he is going to shake the heavens and the earth with his audible voice. Everybody upon planet Earth will know that there is a God in heaven. There will be no excuse for the inhabitants of this age to not repent and follow him, who is the author and creator of all existing things.

Hebrews 12:25 See that ye refuse not him that speaketh. For if they escaped not who refused him that spake on earth, much more shall not we escape, if we turn away from him that speaketh from heaven: 26 whose voice then shook the earth: but now he hath promised, saying, Yet once more I shake not the earth only, but also heaven. 27 And this word, Yet once more, signifieth the removing of those things that are shaken, as of things that are made, that those things which cannot be shaken may remain.

We have come into the time when God is about to sound the trumpet. The sounding of the trumpet will be his audible voice speaking to the human race. Jesus declared that it would wake up the ten virgins, the five foolish, and the five wise. The majority of the believers right now in the church are asleep, but God is about to wake them up with his audible voice. The sad part about it is that only five out of ten will be ready to run with this reality. Through the years the audible voice of God has brought drastic change, direction and warnings to me in my life.

When does God speak audibly? Whenever he so chooses! Never, never, never seek to hear the audible voice of God. We seek first the kingdom of God and his righteousness. We seek God's face every moment of every second of every day. Here are some of my amazing experiences with hearing the audible voice of God.

TV Ministry Began When I Heard God's Audible Voice!

Right after my wife gave birth to Daniel in 1983, we had some good friends (Paul & Mary Birt) come and stay with us. They were our spiritual parents to an extent. Mary was helping my wife clean the house and care for Michael. I basically stayed out of their way. While they were cleaning the kitchen, I was upstairs in my prayer room spending time with the Lord and meditating on the Word. When I was finished, I got up and started to come down the stairs.

As I was coming downstairs, I heard the **audible** voice of God. His voice literally filled my eardrums. This is what He said to me, and I quote, **"Go on TV!"** That's what I heard. The **audible** voice of God was so real, that I instantly fell to my knees trembling. I said, "Lord, the church does not have the money to put me on TV!" Then He began to communicate with me in His still quiet voice. He spoke to my heart and said, The church will not pay for your TV time. You will believe and trust Me for it! I said, Yes, Lord! He then quickened to my heart that the first TV station I would be on would be Channel 25 out of Hagerstown, Maryland. The Spirit literally informed me about the specific time I would be on would be Sunday Mornings at 6:30 a.m. Once again, I told the Lord I would obey Him.

After hearing the Lord telling me to go on TV, the very next day I called Channel 25, WHAG in Hagerstown, Maryland, asking to be transferred over to their sales department. When someone else answered the phone, I told this person that I was interested in purchasing a half-hour slot on their channel. I did not tell them what day of the week or time I wanted. I simply said that I was going to produce a half-hour program. (How I was going to produce these programs I did not know). The sales personnel was a lady who informed me that they did not have any time available, and did not know when another slot would be available. I asked her if she would go to their programming department and discuss with them if there was anything they could do. She said she would, even though she thought it would not make any difference because they had no time available.

Approximately three days later, the sales personnel called me back, telling me that they had called a special meeting to discuss my request. She informed me that normally they do not have their TV station on the air until seven o'clock on Sunday mornings, but they had unanimously agreed to bring their station on the air at 6:30 a.m. just for me! From the very first day of our broadcast we had a tremendous response. All the finances that we needed to stay on the air came in.

Eventually, we were on seven TV stations one day a week. Then I was on with Dr. Lester Sumrall's network five days a week. Dr. Sumrall later came to our church and ministered for us. Until the day Dr. Sumrall died, my ordination papers were with him and his ministry. Now we are broadcasting around the world with all the modern technology available. It all began when I heard the audible voice of God when he said: Go on TV!

Slamming my Broken Foot Down, God Instantly Healed It!

One day I had to climb our 250 foot AM radio tower in order to change the light bulb on the main beacon. However, in order to climb the tower, I had to first find the keys; which I never did. Since I could not find the keys to get the fence open, I did the next best thing—I simply climbed over the fence.

This idea turned out not to be such a wonderful idea after all! With all of my climbing gear hanging from my waist, I climbed the fence to the very top. At this point, my rope gear became entangled in the fencing. As I tried to get free, I lost my balance and fell backwards off the fence. Trying to break my fall, I got my right foot down underneath me. I hit the ground with my foot being turned on its side and I felt something snap in the ankle. I knew instantly I had a broken foot, my ankle.

Most normal people would have climbed back over the fence,

go set up a doctor's appointment, have their foot x-rayed, and then placed into a cast. But I am not a normal-thinking person, at least according to the standards of the modern day church. When I broke my foot, I followed my routine of confessing my stupidity to God, and asking Him to forgive me for my stupidity. Moreover, then I spoke to my foot and commanded it to be healed in the name of Jesus Christ of Nazareth. When I had finished speaking to my foot, commanding it to be healed, and then praising and thanking God for the healing, there seem to be no change what so ever in its condition.

The Scripture that came to my heart was where Jesus declared, *"The kingdom of heaven suffereth violence, and the violent take it by force!"* Based completely upon this scripture, I decided to climb the tower by faith, with a broken foot mind you. Please do not misunderstand, my foot hurt so bad I could hardly stand it. And yet, I had declared that I believed I was healed.

There were three men watching me as I took the Word of God by faith. I told them what I was about to do, and they looked at me like as if I had lost my mind. I began to climb the 250 foot tower, one painful step at a time. My foot hurt so bad that I was hyperventilating within just twenty to thirty feet up the tower. It literally felt like I was going to pass out from shock at any moment. Whenever I got to the point of fainting, I would connect my climbing ropes to the tower, stop and take a breather, crying out to Jesus to help me. It seemed to take me forever to get to the top.

Even so, I finally did reach the very top of the tower and replaced the light bulb that had gone out. Usually I can come down that tower within 10 minutes, because I would press my feet against the tower rods, and then slide down, just using my hands and arms to lower myself at a very fast pace. However, in this situation, my foot could not handle the pressure of being pushed up against the steel. Consequently, I had to work my way down very slowly. After I was down, I slowly climbed over the fence one more time. I hobbled my way over to my vehicle, and drove up to the church office. The men who had been watching this unfold, were right behind me.

I hobbled my way into the front office; which is directly across the street from the radio tower. I informed the personnel that I had broken my foot, showing them my black and blue, extreemly swollen foot. It did not help that I had climbed with it! I told them that I was going home to rest. At the same time, however, I told them that I believed I was healed.

Going to my house, which is directly across from the main office of the church parking lot, I made my way slowly up the stairs to our bedroom. I found my wife in the bedroom putting away our clothes. Slowly and painfully I pulled the shoe and sock off of the broken foot. What a mess! It was fat, swollen, black and blue all over. I put a pillow down at the end of the bed, and carefully pulled myself up onto the bed. Lying on my back, I tenderly placed my broken, black and blue, swollen foot onto the pillow. No matter how I positioned it, the pain did not cease. I just laid there squirming, moaning and sighing.

As I was lying there trying to overcome the shock that kept hitting my body, I heard the **audible** voice of God. He said to me: **"What are you doing in bed? "**God really got my attention when I heard him with my natural ears. My wife would testify that she heard nothing. Immediately in my heart I said: Lord I'm just resting. Then He spoke to my heart with the still small voice very clearly, Do you always rest at this time of day? No, Lord, I replied.(It was about 3 o'clock in the afternoon)

He spoke to my heart again and said this, I thought you said you were healed?

At that very moment the gift of faith exploded inside of me. I said, "Lord, I am healed! "Immediately, I pushed myself up off of the bed, grabbed my sock and shoe, and struggled to put them back on. What a tremendous struggle it was! My foot was so swollen that it did not want to go into the shoe. My wife was watching me as I fought to complete this task. You might wonder what my wife was doing this whole time as I was fighting this battle of faith. She was doing what she always does, just watching me and shaking her head. I finally got the shoe on my swollen, black and blue foot. I put my foot down on the floor and began to put my body weight upon it. When I did, I almost passed out. At that moment, a holy anger exploded on the inside of me. I declared out loud, "I am healed in the name of Jesus Christ of Nazareth!" With that declaration, I took my right (broken) foot, and slammed it down to the floor as hard as I possibly could.

When I did that, I felt the bones of my foot break even more. Like the Fourth of July, an explosion of blue, purple, red, and white, black exploded in my brain and I passed out. I came to lying on my bed. Afterward, my wife informed me that every time I passed out, it was for about ten to twenty seconds. The moment I came to, I jumped right back up out of bed. The gift of faith was working in me mightily. I got back up and followed the same process again, "In the name of Jesus Christ of Nazareth I am healed," and slammed my foot down once more as hard as I could! For a second time, I could feel the damage in my foot increasing. My mind was once again wrapped in an explosion of colors and pain as I blacked out.

When I regained consciousness, I immediately got up once again, repeating the same process. After the third time of this happening I came to with my wife leaning over the top of me. I remember my wife saying as she looked at me, "You're making me sick. I can't watch you do this." She promptly walked out of our bedroom, and went downstairs.

The fourth time I got up declaring, "In the name of Jesus Christ of Nazareth I am healed," and slammed my foot even harder! Once more, multiple colors of intense pain hit my brain. I passed out again! I got up the fifth time, angrier than ever. This was not a demonic or proud anger. This was a divine gift of violent I-will-not-take-no-for-an-answer type of faith. I slammed my foot down the fifth time, "In the name of Jesus Christ of Nazareth I am healed!"

The minute my foot slammed into the floor, for the fifth time, the power of God hit my foot. I literally stood there under the quickening power of God, and watched my foot shrink and become normal. All of the pain was completely and totally gone. I pulled back my sock, and watched the black and blue in my foot disappear to normal flesh color. I was healed! Praise God, I was made whole! I went back to the office, giving glory to the Lord and showing the staff my healed foot.

CHAPTER FOUR

#7 Unction

The **7th way** God speaks to us is what I would call a **divine unction**. An **unction** is different than perceiving something by the spirit. Instead of divine **unction** we could say a **divine urgency**. It is like a holy fire burning in your belly, and in your veins. It's something that you **must** do, or say **right now**. We can see this in the life of Jesus when he was twelve years old. Joseph and Mary had been looking for him. When they finally found him, they questioned why he did this to them? He responded with an amazing statement.

Luke 2:49 And he said unto them, How is it that ye sought me? wist ye not that I must be about my Father's business?

This is a divine **unction**, a Holy Ghost urgency. It's a fire burning in your belly that must come forth. Jeremiah the prophet experience this in his life. He had experienced much persecution because of his obedience to God. Jeremiah finally came to the place where he was extremely disinherited because of the persecution and the lack of response he was getting. He declared that he was not going to speak anymore, but this divine **unction** to speak, preach and warn God's people was so strong in him, that he said it was like a fire shut up in his bones.

Jeremiah 20:9 Then I said, I will not make mention of him, nor speak any more in his name. But his word was in mine heart as a burning fire shut up in my bones, and I was weary with forbearing, and I could not stay.

In the book of 1st John chapter 2:20, John tells us that we have an **unction** from the holy one, and that we know all things. The holy one is the Holy Ghost and the **unction** is the way that God speaks to us, revealing to us all those things which God has for us. This is an **unction**, or an **urgency** that comes from God. It is not just an impression, or a perception, or the still small voice. Now all of these different ways in which God speaks will work together in harmony at times to reveal to us the perfect will of the Father. As you continue to read this book you will discover the many different ways in which God speaks to us. You will also discover that in these different ways in which God speaks, they might also be accompanied with a divine and holy **unction**. You might have a vision, or prophetic word, and in that experience you will discover an overwhelming unction, a supernatural hurry up, a divine urgency! Sometimes this unction can almost overwhelm you. The spirit of God takes a hold of you in order to speak, or do something **Now**. I am not talking about sometime later, I mean **RIGHT NOW**! With this divine unction, this urgency the gift of faith will most likely also be in operation.

Hebrews 11:1 Now faith is the substance of things hoped for, the evidence of things not seen.

I do not pray or ask these things to happen to me, but as I'm walking with God, as I'm pursuing God, as I'm hungering after God, when all I want is his will, that is when these things begin to happen on a regular basis! I'm not implying that God will not speak to you at all if you are not where you need to be spiritually. I can guarantee that the more you want the will of God, the more you hunger for the will of God, the more you pursue God, the more he will manifest himself to you in your life.

Matthew 5:6 Blessed are they which do hunger and thirst after righteousness: for they shall be filled.

James 4:8 Draw nigh to God, and he will draw nigh to you.

Blessed are those who hunger and thirst after righteousness. That means hungering and thirsting to live right, to do right, to think right, to be in-line with God's will, the more clear God's voice will be to you. The more you want to be in the will of God and the more of the word of God you have in your heart, the less you sin against the Holy Spirit, the more that God would speak to you in a more clear and precise fashion. Jesus at 12 years old boldly told Mary and Joseph that he **must** be about his Father's business. If you study the word **MUST** in the Greek, you will discover that it is speaking about being spiritually violent. Jesus when he referred to John the Baptist said: *The kingdom of heaven suffers violence, and the violent take it by force.* When Jesus said I **MUST** be about my father's business, the word **MUST** signified a dynamic spiritual violence.

He meant, I will not take no for an answer! This is the divine unction that I am speaking about which is the **seventh way** in which God speaks to us. If you look up the word **must**, you will discover that it is used in Matthew, Mark, Luke and John. This word is used 38 times all together in the four Gospels. It is used 83 times in the whole New Testament. **Must** is referring to that which God has placed in our heart which is a compelling, urgent, a right now word. Let us just look at a small handful of scriptures were Jesus used the word must. Remember this is referring to a divine unction, a holy urgency, **a right now word**.

Matthew 16:21 From that time forth began Jesus to shew unto his disciples, how that he MUST go unto Jerusalem, and suffer many things of the elders and chief priests and scribes, and be killed, and be raised again the third day.

Mark 13:10 And the gospel MUST first be published among all nations.

Mark 14:49 I was daily with you in the temple teaching, and ye took me not: but the scriptures MUST be fulfilled.

Luke 4:43 And he said unto them, I MUST preach the kingdom of God to other cities also: for therefore am I sent.

Luke 13:33 Nevertheless I MUST walk to day, and to morrow, and the day following: for it cannot be that a prophet perish out of Jerusalem.

Luke 22:37 For I say unto you, that this that is written MUST yet be accomplished in me, And he was reckoned among the transgressors: for the things concerning me have an end.

John 4:4 And he MUST needs go through Samaria.

John 9:4 I MUST work the works of him that sent me, while it is day: the night cometh, when no man can work.

John 10:16 And other sheep I have, which are not of this fold: them also I MUST bring, and they shall hear my voice; and there shall be one fold, and one shepherd.

There was a divine urgency, a Holy Ghost unction in the heart of Jesus to fulfill the will of the Father. *Psalm 40:7 Then said I, Lo, I come: in the volume of the book it is written of me,* This is also revealed to us in the book of Hebrews. *Hebrews 10:7 Then said I, Lo, I come (in the volume of the book it is written of me,) to do thy will, O God.*

Now this divine **unction** should be an underlying factor in your whole Christian walk. What I mean by that is that for over 40 years has been an urgency in my heart to fulfill the will of God. Paul the apostle declared that he had no choice, but that he had to preach the gospel. Still at times a very strong and divine urgency will overwhelm me, an unction, a Holy Ghost must, a do it now reality hits me. It's a very serious situation in which God is trying to get my attention, in order to save lives.

My Wife and My Children Would have Died

Cutting Corners Almost Killed My Wife and My Children! We had built a homemade swimming pool at our new house. (I'm always trying to save money – which can lead to disaster.) The pool was 24 feet across and 4 feet deep. Now our house was built on the side of a small mountain. This pool was in the backyard, where right beyond it there is a very steep slope to the road below us. One day, my son Steven and my daughter Stephanie were swimming in this homemade pool. Stephanie was about 10 years old and Steven was 12. I was at my office when my wife called me on the phone. She said to me, Honey, something just doesn't look right with that swimming pool. There some water leaking out of the side. It must have been God who quickening both of us. A divine Holy Ghost **unction, urgency, a must right now** came upon me.

I told my wife, "Baby Doll Go get the kids out of the pool right now!" It is not in her nature or personality to do anything real quick, but in this instant the same Holy Ghost urgency, unction, this holy hurry up, came upon her. Thank the Lord, she did. She ran out and yelled for my son and daughter to come to her. They usually do not respond so quickly either, but his time they literally ran and swam to her. The pool up to this moment completely looked normal with no problems whatsoever. Thank God my wife was not standing at the part of the pool that is towards the steep slope. This in itself was a miracle. The kids swam, ran across the pool and came to her right away. She reached over the 4 foot wall and pulled out our daughter first and then she help Steven get out. Now she will tell you that was a miracle in itself because of how much they weighed. It was like a supernatural strength came upon her, enabling her to lift them up, and pulled them out.

Now at that very instant, I mean at that very moment when she had both Steven and Stephanie out of the pool, the whole swimming pool completely broke loose and collapsed. The wooden walls and steel cables all came undone, swirling like a gigantic, uncontrollable snake. Over 13,500 gallons of water came flooding out; approximately 112,725 pounds of water broke loose. All of the boards, the four heavy steel cables that wrap around the pool, the pool lining and all the water broke loose. It rushed down the hill like a mighty flood onto the asphalt road over 80 feet below. It tore up the side of that hill creating great groups in the dirt and flooded the road below.

If my children would have still been in that pool, they would have been swept away, broken and tumbling in the flood of the water, steel cables, pool lining and the retaining boards. They both would have surely been killed, along with my wife, if she had been standing on the down side of the pool. Thank God for his mercy and protection! When the divine unction of God hits us, a supernatural urgency, a Holy Ghost hurry up, we need to respond immediately. If we do not respond right away then most likely something tragic and terrible will happen.

For as many as are led by the spirit of God they are the sons of God!

Throughout the Scriptures you will see again and again when this holy unction, divine urgency came upon people. We can even see it when it comes to God sending angelic beings to rescue his people. One wonderful example is when the Lord sent the Angels to rescue Lot and his family. Lot did not want to leave behind his family members, so he began to drag his feet. I believe he was fighting against the divine unction, Holy Ghost urgency that the Lord had put in his heart. Finally God had the Angels intervene by dragging him and his family out of the city of Sodom.

Genesis 19:15 And when the morning arose, then the angels hastened Lot, saying, Arise, take thy wife, and thy two daughters, which are here; lest thou be consumed in the iniquity of the city. 16 And while he lingered, the men laid hold upon his hand, and upon the hand of his wife, and upon the hand of his two daughters; the Lord being merciful unto him: and they brought him forth, and set him without the city.

In Matthew 16:21 Jesus began to tell his disciples how that he **must** go on to Jerusalem. That he was going to have to be betrayed, falsely accused, tortured and crucified. Peter rebuked Jesus telling him that this could not be so. Jesus at that very moment turned around and said to Peter: **get behind me Satan, for you do not desire that which is of God, but you're clinging to the things of the flesh.** We are living in a very dangerous time when ministers, preachers of the gospel are trying to calm the people down, literally telling them that they do not have to be unfire for God. They are telling them that they do not have to be zealous for the Lord, or that they do not have to lay everything at the feet of Jesus. They literally are implying that if you preach a give God everything message, that you are being legalistic. They are robbing God's people from that which causes God to manifest himself to them. When God sees people responding to this divine urgency he will begin to supernaturally move on their behalf. This urgency is what some would call the **zeal of the Lord**. The reason why Christ was able to fulfill the will of the Father is because this urgency, this unction, the zeal of the Lord flowed through his veins like a mighty river.

Isaiah 9:7 Of the increase of his government and peace there shall be no end, upon the throne of David, and upon his kingdom, to order it, and to establish it with judgment and with justice from henceforth even forever. The zeal of the Lord of hosts will perform this.

Psalm 69:9 For the zeal of thine house hath eaten me up; and the reproaches of them that reproached thee are fallen upon me.

Isaiah 59:17 For he put on righteousness as a breastplate, and an helmet of salvation upon his head; and he put on the garments of vengeance for clothing, and was clad with zeal as a cloke.

John 2:16 and said unto them that sold doves, Take these things hence; make not my Father's house an house of merchandise. 17 And his disciples remembered that it was written, The zeal of thine house hath eaten me up. 18 Then answered the Jews and said unto him, What sign shewest thou unto us, seeing that thou doest these things?

The Holy Spirit, God the Father, Jesus Christ are all striving to bring us into a place of Holy Ghost unction. They want this divine urgency, the zeal of the Lord to rise up within us. In the book of Revelation as Jesus Christ is speaking to the church of the Laodiceans he reveals that he cannot help them because of their lukewarm condition. That not only can he not help them, but that they are very revolting to him when they are lukewarm in their heart, and attitude.

Revelation 3:15 I know thy works, that thou art neither cold nor hot: I would thou wert cold or hot. 16 So then because thou art lukewarm, and neither cold nor hot, I will spue thee out of my mouth.

Christ and the Holy Ghost in us, gives us the ability to obey the will of the Father, to get up and go, to move on out. We are talking about a divine unction, Holy Ghost hurry up, supernatural urgency that will overtake you as you surrender your life, mind, heart, spirit, soul and body to the will of the Father. Many times through the years this divine urgency comes upon me like an invisible mantle. In these times of the divine flow of the unction of the Holy Ghost God enables me to do the supernatural and the miraculous. In one service I found myself in the situation where a young lady was about to be seriously hurt when the Holy Ghost unction overtook me.

Brittany would have been consumed by fire

I have discovered through the years that when the spirit of God quickens my heart with the divine urgency, Holy Ghost unction to do something, it is not the time to think, but it is time to obey and act. I cannot tell you how many times I have immediately responded to the spirit of God to a certain situation. As I look back, I realize if I had not quickly done that which the spirit of God quickened to my heart, the end results would have been terrible and devastating. This is one of those situations.

Our youth had been practicing a wonderful Christmas Carol, in which we had a large children s choir. The men of the church had built small risers in which the youth and the children could stand upon. Starting from the front to the back, it took each child up approximately six inches. In one part of the production all the children held lit candles. Almost all the lights were turned off in the sanctuary during this time. It was a beautiful scene, with all the children having their candles lit and singing wonderful Christmas carols to the congregation.

One of our youth was a young attractive teenager who was approximately fourteen years old. Her name was Britney, who had long brown hair. She was standing approximately three rows deep on the third riser. I believe I was sitting on the front row of the chairs in a sanctuary, simply enjoying this wonderful performance of the youth. As I was watching the candlelight, singing performance I noticed something very peculiar. A very light blue haze appeared over the top of Britney's head. Immediately I knew in my heart by the Holy Ghost that her hair was on fire. One of the teenagers behind her had accidentally put her candle up against Britney's hair. Britney must have used some type of hairspray to be prepared for tonight's performance, and this hairspray was extremely flammable. In my heart I knew that this could be a very devastating situation. I discovered later, that this thought was truly from God. Here is some devastating information about the tragedies resulting from hair fires.

*One of the most common characteristics of hair fires is that they are unexpected. Rarely does anyone set his or her hair on fire intentionally. Therefore, when a hair fire happens, the person is caught completely off guard and very often their instinctive reactions make it worse. The most immediate preferred reactions would be to immediately douse the head with water or to smother the fire with a towel, blanket or other suitable material. However, what typically happens is that the person will run about or drop and roll, which only fans the fire with air. Another reaction to a hair fire is to attempt to put out the fire by the use of hands, which typically results in hand and arm burns. – [Burns typical of a hair fire due to drop down]. Because burning hair will often "drop down," the person receives burns to the neck, shoulders and chest, sometimes to a greater degree than burns to the scalp. The individual's clothing may also catch on fire exacerbating these types of neck, shoulder and chest burns.

Another characteristic of a hair fire is that the person often believes they have successfully extinguished the fire and will stop their efforts to put out the fire only to find that it "re-ignites" In reality, the hair fire does not "re-ignite," but was never completely put out in the first place. If any small portion of the hair remains on fire, it will "re-ignite" the remaining hair. The final characteristic of hair fires is severe disfigurement requiring extensive plastic surgery to correct.

Of course I had no knowledge of any of this at the time, all I had was a divine unction, a quickening, and a super natural urgency entering my heart to get to Britney. I immediately jumped up out of my chair, running for the choir, maneuvering pass all the other people in the play, and getting past all the props. In my supernatural rush to get to Brittany, not one time did I stumble, trip over a cord, bump into a person, or knock anything over. It is hard for me to explain to people this supernatural realm I enter in when the spirit of God takes me over.

When I finally reached the bleachers, Britney's hair was glowing bluer than ever. Somehow I got in between the children, not knocking one of them off of the risers in order to get to Brittany. Of course everybody saw all my actions, and had no idea what was happening. To this day many of them that were at this performance never knew what happened. When I finally stood in front of Britney, in my heart I knew what I needed to do. I could not use my hands to put out her hair fire. Instead, somehow I grabbed the back of her head, (with her hair all burning blue now) pulling her head down to my chest. I took my suit jacket and completely enveloped her head into my chest. Miraculously, yes supernaturally I was able to get her hair extinguished in a matter of seconds.

Britney had no idea what was going on until after the service. Once the fire was out, I did not even say a word to her or anyone. I just simply helped her stand back up straight, spun around, and went back to my chair. As I think back on this particular situation, I'm sure it looked a little bit comical. The performance never stopped. The play continued, with the choir singing, holding their candle lights. In the minds of the people it was just a little burp in the performance. Thank God for the Holy Ghost, the divine quickening, the unction of the spirit and divine intervention. It was even supernatural that neither one of us received any burns whatsoever.

Christ always responded immediately when the spirit of God put an urgency, an unction into his heart. One day he was walking along with a massive crowd of people when he came underneath a sycamore tree. When he looked up into that sycamore tree he saw a little man who was a local tax collector. Remember that Christ was in great demand at this period of his ministry, and that a lot of people were vying for his attention. Christ was never motivated by popularity, finances, and people in upper political or spiritual positions. He was constantly being led and guided by the Holy Ghost. In this particular situation and unction of the Lord hit him to go to this particular man's house. He said:

Luke 19:5 And when Jesus came to the place, he looked up, and saw him, and said unto him, Zacchæus, make haste, and come down; for to day I must abide at thy house.

Did you notice that he used the word **must**. He said I **must come to your house today.** This was the divine unction of the Holy Ghost that was leading him, and guiding him. I have had similar situations in my own personal life. I wish I could tell you that I have always responded properly, but I have not. As a result of not responding to the unction of the Holy Ghost, people's lives have been lost for eternity.

He Lost His Soul Because I Disobeyed*

It was the Fourth of July weekend. I had stopped at the local convenience store to pick up some items to take to my wife's family reunion. Every Fourth of July, all of her relatives on her mother's side would get together. We were running late, as usual. I was trying to get some things done before we left. As I entered into the convenience store, I saw the owner of the property standing behind the counter. I had spoken to him a little bit in the past but never in great depth. The minute I saw him, the Spirit of God quickened my heart, a Holy Ghost urgency came upon me to speak to him about Christ; the only problem was that I was running extremely late. My wife and children would be upset with me if I did not get home right now. So even though I had this divine urgency in my heart, I argued with God, telling him that as soon as I got home from my wife's family reunion, I would stop and speak to him. Tremendous conviction began to flood my soul, but I am sorry to say that I pushed it aside. One would think that I would have learned my lesson from the last devastating experience; the time that I was supposed to talk to Billy but did not. Billy had died shortly afterwards in a drunken head-on collision accident.

I went home and very quickly, loaded up all of the picnic supplies and food. Yes, I said in my heart that when I get back from the picnic I would go to speak the owner of the convenience store. I got my family into the car and we went to Kathleen's Fourth of July family reunion. Approximately four hours later that day, we returned back home. On the way, I decided to obey God and what he had placed upon my heart four hours earlier. I pulled into the convenience store with all sincere intentions of speaking to the owner. When I pulled into the parking lot, I noticed there was something wrong. They did not have any business which was highly unusual especially on the Fourth of July. Not a single vehicle was in the parking lot to be seen.

A very bad feeling came over me. I walked up to the store doors and discovered them locked. To my dismay, there was a notice on the door that said, "CLOSED DUE TO DEATH IN THE FAMILY." That afternoon, the owner of the store had died from a massive heart attack. I should have shared Jesus with him when the Lord when the unction of God had come upon me earlier that day. Lord have mercy! The moment the unction of God comes upon us, we need to obey!

Jesus said to Zacchæus, I have to come to your house today. Most times you will discover that when God gives you and unction of the Holy Ghost, that you will not know all of God's plan for this situation. We're not called to think, or lean unto our own understanding. In order for God to speak to us, and through us, we must be available for him 24 hours a day. I triy to live a life in which I am available for God no matter what the situation. You might wonder what you should do through the day if you do not have any divine guidance. I simply go about my normal routines, that which I know needs to be done or accomplished. Many times in my daily routines all of a sudden God will speak to me by a divine unction, or the still small voice, or a holy perception, a conviction, or by my conscience. Remember there are at least **20 ways** that God will speak to his people. Many times I have said to the Lord: Lord I know that you're intelligent, but I don't know about me. Please speak to me what you want me to do. Your will be done and not mine. You have to make yourself available to God, on-call in every situation, at every opportunity. Isaiah the prophet said: **here I am Lord, send me**. The Divine Unction of God saved Our Lives!

Death & Destruction over the Mississippi!

My family and I was saved from a terrible death at the Mississippi river! Many times in my life I have had vivid experiences, perceiving that God is about to do something or that something is about to take place right before it happens!

On August 1, 2007 my wife, three sons, daughter and I were traveling on Highway I 35 West. We were in our Toyota crew cab pickup truck, pulling a 35 foot fifth wheel trailer. We were on vacation and headed for Yellowstone National Park. At the time, we were headed towards the downtown area of Minneapolis, Minnesota. As I was driving, I sensed in my heart that we needed to get off this highway, even though our GPS was taking us the shortest route to where we were headed. I have discovered and personally experienced twenty major ways that God leads and guides. All twenty of these specific ways in which God leads and guides can be discovered in the Scriptures. What I felt is what I call a divine unction of the Holy Ghost. It is more than a perception or a feeling. It is more like an overwhelming urgency that flows up out of your belly.

I informed my family that something definitely was wrong, that there was an urgency in my heart and we needed to get off I 35 West immediately. This is the only time I can remember having experienced this divine unction, urgency to get off a road or highway. I took the nearest exit off of I 35 W. and went north towards Canada. After a while, we connected to another highway that would take us West, over the Mississippi River towards Dakota. A little Later in the day, we pulled into a store to take a break from driving. As we entered this facility, we noticed that there were people gathered around the television.

We could see that some major disaster had taken place. The viewer's informed us that a bridge had collapsed over the Mississippi River, when a lot of heavy traffic was loaded on top of it. We could see on the TV screen cars, trucks, buses everywhere that had fallen into the Mississippi. There is death and destruction everywhere.

The hair on the back of my neck stood up as I realized this bridge that had collapsed was on I 35 W. It was the same highway in which the spirit of God quicken my heart with a divine unction, urgency to get off. As we discussed this situation, and the precise time when the bridge collapsed, we discovered that we would've been on this bridge with our truck and our fifth wheel trailer. If I had not left the highway at the unction, and the urging of the Holy Ghost most likely we would have found ourselves in the bottom of the Mississippi River. Thirteen people died that day and many were seriously injured, not including all the terrible destruction, and horrible nightmare that took place with all those who were a part of this tragedy. Thank God for the divine intervention and leading of the Holy Ghost.

In order for the spirit of the Lord to lead and guide us we must not have any other agenda, no other purpose, no other plan, just simply God's will to obey. John the Baptist said: but I must decrease, in order for Christ to increase. To be a disciple of Christ means to be led by the spirit. We become a nobody in our own eyes. For many years when I have perceived that people were beginning to look to me instead of Christ I told them I'm not your answer. If I can help it I never let people think that I am there solution. If you allow people to put you on a pedestal you are simply an accident going somewhere to happen.

He Died Because He Did Not Heed My Warnings!

One night (back in 1975) while I was praying alone in my barracks, when a holy **unction**, and urgency came upon me to pray for a Muslim man that I knew. As I responded to this **unction** of the Holy Ghost I entered into deep travail for his soul. I began to weep almost uncontrollably for this man, whose name was Hussein. He was a military friend of mine that I used to do drugs with. As I prayed the Spirit of God spoke to my heart, telling me the devil was going to kill him in the very near future if he did not repent, and cry out to Jesus. The spirit of God told me that Hussein had only a very short period of time left on the earth before the enemy would snuff out his precious life.

This **unction**, this deep urgency of God was so strong within me that I got up off of the floor of my dorm room, where I had been praying. I immediately went to his room and knocked on his door. Hussein opened his door and saw me standing there weeping uncontrollably. I was so moved in my heart that I could not speak for a while. He asked what was wrong with great concern in his voice. "Mike, Mike, what's wrong?" I could barely speak in English because I was weeping so hard. I finally was able to tell him that I had been in prayer in my room, when the Spirit of God literally told me that the devil was about to kill him. I told him that his time to get right with the Lord was running out. I explained that he was going to be dead in the very near future, and that he would end up in hell without Jesus. I began to plead with him with great urgency and compassion, with tears flowing down my face to get right with God. I encouraged him to cry out to God, repent for his sins, and give his heart to Jesus Christ.

It was obvious the Spirit of God was moving upon him in a very real way. He said that he believed what I was saying was true, but that he just was not ready to make that kind of commitment at this time. Soon after this experience I left the Navy, headed out to minister to the Yupik Indians. I kept in touch with some of the people that I knew on this military base. It was approximately two months later that I was speaking to one of my friends on the base when he asked me if I had heard about what happened to Hussein.

I informed him, no that I had not heard anything. He told me that they had discovered him dead, with his head in the toilet. They think that he had either gotten his hands on some bad drugs or he had simply overdosed. Oh how it must break the heart of God when souls are lost because they will not respond to his love and beckoning call.

He Was Going to Rape & Murder My Wife!

I was working for the Broken Arrow school district as a janitor while my wife and I attended a Bible school in Oklahoma. One night at about 7:00 p.m. while I was waxing and buffing the floors in a classroom, the **unction's** of the Lord came upon me mightily. It was a divine urgency that overwhelmed my heart and my soul. Immediately I stopped what I was doing. I began to pray fervently in the spirit and also in English. I asked the Lord what was going on. He spoke to me in an almost audible voice saying, there is a man at your house right now who is there to rape and murder your wife!

For the last couple months there had been a lot of rapes and murders going on in the Tulsa and Broken Arrow, Oklahoma area. There was literally a man hunt trying to find this man before he committed another atrocious crime. But up to this time they had been completely unsuccessful in finding him.

When I heard the voice of the Lord say this to me it shook me to the very core of my being. I did not have a phone to call her to see if she was okay. In those days there is no such thing as cell phones. And we did not have a phone in our apartment. I knew it would be too late by the time I got in my truck and drove home. I did the only thing I could I began to cry out to God for her deliverance and safety. I took authority over the demonic powers that were operating in this man. I kept praying and interceding. If you would have walked into that classroom at that moment you would've seen a man completely consumed in prayer on his knees, and in deep intercession. This continued for quite a while until all of a sudden the peace of God that passes all understanding came upon me. At that moment I knew that I knew in my heart God had divinely intervened, and that she was okay. The peace that passes all understanding had come upon my mind and my heart.

I do not get off work until after midnight, so it was rather late when I walked through the door of our apartment. When I came through the door the first thing I said to my wife was "Who came to the house tonight?" She looked at me a little surprised. She told me a man came by who said he was from children's services. I asked her what he wanted. He said they were doing a survey, and that he needed some questions to be answered. He began to ask her numerous questions about her life.

It turns out while that at that very moment he was asking my wife these personal questions, I was in deep intercessory prayer in the classroom where I was working. During that time we had another couple staying with us temporarily in our apartment. The husband's wife, Pam, came out of the back room as the stranger was talking to my wife. Now Pam is just a very small petite woman that nobody in their right mind would be at all intimidated or concerned about. This man seemed to get extremely nervous and fearful at that moment. He said he needed to get some literature from his car, and that he would be right back. He quickly left through the door of our apartment. Thank God he never did come back. My wife said they saw him driving his car away.

The next day I called the children's services to investigate what had happened. I told them precisely what had happened. They adamantly declared that they never send anyone out after five o'clock. They also said that they did not have any man working for them who go to people's homes and ask questions.

God had supernaturally and divinely intervened by placing within me a holy unction to cry out to him. Now it might be assumed that this man simply left because there is another woman in the house. Personally I do not believe this is the case. A man so possessed by devils could have easily intimidated both of the ladies, and taken advantage of them. Praise God for divine intervention and guidance.

1 John 2:20 (KJV) But ye have an unction from the Holy One, and ye know all things.

John 3:30 (KJV) He must increase, but I must decrease.

John 10:16 (KJV) And other sheep I have, which are not of this fold: them also I must bring, and they shall hear my voice; and there shall be one fold, and one shepherd.

1 John 2:20 (KJV) But ye have an unction from the Holy One, and ye know all things.

Luke 2:49 (KJV) And he said unto them, How is it that ye sought me? wist ye not that I must be about my Father's business?

Matthew 16:21 (KJV) From that time forth began Jesus to shew unto his disciples, how that he must go unto Jerusalem, and suffer many things of the elders and chief priests and scribes, and be killed, and be raised again the third day.

Luke 19:5 (KJV) And when Jesus came to the place, he looked up, and saw him, and said unto him, Zacchaeus, make haste, and come down; for to day I must abide at thy house.

#8 Prophecies

Another important way that God speaks to us is through prophecy. God is still speaking to the human race through prophetic words, in which he will use people, even people who are not mature to speak into our lives. Now, we need to be very careful with this because there are a lot of fleshly and false prophetic words being delivered in this day and hour. First 1/3 rd of the prophetic words given in the Bible were all pertaining to the future. To see this you can look at the prophecies in Isaiah 53, where it talked about Christ, or look at the prophecies of Jeremiah, which were very precise and accurate. Jeremiah said in 70 years the children of Israel would return to Jerusalem, and rebuild it.

Jeremiah 29:10 For thus saith the Lord, That after seventy years be accomplished at Babylon I will visit you, and perform my good word toward you, in causing you to return to this place.

It came to pass exactly as he prophesied by the spirit of God. In Genesis chapter 3 God prophetically said that the seed of the woman would crush the head of the serpent. The seed of the woman would bruise his own heel in this process. That was a proclamation about Jesus Christ over coming the devil. So at least one 3rd of the Bible is prophetic words spoken before it happened. Almost all the prophetic words in the Bible have already been fulfilled. When Paul prophesied to Timothy he said: for the day will come when people become morally bankrupt. And this is pertaining to those within the church.

2 Timothy 3:1 This know also, that in the last days perilous times shall come. 2 For men shall be lovers of their own selves, covetous, boasters, proud, blasphemers, disobedient to parents, unthankful, unholy, 3 without natural affection, trucebreakers, false accusers, incontinent, fierce, despisers of those that are good, 4 traitors, heady, highminded, lovers of pleasures more than lovers of God; 5 having a form of godliness, but denying the power thereof: from such turn away. 6 For of this sort are they which creep into houses, and lead captive silly women laden with sins, led away with divers lusts, 7 ever learning, and never able to come to the knowledge of the truth.

This has already come to pass in our generation. Jesus gave prophetic words in *Matthew 24* when he began to talk about the last days. They asked him 3 questions in which we do not have the time or space to go into in this book. That was a prophetic futuristic word that Christ spoke, which is being fulfilled right before our very eyes. Personally I believe that the future prophetic words that the prophet spoke, even Christ himself were not really given to us in order to understand what was about to happen. I believe it is God sending his word into the future to bring to pass that which he knew or wanted to happen.

2 Corinthians 4:13 We having the same spirit of faith, according as it is written, I believed, and therefore have I spoken; we also believe, and therefore speak;

God has never done anything without saying it first. There are prophetic words given to us from people that are truly inspired by God, but then there's some that are operating in the flesh, or their inspired by evil spirits. Did you know that the enemy can speak through born again believers. You might say: oh the devil doesn't speak through born-again people. Oh yes he does. If you truly have any humility and meekness in your heart at all you will admit that the devil has used you and I at times to say things to people that we had no right to say! This is why we have to carefully examine whatever somebody speaks over us. We have to make sure it lines up with the Scriptures.

1 John 4:1 Beloved, believe not every spirit, but try the spirits whether they are of God: because many false prophets are gone out into the world.

2 Timothy 3:16 All scripture is given by inspiration of God, and is profitable for doctrine, for reproof, for correction, for instruction in righteousness: 17 that the man of God may be perfect, throughly furnished unto all good works.

I have seen people get a prophetic word, and then they have quit their jobs and run off to another country. When they get there nothing works out, and it is a complete and total disaster. Every prophetic word has to be confirmed in your heart, and the Scriptures. The question I ask is why people are looking for a prophecy or prophetic word over their lives? Honestly in over 40 years of walking with Christ I have never sought for someone to give me a prophetic word. Yes I have spoken many prophetic words over people, but I never sought for a prophetic word. Why? It is because I have the Word of God, the truth. Have I ever received prophetic words about my life? Absolutely. Have they helped me? Yes, many times they have given me direction and confirmed that which the spirit of God had already spoken to me. Some people write down or record the prophetic word that they received from a person, which is perfectly fine, but it also can cause them many problems if they do not handle them right.

Now is the mistake that many people are making when it comes to the prophetic word they have received. I watch people almost end up worship this prophetic word that was given to them, like as if it was the Bible! Realize that no prophetic word equals the authority of the Bible. Many false religions and denominations have started because someone received a prophetic word, and exalted it above the Bible or equal to the Bible. Paul the apostle warned us by a bold declaration in the book of Galatians.

Galatians 1: 8 But though we, or an angel from heaven, preach any other gospel unto you than that which we have preached unto you, let him be accursed. 9 As we said before, so say I now again, If any man preach any other gospel unto you than that ye have received, let him be accursed.

Are prophetic words spoken by people still for today?

Absolutely, the Scriptures very clearly deals with this fact of personal prophecies, and that they are still viable in the believers life. This is revealed to us in first Timothy as the apostle Paul is giving instructions to Timothy.

1 Timothy 1:18 This charge I commit unto thee, son Timothy, according to the prophecies which went before on thee, that thou by them mightest war a good warfare;

There are times that prophetic words will help us in the spiritual battles that we encounter in daily living. Paul told Timothy: by these prophetic words he could fight a good fight in the mist of his battles. God knows what we are going to be going through, even in the real dark times of our lives. Yet God will give to us a prophetic word that will give us direction and encouragement. This prophetic word might come to you in a time of prayer, dreams, or by other people. Here is an example. I gave a prophetic word one time to a husband and a wife who were members of the church I was pastor of.

I Prophesied in Three Days!

In one particular service, there was a married couple who had come forward for prayer. The husband and wife were both working for a youth and children s camp ministry. He was a rodeo clown for the children s camp. As I came to this couple, the Spirit of God quickened me, and I prophesied by the spirit of the Lord that in three days he would lose his job and position with that ministry. I also told them prophetically that at the time it would seem to be devastating, but that he should not despair, because God was about to open up new doors of opportunity for him and his family.

Sure enough just as I prophesied, within three days they called him into a meeting. In this meeting they informed him that they were going to let him go. He was fired right there on the spot! They fired him because he and his wife spoke in tongues, and this ministry they work for was not a Pentecostal or full Gospel ministry.

Yes, it was extremely devastating for them, but because the Lord had already told them that this was going to happen and that they were going to have a bright and prosperous future, with a new occupation, they were able to endure this trial. God supernaturally gave this man and his wife favor and they opened up another business that became prosperous.

Paul told Timothy to fight a good warfare with the prophetic words that were given to him. Paul also told Timothy not to neglect the gift that was imparted to him by a prophetic word. Amazingly there can be an impartation by God speaking a prophetic word over your life by true ministers of the gospel. In my book How Faith Comes, I share that this is also one of the ways that faith can be imparted.

1 Timothy 4:14 Neglect not the gift that is in thee, which was given thee by prophecy, with the laying on of the hands of the presbytery.

Jeremiah was one of the only true prophets that was left in Israel in his lifetime. God said that the prophets of his day and age were prophesying of their own imagination.

Jeremiah 23:16 Thus saith the Lord of hosts, Hearken not unto the words of the prophets that prophesy unto you: they make you vain: they speak a vision of their own heart, and not out of the mouth of the Lord. 17 They say still unto them that despise me, The Lord hath said, Ye shall have peace; and they say unto every one that walketh after the imagination of his own heart, No evil shall come upon you........:21 I have not sent these prophets, yet they ran: I have not spoken to them, yet they prophesied.22 But if they had stood in my counsel, and had caused my people to hear my words, then they should have turned them from their evil way, and from the evil of their doings.....:32 Behold, I am against them that prophesy false dreams, saith the Lord, and do tell them, and cause my people to err by their lies, and by their lightness; yet I sent them not, nor commanded them: therefore they shall not profit this people at all, saith the Lord.

One time I had a so-called prophet come and minister in our

church. In one of the services he told the congregation he was going to teach them how to prophesy. Now this is not something you can teach people to do. You cannot teach people how to prophesy, any more than you can teach people how to speak in tongues. I was a young pastor at this time but I knew better than to believe you can teach people how to prophesy. He had the congregation breakup in groups of 4 to 6 people. Then he told them that they were to pray, asking God to give them a prophetic word. He told them that a thought would come to their mind, and whatever came to their mind, was God! I stood back watching and listening to this bizarre and strange instruction. He went to one of the groups asking if anybody had received something. One of the men in the group said that only one word came to his mind. This so-called prophet asked him what that word was. He said it is the word baby, yes baby. Then it became a guessing game, trying to interpret what the word baby could mean. Of course this did not produce any kind of positive results, or true divine revelation. The whole meeting was nothing but a disaster.

In second Peter it is revealed to us how prophecy truly works. This is actually the way that God used men to speak and write the whole old and New Testament of the Bible.

2 Peter 1:21 For the prophecy came not in old time by the will of man: but holy men of God spake as they were moved by the Holy Ghost.

If you are truly going to be led and guided by the spirit of God, you must agree and believe that all Scripture in the Bible has been inspired by God. The minute you rationalize away, or argue, or water down any of the word of God, you are headed for destruction.

2 Timothy 3:15 And that from a child thou hast known the holy scriptures, which are able to make thee wise unto salvation through faith which is in Christ Jesus.16 All scripture is given by inspiration of God, and is profitable for doctrine, for reproof, for correction, for instruction in righteousness:17 That the man of God may be perfect, thoroughly furnished unto all good works.

Now prophetic words do not always pertain to the future. In the midst of this prophetic word you might discover the operation of the word of knowledge, a word of wisdom, or the discerning of spirits. All of these gifts of the spirit work together by the one and same Holy Spirit. Holy men of God spoke as they were moved by the Holy Ghost. These men did not have their own agenda, they were not in it for financial rewards, they were not looking for positions, power, prestige, or recognition! These were men of God who simply wanted nothing but the will of God.

Jesus himself never did anything without the Father's influence and direction. Every word, deed, and action that Jesus took was underneath the direct leading of the Spirit of God. Christ is our supreme example of how we are to talk, walk, and live our lives in this world. Actually the greatest challenge of our faith is to be led by the spirit of God, moment by moment. It is so easy to get out of God's will, especially when you do not have a desire to be led by the Spirit. For as many as are led by the spirit of God, they are the sons of God. That means they are the mature, spirit filled, God inspired believers.

I was teaching in a little country in South America, called Surinam, and I perceived that there was a lot of abuse of this gift called prophecy. Everybody wanted a prophetic word. There was one man about my age who I had spoken to, that I could see that he was desperately wanting a prophetic word from the Lord. In one particular meeting where I was ministering, I pointed to this man under the leading of the Holy Ghost, calling him up to the front of the gathering. I said: sir I have a prophetic word for you. You could see that this was really causing him to be extremely excited. I told him the prophetic word that I was about to give him would forever change his life. That if he would believe this prophetic word, receive it, and put it to work in his life he would enter into a row of such victory as he had never known in his life before. I told him that it would transform him, and change him into a completely different man. As I continued to tell him what this prophetic word was going to do for his life, you could see that he could hardly contain himself. As he stood right in front of me, I asked him if he was ready to receive this word? He told me with great excitement, yes, I am ready. I said okay, here's what you have to do. I said you have to close your eyes, put your hands out in front of you as if you are about to receive something from the Lord. Immediately he closed his eyes, putting out his hands with his palms turned upward. I asked him if he was ready? He said yes! As his eyes were closed, and his hands were stretched out in front of himself, I took my Bible and place it into his hands. I told him, now open your eyes. He opened his eyes, and saw my Bible in his hands. I told him, that prophetic word in your hands will radically transform and change you, if you will receive it, believe it, and act upon it. There will be those who will read this story, and find fault with what I did. They will think that I was simply messing with his mind, when in reality I gave to him a powerful truth by the Holy Ghost that will absolutely radically change his life, if he will simply believe it, receive it and do it.

How Do I Know If the Prophetic Word Is of God?

#1 It will never contradict Scripture.

Scripture is the final authority and if it contradicts scripture then you must rejected it.

2 Timothy 3:16 All scripture is given by inspiration of God, and is profitable for doctrine, for reproof, for correction, for instruction in righteousness:

#2 By their fruits you will know them.

Fruit is so vitally important when it comes to discerning whether or not the word given to you is truly of God. If the one who is giving you the prophetic word is living in outright sin or immorality, you should be very hesitant to accept it.

Matthew 7:16 Ye shall know them by their fruits. Do men gather grapes of thorns, or figs of thistles?

#3 It always lead you to a place of absolute devotion to God.

If the prophetic word does not take you closer to Christ and the

Father, run from that prophetic word as fast as you can.

Deuteronomy 13:1 If there arise among you a prophet, or a dreamer of dreams, and giveth thee a sign or a wonder, 2 and the sign or the wonder come to pass, whereof he spake unto thee, saying, Let us go after other gods, which thou hast not known, and let us serve them; 3 thou shalt not hearken unto the words of that prophet, or that dreamer of dreams: for the Lord your God proveth you, to know whether ye love the Lord your God with all your heart and with all your soul.

#4 It will produce righteousness and true holiness.

Without holiness no man will see God. God's ultimate purpose is to create his image and his likeness in us. Before the throne of heaven stands angelic beings who cry **Holy, Holy, Holy**, day and night. Every prophetic word will direct us to Gods true nature and Holiness.

Jeremiah 23:22 But if they had stood in my counsel, and had caused my people to hear my words, then they should have turned them from their evil way, and from the evil of their doings.

#5 It will not glorify and exalt the one it is given to.

Any time a so-called prophetic word builds up your ego, exalts you, makes you think highly of yourself, I guarantee it is a lying spirit. The Holy Ghost did not come to exalt us, but Jesus Christ.

John 3:29 He that hath the bride is the bridegroom: but the friend of the bridegroom, which standeth and heareth him, rejoiceth greatly because of the bridegroom's voice: this my joy therefore is fulfilled. 30 He must increase, but I must decrease.

John 7:18 He that speaketh of himself seeketh his own glory: but he that seeketh his glory that sent him, the same is true, and no unrighteousness is in him.

John 16:13 Howbeit when he, the Spirit of truth, is come, he will guide you into all truth: for he shall not speak of himself; but whatsoever he shall hear, that shall he speak: and he will shew you things to come.

#6 Yes it will encourage, but at times warn, correct and chastise.

We live in a day and age when many are seeking to be tickled and pampered. If you are a serious student of the Scriptures you will discover there is much correction, warning and chastisement in the Bible, given to the believer. Many so-called prophets of the modern-day church bring very little if any correction to people's lives. When we do bring correction, it must be it with a true motivation of love for that person or people.

2 Timothy 4:2 preach the word; be instant in season, out of season; reprove, rebuke, exhort with all longsuffering and doctrine. 3 For the time will come when they will not endure sound doctrine; but after their own lusts shall they heap to themselves teachers, having itching ears; 4 and they shall turn away their ears from the truth, and shall be turned unto fables.

#7 Most true prophetic words will state the conditions for their fulfillment.

If we study most of the prophetic Scriptures in the Bible, you will discover there were almost always conditions. This is old covenant and new covenant reality. Many of the prophetic words that people are giving today are unconditional. That flies in the face of biblical and prophetic words given by the prophets.

2 Chronicles 7:14 if my people, which are called by my name, shall humble themselves, and pray, and seek my face, and turn from their wicked ways; then will I hear from heaven, and will forgive their sin, and will heal their land.

#8 Does the Prophet who is giving you this word have a good track record of fulfilled prophecies.

This should be one of the most obvious ways to determine whether or not the person speaking to you is of God. To a great extent this reality is being excused away in the modern day church when it comes to prophecy. In almost all the books the Lord has me write, I share stories that give evidence to the reality of God in my life. This should not be considered abnormal, but normal Christianity.

Deuteronomy 18:22 When a prophet speaketh in the name of the Lord, if the thing follow not, nor come to pass, that is the thing which the Lord hath not spoken, but the prophet hath spoken it presumptuously: thou shalt not be afraid of him.

#9 It should bear witness in your heart, and with the Holy Ghost.

When someone gives you a prophetic word, if it is of God, there should be a quickening in your heart. This quickening could also be a conviction that what is said is true. In your heart there should be a large and strong YES, AMEN, this is of God.

1 John 2:27 But the anointing which ye have received of him abideth in you, and ye need not that any man teach you: but as the same anointing teacheth you of all things, and is truth, and is no lie, and even as it hath taught you, ye shall abide in him.

#10 Is the doctrinal beliefs of the giver of the prophecy, in line with biblical theology.

If someone gives to you a prophetic word, and yet their biblical perspective is twisted and perverted, you need to take this to heart. If there theology is wrong, most likely they are listening to the wrong voices. I can almost guarantee they will give you a prophetic word that is not accurate.

2 Peter 2:1 But there were false prophets also among the people, even as there shall be false teachers among you, who privily shall bring in damnable heresies, even denying the Lord that bought them, and bring upon themselves swift destruction.

#11 A true prophetic word will never deny the deity, and authority of Jesus Christ.

We are living in a very dangerous time when many are beginning to deny the importance of the words of Christ, and even his deity.

Personally I have a family member who I had led to the Lord years ago who has embraced the lie that Jesus Christ is not God who came in the flesh. This has led him to now believe there is no hell or judgment. He has completely given himself over to the damnable lies of universalism. No matter what Scriptures I give him, he is completely blind and deaf to them. I say this with great sorrow in my heart. Run from those who deny the deity of Jesus, the authority of his word, and his divine nature.

1 John 4:1 Beloved, believe not every spirit, but try the spirits whether they are of God: because many false prophets are gone out into the world. 2 Hereby know ye the Spirit of God: Every spirit that confesseth that Jesus Christ is come in the flesh is of God: 3 and every spirit that confesseth not that Jesus Christ is come in the flesh is not of God:

#12 Always take what has been spoken over you before the Lord in prayer!

The Scriptures are very straightforward when it comes to us praying about everything. Especially when it comes to a prophetic words whether given by a person, dream, vision or divine encounter.

Philippians 4:5 Let your moderation be known unto all men. The Lord is at hand. 6 Be careful for nothing; but in everything by prayer and supplication with thanksgiving let your requests be made known unto God. 7 And the peace of God, which passeth all understanding, shall keep your hearts and minds through Christ Jesus.

He became a Reprobate and an Outlaw

One Sunday morning, the Spirit of God moved in our service in a powerful and amazing way. Many people came forward to be prayed for that particular morning. Now in the prayer line there was a young evangelist who had been attending our church for some time. This particular morning the spirit of prophecy was flowing like a mighty river. I came up to this young man, and I laid my hands upon him, in which he immediately fell under the power of God. I continued to go down the line ministering to the people. When I was about three people down from him the Spirit of God arrested me, and took a hold of me. I found myself back at this man's feet. I ended up straddling him with my left foot on his right side, and my right foot on his left side. Then I reached down and grabbed his shirt with my left hand. With my right hand I began to slap his face very hard. I must have slapped him at least five times, on both sides of his cheeks. I was not truly aware of what I was doing in the natural. It was the mighty river of God flowing through my innermost being.

When I am in this place of the spirit I am not leaning at all upon my natural intellect or mind. When I was done slapping him, I went back to praying for the other people.

After a brief period once again the spirit of God arrested me, he took me back to this young evangelist once again. I spoke by the Spirit of God to him. The Spirit of the Lord told him, "Even as my servant has slapped your flesh, so you must slap your flesh. If you do not crucify your flesh, you will become a reprobate to the gospel and a fugitive from the law!" Now when the Spirit of God moves upon me this way, I sometimes do not completely remember the things that I say.

Three days later I received a phone call from one of the ladies in the church. She was weeping and said that her twenty some year old daughter had up and ran away with this particular evangelist. Not only had this young evangelist ran away with this lady's daughter, but it turned out that he was also involved with another young lady in the church. It was revealed that they had been involved in a sexual relationship also. I prayed with her over the phone.

Approximately one month later I received another phone call from this same lady whose daughter had ran away with this evangelist. She informed me that her daughter had been being beaten by this man, and that they had gone out one night drinking, when they were pulled over by a policeman. This evangelist got in an argument with the officer, which ended up with him physically fighting this policeman. Before he knew what he was doing, he had grabbed the police officer's revolver out of his holster and aimed the gun at the cop. He then left her daughter and the police officer, and ran for his life. Supposedly, he was headed for Canada. The last time I had heard, he was a fugitive of the law. Now I cannot verify all of this story, this is simply what was told me by the girl's mother.According to her story, everything that I had prophesied over this young evangelist if you did not crucify his flesh came to pass. If only we would harken to the correction of God's voice and spirit, how much trouble and disaster we could prevent. May God have mercy on us!

Three Precise Prophecies I gave that came to Pass!

One of the mothers in the church (Mary) came to the front for prayer. The Spirit of the Lord quickened me and I prophesied that all of her children would be saved. I also said and that her husband would also be saved, but it would be as if he was snatched from the flames of hell. A number of years later, she shared with me that everything I said came to pass. Her husband ended up with cancer. He was not open to the things of God, but as he lay on the bed of death, he cried out to Jesus. He was gloriously saved, with a deep hunger for the things of God. Shortly thereafter, he slipped off into eternity. He had been snatched from the flames of hell. Here is her story in her own words.

Mary's Testimony: My name is Mary J. Rockwell. I would like to share three quick testimonies in which I saw God speak in precise and prophetic, powerful ways in connection to Pastor Mike:

Testimony 1: Years ago my mother was very sick and in the hospital in New York state. I had asked Pastor Mike to pray for me prior to leaving Maryland to go see her. He told me when I saw her I was to pray over her and say, "I command all tormenting mental spirits to leave her now in the name of Jesus. He said that after I spoke this word of authority in the name of Jesus then I was to Clap my hands together three times and say: Now!

When I arrived at the hospital three of her doctors told me that she was going to die. My sister had called a pastor and began planning for her funeral. She had not eaten for days and had huge bags of fluid in the whites of her eyes and all over her face and didn't even look human. She was in a coma like condition. She was hooked up to IVs and monitors. I waited until she and I were the only ones left in the room. I pulled the curtain around us, put my hands on her head and prayed and commanded just as the Lord told me to according to the prophetic word from Pastor Mike. Then I clapped my hands three times and I said, "Now". As I did this I felt a surge leave my hands and go into her body. The next morning I went in to see her. The IVs had been removed, and she had come out of her coma. She was eating, and all the pockets of fluid had disappeared from her face and eyes! The doctors were absolutely amazed because according to all of their medical knowledge she should've been dead. They released her that morning. She lived another three or four years.

Testimony 2: I had fallen and broken both my wrists. The doctor had put a cast on one but I wouldn't let him cast the other. I went to Pastor Mike's home and he met me in the driveway. I asked him to pray for my healing, so he did. He told me prophetically that I was healed. I went home and within a week I felt that my wrists were healed. I told the doctor either he remove the cast or I would have my husband cut it off. The doctor had told me I would have to keep it on for weeks, but he reluctantly removed it. That same week I painted three ceilings by hand. The Lord had totally healed my wrists!

Testimony 3: When my children were still in school, I went up to the altar for prayer. Pastor Mike prayed and said, "Your prayers have reached the very throne room of heaven. God said, "You will live to see all of your children serve the Lord. Your husband will be saved but he will be literally pulled out of the pit of hell at the very end." My husband, at age seventy-two, contracted cancer from exposure to deadly chemicals while serving in the Marines in Vietnam. I had assumed that he knew the Lord. I prayed for him and said, "I could lay hands on you until you are bald, but you need to cry out to Jesus for yourself." He could not say the name, Jesus so I knew instantly that it was a demonic block. That it was obvious he was not yet born again.

I called a local pastor and was about to relate that to him when he told me that my husband's perception of salvation was wrong and he didn't believe he was really saved. He went to the hospital and prayed with him. My husband called me on the phone and said he had just received Jesus Christ as his Lord and Savior. His one regret was that he hadn't done enough for the Lord. The Lord had spoken to two young ladies who lived miles away from us to come and pray with him. When they came, my husband prayed for them and they wept and wept. It was not very long after that that he went home to be with the Lord. It was even as Pastor Mike prophesied. He was snatched out of the flames of the pit of hell right at the end of his life.

Three people who were there when Pastor Mike prayed for me called me on the phone and each of them reminded me of the prayer that Pastor Mike had prayed over me many years prior to that. Each of them inquired if my husband was saved and I told them it was just as Pastor Mike had prayed many years before. Since then, two of my four children are serving the Lord...two more to go!

A Prophetic Word That I Gave Saved Him $45,000

I had a precious brother who came to me the other day and made a bold statement. He declared, you saved me $45,000. I was surprised that he made this statement. I said to him, what exactly are you talking about? He told me that right before the economy fell through that I gave him a prophetic word that he needed to trade in his 401(k)! Honestly I did not even know that he had any 401(k)s. I do not even remember prophesying this to him. Many times this is the case when I am moving in the spirit, I will make statements or give prophetic words to people and not remember what I said. This is probably for the best, that way I cannot take the glory for myself. This brother had plenty of experiences with me as his pastor though, so he took to heart what I said to him. He told me that he immediately went and cashed in his 401(k)s. He also informed me that he was extremely glad that he had listened to the prophetic word, because if he had waited any longer, he would have lost $45,000. It is so important that we hear from heaven in order to preserve our lives.

Prophesied to a Brother that his family would Re-unite!

One day I received a phone call from a gentleman who wanted to rent a room from me. I have a house where I keep single men, helping them to get back on their feet. As I was speaking to him, he told me he knew who I was. I asked him: how's that? He informed me that a number of years ago he had visited our church. When he began to describe to me his family, immediately I remembered him. He came to our church with his family all dressed up, in strict religious style.

At the end of that service he informed me in his opinion that our church would never grow. I asked him why he would say such a thing. He said: if you would be preaching a religious and even restrictive philosophy there would be a chance of growth. But because you are preaching the divine nature of Christ, the fruits of the spirit, and the character of God, true holiness of the heart, most who come will not stay. He told me people like a religion they can take pride in. That was the last time I had seen him or his family.

Now here he was some years later. He informed me that he had lost his wife, and his children were scattered. Three sons and a daughter were spread out among relatives. He had fallen back into drugs and alcohol, going astray. As I was speaking to him, the spirit of the Lord gave me a word of wisdom. I told him by a prophetic word of the Lord, "I will rent a room to you at the house that is located on the church's property. Your wife will come back in approximately a month, then your children will come home, and your family will be restored." I told him to begin to attend our services, cry out to God, and he will answer you.

He moved into the room, that I had made available, with no security or money. I knew that God wanted to do a miracle for him and his family. He began to attend our services. Approximately three Sundays later, his wife shows up at one of our services. She had her hair dyed black, with black mascara on her eyes, looking Gothic. I was not moved by her rough appearance, for I had heard the word of the Lord. During the time of preaching and teaching, the spirit of God moved on her in a mighty way. She began to cry, with mascara running down her face. When I gave the altar call, she responded wholeheartedly. Oh, what a wonderful and beautiful instant change we saw in her.

She started coming to the services, and we saw her aggressively going after God. During the worship time she would be standing on her tippy toes, her arms stretched towards heaven, tears rolling down her face, hungry for Jesus. In a very short time all of the Gothic dress was completely gone. Within a very short time they had gathered all their children back to themselves. I rented an apartment to them, which had four bedrooms. God had restored his family, even as I had prophesied by the spirit of the Lord.

During this time period we ended up opening up a thrift store, where his wife would work through the day. Her husband, when he was not seeking work, or doing work, would help at this thrift store. My children grew close to their children, many times babysitting them when the parents went away. God is so good, and is more than willing to give us opportunity after opportunity to get right with him. He wants to restore every family. He wants to heal every marriage. He wants to set the captives free. We have a choice whether or not we will follow Christ or forsake him, and go our own way.

CHAPTER FIVE

#9 Tongues & Interpretation

We just finished teaching about the eighth way in which God leads and guides us. Now we will look at the **ninth way** which is tongues and interpretation. Interpretation according to the Scriptures equals that of prophecy. It reveals this to us in first Corinthians chapter 12 verse 10.

1Corinthians 12: 7 But the manifestation of the Spirit is given to every man to profit withal.8 For to one is given by the Spirit the word of wisdom; to another the word of knowledge by the same Spirit;9 To another faith by the same Spirit; to another the gifts of healing by the same Spirit;10 To another the working of miracles; to another prophecy; to another discerning of spirits; to another divers kinds of tongues; to another the interpretation of tongues:

I'm not really going to spend a lot of time speaking about this particular gift, because everything I wrote about prophecy would apply to tongues and interpretation. My wife flows in the gift of diversity of tongues. That simply means that she speaks in more than one. Sometimes it sounds like she speaking in Chinese, other times German, or French. I've heard her at times praying to the Lord where she would switch into six different languages. Sometimes when she has spoken in tongues it literally could be understood by someone who spoke and knew that language. Here is one example.

Singing in Arabic by the Holy Ghost

During worship one Sunday morning in 1981, my wife

Kathleen began to praise God in tongues. It was a very beautiful language. I love to listen to my wife speak and worship God in heavenly tongues because she operates in the what the Bible calls the gift of the diversity of tongues. On that particular Sunday morning, we had a first-time visitor that we had never seen before. He looked as if he was from the Middle East. At the end of the service this gentleman came over to me with a look of amazement on his face. He asked me where my wife had learned to sing in such beautiful and perfect Arabic. I informed him that she did not know how to speak in Arabic, that this was the spirit of God singing through her. When he informed me that she had been singing in perfect Arabic, I asked him what she had said? He told me that she was giving worshiping, praising and and giving glory to God. You can read in the book of acts you'll discover that this is nothing new.

Acts 2: ………...4 And they were all filled with the Holy Ghost, and began to speak with other tongues, as the Spirit gave them utterance.5 And there were dwelling at Jerusalem Jews, devout men, out of every nation under heaven.6 Now when this was noised abroad, the multitude came together, and were confounded, because that every man heard them speak in his own language.7 And they were all amazed and marveled, saying one to another, Behold, are not all these which speak Galilaeans?8 And how hear we every man in our own tongue, wherein we were born?9 Parthians, and Medes, and Elamites, and the dwellers in Mesopotamia, and in Judaea, and Cappadocia, in Pontus, and Asia,10 Phrygia, and Pamphylia, in Egypt, and in the parts of Libya about Cyrene, and strangers of Rome, Jews and proselytes,11 Cretes and Arabians, we do hear them speak in our tongues the wonderful works of God.12 And they were all amazed, and were in doubt, saying one to another, What meaneth this?

God is the author of all languages. In the book of Genesis chapter 11, it is revealed to us that in order to get the human race to spread across the earth as he had commanded them, God gave them different languages.

Genesis 11:8 So the Lord scattered them abroad from thence upon the face of all the earth: and they left off to build the city.9 Therefore is the name of it called Babel; because the Lord did there confound the language of all the earth: and from thence did the Lord scatter them abroad upon the face of all the earth.

Now when my wife speaks in diversity of tongues, and I give the interpretation, it is not what you would call and exact translation. What I am saying is that in my interpretation of the tongues, my voice inflections or body actions will not always be exactly the same as hers. Sometimes my interpretation might be longer or shorter than her message of tongues. There are times though that I have operated so deeply in this gift of interpretation that even with my wife being behind me, when I cannot see her, I will move my hands and arms in the same way that she gave the tongues. At times some people have even came to us after the service asking if we had practiced before the meeting for this to happen. Her tongues and the moving of her body, is so matched by my interpretation and demonstration, even though I did not see it, they thought that we had practiced and manufactured this manifestation, but this is not the case. She was moving by the spirit of God in the tongues and in the moving of her hands and her body, and by the spirit I simply did the same things but with the interpretation.

Most times when my wife moves in diversity of tongues and I have the interpretation she is behind me, and I am not seeing what she is doing. These tongues, and the interpretation of these tongues is not coming from our heads or intellect, but from our hearts, by the spirit of God. Jesus said out of your belly would flow rivers of living water. This is pertaining to the baptism of the Holy Ghost. All of these gifts happen by the spirit and are manifested according to our faith in Christ.

THE WHY OF TONGUES?

TONGUES is a Supernatural and divine utterance inspired by

God in an unknown tongue. It is a New Testament experience that is distinctive to this dispensation. Probably tongues has become one of the most controversial and misunderstood subjects of the Bible. Through the years I have run into those who say that the gift of tongues is done away with. To prove this they quote first Corinthians chapter 13.

1 Corinthians 13:8 Charity never faileth: but whether there be prophecies, they shall fail; whether there be tongues, they shall cease; whether there be knowledge, it shall vanish away.

Of course the context is: when that which is perfect is come. I believe that when the Scriptures say, that which is perfect, is referring to the second coming of Jesus Christ. All of the gifts of the spirit, the supernatural manifestations of the Holy Ghost will still be in operation until the coming of Christ.

Acts 2:38 Then Peter said unto them, Repent, and be baptized every one of you in the name of Jesus Christ for the remission of sins, and ye shall receive the gift of the Holy Ghost.39 For the promise is unto you, and to your children, and to all that are afar off, even as many as the Lord our God shall call.

In I COR 14:18 Paul the apostle declared that he spoke in tongues more than them all. In first Corinthians 14:5 Paul said that he wished, or desired that all should speak in tongues. The enemy of our soul hates it when we used the gift of tongues because of potentiality and power that is released through this Gift! You will discover that most people who do not want this gift, or have it, have no idea what it is they're missing.

10 MAJOR REASONS Why We Should Pray in Tongues!

I hope this teaching will encourage you to believe God to be baptized in the Holy Ghost, with the gift of speaking in tongues.

#1 It authenticates, substantiates, and verifies God's presence.

Mark 16:17 And these signs shall follow them that believe; In my name shall they cast out devils; they shall speak with new tongues;

Mark 16 proclaims these signs, including tongues. This is the evidence of the presence and power of Holy Ghost.In the old covenant the manifestation of God's presence was a Fire by night, and a cloud by day.But now in the New Testament, the evidence of the spirit of God and rolling his tabernacle is the gift of tongues.

Acts 2:3 And there appeared unto them cloven tongues like as of fire, and it sat upon each of them.4 And they were all filled with the Holy Ghost, and began to speak with other tongues, as the Spirit gave them utterance.

1 Corinthians 14:22 Wherefore tongues are for a sign, not to them that believe, but to them that believe not: but prophesying serveth not for them that believe not, but for them which believe.

The fire by night and the cloud by day has been replaced and this dispensation with tongues of men and of angels. This is the proof and evidence of the infilling of the Holy Spirit.

#2 A supernatural means of communicating directly to God.

1 Corinthians 14:2 For he that speaketh in an unknown tongue speaketh not unto men, but unto God: for no man understandeth him; howbeit in the spirit he speaketh. ... :27 If any man speak in an unknown tongue, let it be by two, or at the most by three, and that by course; and let one interpret. 28 But if there be no interpreter, let him keep silence in the church; and let him speak to himself, and to God.

This God-given prayer language is like an invisible supernatural umbilical cord of divine fellowship linking us directly to the Heavenly Father.

 *another amazing reality is that the devil cannot and does not understand what you are praying, therefore the demonic world cannot interfere, hinder or obstruct your prayers like he did to Daniel.

Daniel 10:12 Then said he unto me, Fear not, Daniel: for from the first day that thou didst set thine heart to understand, and to chasten thyself before thy God, thy words were heard, and I am come for thy words.13 But the prince of the kingdom of Persia withstood me one and twenty days: but, lo, Michael, one of the chief princes, came to help me; and I remained there with the kings of Persia.

#3 When you pray in tongues you are praying the perfect mind and will of God.

ROM 8:26 Likewise the Spirit also helpeth our infirmities: for we know not what we should pray for as we ought: but the Spirit itself maketh intercession for us with groanings which cannot be uttered.27 And he that searcheth the hearts knoweth what is the mind of the Spirit, because he maketh intercession for the saints according to the will of God.

(The Holy Ghost who knows all things, can pray through us about things which our natural mind knows nothing about.)

*Praying in the Holy Ghost, tongues also eliminates the possibility of selfishness entering into our prayers, or wrong praying which is out of line with the Word and the will of God!

#4 It is a wonderful way of praising and giving thanks to God.

1 Cor14:15 What is it then? I will pray with the spirit, and I will pray with the understanding also: I will sing with the spirit, and I will sing with the understanding also.16 Else when thou shalt bless with the spirit, how shall he that occupieth the room of the unlearned say Amen at thy giving of thanks, seeing he understandeth not what thou sayest?17 For thou verily givest thanks well, but the other is not edified.

Paul says that when you sing in tongues you are giving thanks and praise to God. This is something that you should practice on a daily basis.

#5 Helps us to become God inside conscious.

As you pray in his heavenly language it will cause you to become God inside mine did. In your heart you know that it is not truly you speaking, but the spirit of God within you. This is definitely going to affect the way you live.

"We have a tendency of forgetting the Greater One in us."

1 John 4:4 Ye are of God, little children, and have overcome them: because greater is he that is in you, than he that is in the world.

#6 Spiritual edifies us, beyond the physical or mental realm.

1 Corinthians 14:4 He that speaketh in an unknown tongue edifieth himself; but he that prophesieth edifieth the church.

(Praying in tongues enriches, cultivates, develops, improves us spiritually) *Out of your belly - a flowing stream that should never dry up.

John 7:37 In the last day, that great day of the feast, Jesus stood and cried, saying, If any man thirst, let him come unto me, and drink.38 He that believeth on me, as the scripture hath said, out of his belly shall flow rivers of living water.39 (But this spake he of the Spirit, which they that believe on him should receive: for the Holy Ghost was not yet given; because that Jesus was not yet glorified.)

#7 It is a refreshment, from turmoil, perplexity, insecurity.

ISA 28:9 Whom shall he teach knowledge? and whom shall he make to understand doctrine? them that are weaned from the milk, and drawn from the breasts.10 For precept must be upon precept, precept upon precept; line upon line, line upon line; here a little, and there a little:11 For with stammering lips and another tongue will he speak to this people.12 To whom he said, This is the rest wherewith ye may cause the weary to rest; and this is the refreshing: yet they would not hear.

Praying in the Holy Ghost will bring you into a place of rest and refreshment, in your walk with God. The Scripture says that it will free you from turmoil, perplexity, insecurity. It brings tranquility, relaxation, restoration and spiritual reviving in your heart. It invigorates and renews your walk with God. A tremendous spiritual pick-me-up you might say.

#8 Keeps our bodies under the control of the Holy Spirt.

James 3:1My brethren, be not many masters, knowing that we shall receive the greater condemnation.2 For in many things we offend all. If any man offend not in word, the same is a perfect man, and able also to bridle the whole body.3 Behold, we put bits in the horses' mouths, that they may obey us; and we turn about their whole body.4 Behold also the ships, which though they be so great, and are driven of fierce winds, yet are they turned about with a very small helm, whithersoever the governor listeth.5 Even so the tongue is a little member, and boasteth great things.

The Tongue is a rudder and bridle of our human body, mind and emotions.

#9 Teaches you how to yield yourself to God, thereby opening the door for the other gifts to flow.

Because it is considered one of the least of the gifts, it is like stepping stones into the deeper realms of the spirit.

"It is a major KEY to the MANIFESTATION of the GIFTS of the Holy Ghost"

#10 It charges, fortifies, stimulates, invigorates your faith.

This last particular point about the purpose of praying in your heavenly language needs to be dealt with in much greater detail.

*Praying in the Holy Ghost is one of the greatest spiritual exercises there is. Takes faith to pray in, believe it is accomplishing, etc. Prepares us for whatever the future holds in store for us. Gets us ready.

Jude 20 But ye, beloved, building up yourselves on your most holy faith, praying in the Holy Ghost.

If you will study this Scripture in other translations it declares that we must fortify, strengthen, and establish our most holy faith! How do we do this? By praying in the Holy Ghost. I do not believe this is only speaking about praying in the gift of tongues which you received when you received the baptism in the Holy Ghost. But it is also speaking about the Holy Ghost leading you in your prayer time. The spirit of the Lord himself will put the words into your mouth that need to be spoken.

2 Samuel 23:2 The Spirit of the Lord spake by me, and his word was in my tongue.

Psalm 45:1......my tongue is the pen of a ready writer.

When you build yourself up in your most holy faith, this spiritual response is that it will take a hold of the holiness of God, it takes a hold of the will of God, and it takes a hold of the character and the divine nature of God. There is a teaching that I have done which reveals 10 biblical benefits that take place when you pray in tongues! Out of the 10 gifts of the Holy Ghost revealed within the Scriptures, tongues is one of the simplest that Christ has given to the church. This tongues that I'm referring to is not the same diversity tongues that needs to be interpreted. It is your own personal prayer language that the Holy Ghost will give you to communicate to God.

Romans 8:26 Likewise the Spirit also helpeth our infirmities: for we know not what we should pray for as we ought: but the Spirit itself maketh intercession for us with groanings which cannot be uttered.

The exercising of this God-given language opens the door wide for the manifestation of the other 9 gifts of the spirit. It takes faith to believe that God is speaking through you in this super natural language which sometimes sounds like baby talk. I asked the Lord one time why would he give his people a language that sounded ridiculous? He spoke to my heart and said I do it to humble my people. You must be as a child to enter into the kingdom of heaven.

Ephesians 6:18 Praying always with all prayer and supplication in the Spirit,

How God Supernaturally Healed Me of Being Tongue-Tied!

Let me share an amazing story about how I was baptized in the Holy Ghost, and the difference it made in my life. After I gave my heart to Christ a divine hunger and thirst for the Word of God began to possess me. I practically devoured Matthew, Mark, Luke, and John. Jesus became my hero in every sense of the word, in every area of my thoughts and daily living. He became my soul reason for getting up every day and going to work, eating, sleeping, and living. I discovered that everything I did was based on a desire of wanting to please Him. One day I was reading my Bible and discovered where Jesus said that it was necessary for him to leave. That because when he would go back to the Father, he would send the promise of the Holy Ghost to make us a witness. Furthermore, I learned it was His will for me to be filled to overflowing with the Holy Ghost and that the Holy Ghost would empower and equip me to be a witness an ambassador for God.

The Holy Ghost would also lead me and guide me into all truth. With all of my heart I desperately wanted to reach the lost for Jesus Christ in order for they could experience the same love and freedom that I was now walking in. I searched the Scriptures to confirm this experience. In the book of Joel, in the old covenant, the four Gospels and especially in the book of acts I discovered the will of God when it comes to this baptism. I perceived in my heart that I needed to receive this baptism the same way that I had received salvation. I had to look to Christ and trust by faith that he would give to me this baptism of the Spirit. It declared in the book of acts that after they were baptized in the Holy Ghost they all began to speak in a heavenly language. I had not been around what we would call Pentecostal people, so I had never heard anybody else speak in this heavenly language. But that did not really matter to me, because it was within the Scriptures.

Acts 2:39 For the promise is unto you, and to your children, and to all that are afar off, even as many as the Lord our God shall call.

I remember getting on my knees next to my bunk bed where I cried out and asked God to fill me with the Holy Ghost so I could be a witness. As I was crying out to God something began to happen on the inside of me. It literally felt like hot buckets of oil was beginning to be poured upon me and within me. Something then began to rise up out of my innermost being. Before I knew what I was doing, a new language came out bubbling of my mouth which I had never heard before, or been taught to speak. I began to speak in a heavenly tongue.

Now up to this time I had a terrible speech impediment. You see I had been born tongue-tied. Yes they had operated on me, and I had gone to speech therapy, and yet most people could not understand what I was saying. I could not even pronounce my own last name YEAGER properly. My tongue simply refused to move in a way in which I could pronounce my Rs. After I was done praying in this new language, I discovered to my absolute surprise that my speech impediment was instantly and completely gone! From that time on, I have never stopped preaching Jesus Christ. For almost 40 years I have proclaimed the truth of Jesus Christ to as many as I can.

For the First Time She Could Understand Me

About 4 months after I gave my heart to Christ I went back to my hometown, Mukwonago, Wisconsin, and I immediately went to see one of my best friends to share with him my conversion experience. Actually, it was his sister I had been dating for the last three years. I wrote her a letter telling her what happened to me, and how God gloriously had set me free from drugs, alcohol, and all of my worldly living. This caused her to cut me off completely, as if I had lost my mind. Praise God! I had lost my mind by receiving the mind of Christ. My friend's mother was listening while I was speaking to her son, and out of nowhere she said, "Mike, what happened to you?" I told her how I had been delivered from drugs and immorality because I gave my heart to Jesus. She said, "No, that's not what I'm talking about. After many years of knowing you, this is actually the 1st time I can fully understand what you are saying." You see, my speech was so garbled that it was very difficult for people to truly understand exactly what I was saying. Those who know me now would not have recognized the old me. Before I was baptized in the Holy Ghost you would not have been able to understand most of what I said. I'm still trying to make up for the nineteen years when I could not speak properly.

#10 VISIONS

I believe with all my heart that one of the most important realities in a believer's life is that we need to hear from heaven. We need to hear directly from God. The Bible says:

Jeremiah 10:23 O Lord, I know that the way of man is not in himself: it is not in man that walketh to direct his steps.

Proverbs 16:25 There is a way that seemeth right unto a man, but the end thereof are the ways of death.

Now if we lean to the understanding of our mind, we will end up going down a dead end alley. The ways of the natural man will bring nothing but destruction and death. If we are not led by the spirit of God, our life will be meaningless, having no real significance. The Scripture says:

1 Corinthians 3:19 For the wisdom of this world is foolishness with God. For it is written, He taketh the wise in their own craftiness.

If I live my life according to how I think I should live, and not according to God's will,God's plan,God's purposes for my life, it will end up being nothing but a waste of time. What's going to happen after I die and stand before the Lord if I have lived my life this way? I will find out that everything I did in this world had no meaning and had no real significance. I know I'm specifically speaking to believers, but this is even more frightening. I think most people who call themselves believers are living lives that have no meaning and no significance. What I mean by this statement is that when you stand before God, and you give an account of your life, but you have lived your life the way you wanted, you will have nothing to offer to God.

When the disciples looked at Jesus, they saw something different about his life. That's why they said to him: Lord teach us to pray! As believers there's should be something different about our lives, every step, every word, and everything we do. Listen to the amazing response that Jesus gave his disciples.

Matthew 6:9 After this manner therefore pray ye: Our Father which art in heaven, Hallowed be thy name.10 Thy kingdom come, Thy will be done in earth, as it is in heaven.

The foundation of a believer's life is this: **I want your will Father to be done in my life today, and every day, in every area.** Now notice it's a day by day walk. Sometimes, most times for me it's a minute by minute situation. I want Gods will to be done for me today, right now on earth as it is in heaven. If you really do not care about the will of God, then what I'm saying is going to go right over the top of your head. Most believers I have know are more interested in talking about football, NASCAR, politics and the weather. Most likely you are not in this category, because you have taken the time to purchase this book, and to read it. Now, I use to be really deep into hunting and fishing, sports, but when I experienced the reality of Jesus Christ, all of these things became extremely boring to me. When I hear somebody talk about Jesus, then my ears perk up. I want to stop and listen. I want to see what you have to say because that's what I'm looking for. I'm looking for the will of God to be done in my life as it is in heaven.

Tattooed woman saved and filled with the Holy Ghost.

In July of 2015 my wife and I walked into a store where we knew the owner very well. Actually the owner used to work for me as the principle of our Christian school. Standing in front of the counter was a lady who probably was in her late 30s. She was dressed in the style of a Gothic. She had a large tattoo of a human skull on her neck. She also had tattoos on her arms and her legs. This did not bother me in the least, because I came out of that kind of world. I knew that God is not moved by what he sees on the outer man.

Immediately my ears perked up because I heard this lady talking about the things of God. Instantly I perceived there was a spiritual hunger in her heart to know the Lord. I knew by the gift of the word of knowledge that she had been involved in new ageism. That she had been looking for something that was real her whole life, and yet she had not discovered it.

I heard the Lord say to me (in my heart) she is ready right now to be born again and filled with the Holy Ghost. When she had stopped to take a breath of air, I began to talk to her. I began to share with her what the Lord spoke to my heart about her life. She said that it was absolutely true. I asked her if she was ready to receive from the Lord? She said she absolutely was! At that moment I told her that she needed to pray along with me, accepting Jesus Christ, and being filled with the Holy Ghost. She said she would.

I had her pray according to that which God was quickening to my heart. She gave her heart to Jesus Christ right then and there. I asked my Heavenly Father to baptize her in the Holy Ghost, that the evidence of speaking in tongues. I told her that she needed to reach her hands towards heaven, in which she did. As I laid my hands upon her with my wife, instantly she began to speak in a heavenly language.

She is now attending church, and actively pursuing God with her children. Just last week, as I write this experience, she was water baptized for the glory of Jesus.

John 10:27 My sheep hear my voice, and I know them, and they follow me:

Romans 8:14 For as many as are led by the Spirit of God, they are the sons of God.

If you study Romans 8:14 in the Greek, the word **sons** in the Greek is pertaining to those who are mature sons. Those who have the maturity to recognize that God has a right to lead and guide us in whatever direction he so desires. Many within the body are not mature enough, in order for God to direct them in such a way.

1 Corinthians 13:11 When I was a child, I spake as a child, I understood as a child, I thought as a child: but when I became a man, I put away childish things.

Personally I fall short of this many times, but when I fall down, I repent and get back up. I say: Lord I want to hear your voice because without your voice I am lost and undone. Hearing the voice of God is always discovered in the arena of faith, even though at times it will involve your feelings,emotions and even your circumstances. I will tell you that God at times will use circumstances, feelings and emotions to direct your life. These are some of the ways that God will lead you and guide you. We will be talking about these different ways as we progress in this teaching. Please realize that God wants to speak to us 24/7 if we have a desire to hear him.

In this chapter we are talking about the **10th Way** in which God will lead and guide us, which is by the use of **V**isions. If we went from Genesis to Revelation we would discover that much of the will of God is revealed by this divine supernatural experience. The word vision alone appears in the Bible almost 100 times. If we would count every time God gave a vision to one of his people it would number may be in the thousands. This is a major way that God reveals his will, not just to his people, but to the human race. For instance God called Abraham out of the city of the Chaldean s, and told Abraham his plan and his future, for his life by visions.

Genesis :1 After these things the word of the Lord came unto Abram in a vision, saying, Fear not, Abram: I am thy shield, and thy exceeding great reward.

Actually I could write a book on the subject of visions alone. I have discovered that there is at least **five different levels of**

visions, in which God will speak to us, and reveal his will. Let us look at the first type of vision.

#1 It is simply a **very translucent image or vision that happens in your mind! This very soft and light foggy image floats up from your heart, into your brain.** This happens to me all the time. Especially when I go to pray for people. I'll see something going on in someone's life. I'll see a problem or I'll see a physical disability. Sometimes I'll see something happening in the past, or something that is going to happen in the future.

His Hernia Was Instantly Gone!

One night I was at a fellowship gathering with other believers from our little church. Chief officer Lloyd and his wife, Bonnie, had invited us all to come to their house for fellowship.

Now as I was standing in their front room enjoying the fellowship, a kind of foggy image came floating up from my heart into my mind. In this semi-foggy vision I saw a bulge in the lower stomach area of the man standing directly across from me. I did not know that this bulge was actually what they call a hernia. I had only been born again for about a month, and not yet been taught on the gifts of the Holy Ghost. This was the word of knowledge operating by a vision inspired by the Holy Ghost.

As I saw this image in my mind's eye, I said to the Lord in my heart: Lord, if this image is really of you then let that brother come over to me. The very moment this little prayer left my heart, this navy chief (Frank) looked up and walked over me. I then also walked toward him, and we both reached out our hands towards each other, shaking hands. He introduced himself as Frank. As we were making small talk, I brought up the image I just had.

He looked rather surprised and informed me that he was indeed having a terrible time with a hernia. The doctors had operated on it three times up to this point he informed me, but it had torn loose after each operation. I asked him if I could pray for him pertaining to this problem, and he gave me permission. I told him that I would like him to put his hand over this hernia and that I would place my hand over his.

Then I simply prayed but a long prayer. I simply spoke very quietly to this hernia telling it to go away in the name of Jesus Christ, and for his stomach muscles to be healed. The moment I finished praying, it disappeared. The hernia was instantly and literally sucked back into his abdomen; it was gone!

We both stood there, being wonderfully surprised, and rejoicing in the miracle that God had just performed. How this miracle came to pass is that God had given me "a word of knowledge and operating with the gift of faith and healing." Frank and I became good friends afterwards. At times we would go fishing out on the Bering Sea for halibut, but that's a whole another story.

#2 a very strong picture or image floats up from your heart in to my mind. This type of a vision is in between that which is **visible and that which is invisible. You could say that it's almost like an imprint in your mind.**

Pastor Healed of Cancer When She Was Called out with the Word of Knowledge!

In Her Own Words: In the Month of February 2013, I was diagnosed with a large lesion in the upper left Chest area. Pastor mike I came to your fellowship, Jesus is Lord Ministries that Sunday Morning, I had The X-ray results from the study on my chair. I was praying that somehow that the Father God would give ME an opportunity to share with you and ask you to prayer for me.

Well do you know during the time that you were delivering the message you asked me to stand to my feet because God had revealed to you exactly what I was dealing! This was without me telling you anything. You pointed directly to the Left side of my chest and said: I see a growth in your lungs. You then called me forward to be prayed for. You anointed my forehead with oil, and asked me to place my hand on my left chest, you began to pray for me, the power of God hit me, and we both jumped, and you said. "I'm waiting for the praise report" I was scheduled for a CT SCAN of my chest the follow Saturday. .well..

The report from that study read: **THERE IS NO LESION FOUND IN LEFT LUNG AREA"** I did return to Jesus is Lord Church and shared my miracle testimony with you and the congregation. I want to thank you man of God for every time I've fellowship with your Precious Church family, I always get restored, refreshed and watered to overflowing. I've always know that this is a "Well of refreshing water for me"..I'm grateful to Jesus for your prayers, intercession, loving kindness towards me. .Joy over flowing in my soul! Pastor Lauretta Melendez. Owings Mills, Md

Pastor Mike's side of the story: as I was preaching the word of God, and looking over the congregation, something supernatural took place. As I was looking at Pastor Lauretta (by the way at the time I did not know in the natural she was a pastor - the Lord supernaturally told me that she was, in which she confirmed it.) I had very strong picture or image that floated up from my heart into my mind. I could literally see that there was a role in her left lungs. As I saw this girl, by the word of wisdom, and the gift of faith, I knew, that I knew God was going to healer this morning.

I stopped preaching, pointed my finger at her, and told her what the Lord said to me. She began to immediately rejoice, because that is exactly why she had come to our service. I called her up front, anointed her with oil, and laying my hands upon her. I cursed the growth in the name of Jesus, and commanded the growth and the cancer to be gone. Then I told her by the Holy Ghost that she needed to go back to the doctors, and get it confirmed. Praise God, I obeyed what the Lord said to me, she responded accordingly, and God healed her. Jesus Christ is the same yesterday today and forever!

#3 A see-able vision laid over the top of your eyesight. It is a vision that you literally see with your human eyes. I'm seeing the natural, and yet I'm seeing into the spiritual realm.

I saw through his shoes, fungus on his feet!

My wife and I were ministering at a church in the Harrisburg, Pennsylvania area. I had finished ministering the message that God had laid on my heart, and now I was beginning to move in the gifts of the Holy Spirit. God began to confirm His word with wonderful signs and wonders. The word of knowledge, wisdom and discerning of spirits were being manifested as I surrendered and yielded to the Spirit of God. New wine began to flow as people were being touched by the Holy Ghost. As I was finishing up with one of the people we were praying for, I looked over at the pastor who was sitting on the front row of chairs with his wife.

This pastor is a rather large man, in height and weight. The Holy Spirit drew my attention to his feet. Because he is also involved in the farming industry, he was wearing a heavy duty pair of shoes. As I was looking at the shoes, all of a sudden I could see right through them. It actually shocked me to some extent. I could see very clearly his feet and toes. This experience was so real that it pulled me right over to him. I stood in front of this pastor looking at his feet, with a look of surprise on my face. I pointed right down at his feet, stating: what is going on with your toes? He said: what? I repeated my question: what is going on with your toes?

I could see that they were completely covered in fungus! I saw that even the nails of his toes were gone, or completely covered in black, yellow nasty fungus. I told him, fungus! Your toes and your feet are completely covered in fungus! He answered and said: yes, they have been like that for many years. When I used to play football (must have been about forty years earlier) somehow I contracted this fungus, and I have never been able to get rid of it.

I fell to my knees right then and there, putting my hands on his shoes. I spoke to the fungus on his toes, and feet, commanding that in the name of Jesus Christ it had to go. I told the spirit of infirmity to leave his feet now in the name of Jesus. As I spoke the word of God, I knew in my heart by a gift of faith, and the gift of healing that he was healed. I told him, it's gone. In the name of Jesus it is gone, and you are healed. At that moment I got up off the floor and continued to minister to others by the spirit of God.

About a month later I was back in this man's church ministering. I asked him: brother, how is your feet? He told me the fungus was all gone, and that after all those years he was now free. Jesus Christ, by the gifts of the Holy Ghost, had revealed this need, and caused him to be completely healed.

#4 Then there is what we would call an open vision! What I mean by this is that everything disappears, and all you see is that which God is showing you.

I Had An Open Vision!

The Lord began to bring discipline into my life about my spiritual condition. He basically told me that I was a "favorite scripture" preacher, and that I really did not know his Word the way I should. I was so convicted by this confrontation from God that I made a commitment that I would begin to pour myself into the Bible like I never before. I was going to spend hours in God's Word and prayer.

When I got home from vacation, I informed my staff that I would begin to give myself to long hours of prayer and the Word. I began with the book of Ephesians, starting with the very first chapter. I did not want to only memorize it, but I wanted to get it into my heart. This took me close to three weeks and countless hours to memorize.

Then the next mountain I climbed was the book of Galatians. As I was memorizing scriptures and chapters of the Bible, I was get terrible headaches. But I kept working at it because I knew that without pain, there is no gain. When I had conquered the book of Galatians, I moved to the book of Philippians. One day as I was into the second chapter of the book of Philippians, something supernatural and amazing took place. I had what the Bible calls an open vision. This happens when you are wide awake and yet everything disappears around you except what God is showing you.

Now in this open vision there appeared in front of me was a very large body of water. It was pure blue with not one ripple upon it, stretching as far as the natural eye could see in every direction. The room I was in was completely gone and there was nothing but this gigantic blue lake. As I lifted my head to look into the light blue never-ending cloudless sky, I saw a large, crystal-clear rain drop came falling down towards this body of water in slow motion from the heavens. I watched in amazement as it slowly came tumbling down towards this lake. When it hit the surface of this body of water, it caused ripples to flow forth.

These ripples, as they flowed forth from the center of where the drop had hit, began to grow in size and intensity. Then all suddenly as the vision had come it was gone. I stood there in my office in complete amazement, not understanding what had just happened, or why it had happened. I knew this experience was from God, but I did not know what the significance of it was. I knew in my heart that God eventually would show me what it meant. You see, when the Lord gives me a supernatural visitation, I do not try to understand with my natural mind. I just simply give it to the Lord, knowing that in His time He will show me what the experience means, or what He was saying.

I picked up my Bible to get back to my memorizing scriptures. I immediately noticed that there was a change in my mental capacity. It seemed like as if my brain was absorbing the Word of God like a dry sponge soaking up water. Within one hour I literally memorized a whole chapter of the book of Philippians, as if it were nothing. To my amazement, where it took me days to memorize a chapter before, now I could memorize a chapter in an hour. I continued to memorize books of the Bible until there were nine books inside of me. This is not including thousands of other scriptures that I continued to memorize dealing with certain subjects.

I believe I could have memorized the whole New Testament had I not allowed the activities of ministry to overwhelm me and keep me preoccupied. The enemy of our soul knows how to make things happen in our lives to get us sidetracked.

Now why in the world would God open up my heart and my mind in such a dramatic way to memorize the Word? It is because it is by the word of God that our minds are renewed, and we can discover his perfect will for our lives. The Word of God has the capacity to quicken our minds and mortal bodies. God's Word is awesome, quick and powerful. I believe that there is an activation of the things of the Spirit, when we begin to give ourselves to one hundred percent of whatever it is that God has called us to do. There is a dynamic principle of laying your life down, in order to release the aroma of heaven.

#5 This type of **vision** is so real that you **literally feel and experience what you're seeing.** Paul the apostle experience this:

2 Corinthians 12:2 I knew a man in Christ above fourteen years ago, (whether in the body, I cannot tell; or whether out of the body, I cannot tell: God knoweth;) such an one caught up to the third heaven.3 And I knew such a man, (whether in the body, or out of the body, I cannot tell: God knoweth;)4 How that he was caught up into paradise, and heard unspeakable words, which it is not lawful for a man to utter.

The Splendors of Heaven

One night I was all alone in deep prayer in my military barracks. I was on my knees crying out to God when the atmosphere of the room began to change. The hairs on my arms and neck stood up as if electricity was completely surrounding me. To my amazement, suddenly out of the blue, a portal made of pure light opened up into my room. To me this was physical and real. It was not a figment of my imagination in any way form or fashion.

An angel of the Lord came walking through this portal. As he came into my room, I fell as a dead man to my face. This angel commanded me not to be afraid and he took me by my right hand and lifted me up as if I was nothing but a feather. This angel took me back through the white portal that had opened up in my dorm room. He took me to into that place that we call heaven. You can read all about this experience in the book I wrote called "Horrors of Hell, Splendors of Heaven".

Now sometimes you can experience things so real in your mind that even if it's not of God, you convince yourself it is. We must never exalt experiences above the written word and will of the Father. So many sincere men and women of God have prophesied, and declared that certain events would happen, but they never did. These people were totally convinced they had heard from heaven. What do you do if you believe that you have an experienced something from God, and it does not come to pass? First it could be that it is not yet time. The second reason is simply that you missed God. In that situation, you repent! You ask God to forgive you. You verbally acknowledge in public that you missed the will of the Father, and you move on.

If you look at most religions you'll discover that most of them were started by someone who had what they called a supernatural visitation. This visitation they experienced whether it was a dream, a vision, an audible voices, did not line up with the biblical scriptures that God has given to us by His Holy apostles and prophets. These men and women if they had known the word of God, would have taken authority over these visitations which were demonic. Instead they embraced them, declaring that their experiences were from God himself.

Matthew 24:24 For there shall arise false Christs, and false prophets, and shall shew great signs and wonders; insomuch that, if it were possible, they shall deceive the very elect.

God does speak to us by visions and dreams.

Numbers 12:6 And he said, Hear now my words: If there be a prophet among you, I the Lord will make myself known unto him in a vision, and will speak unto him in a dream.

The prophet Isaiah had amazing vision after vision with such clarity of heavenly and spiritual realities, that it is almost virtually impossible to improve on his descriptions. One amazing vision he had was a declaration of the sufferings of Christ discovered in Isaiah 53.

Isaiah 53:3 He is despised and rejected of men; a man of sorrows, and acquainted with grief: and we hid as it were our faces from him; he was despised, and we esteemed him not.4 Surely he hath borne our griefs, and carried our sorrows: yet we did esteem him stricken, smitten of God, and afflicted.5 But he was wounded for our transgressions, he was bruised for our iniquities: the chastisement of our peace was upon him; and with his stripes we are healed.

God in his imparting divine visions to his people, is not just not just for the old testament. He granted to many of those in the book of Acts divine visitations, by means of a vision. Peter shared such a vision that he experienced when he was in Simon the tanner's house.

Acts 10:9 On the morrow, as they went on their journey, and drew nigh unto the city, Peter went up upon the housetop to pray about the sixth hour:10 And he became very hungry, and would have eaten: but while they made ready, he fell into a trance,11 And saw heaven opened, and a certain vessel descending upon him, as it had been a great sheet knit at the four corners, and let down to the earth:12 Wherein were all manner of fourfooted beasts of the earth, and wild beasts, and creeping things, and fowls of the air.13 And there came a voice to him, Rise, Peter; kill, and eat.14 But Peter said, Not so, Lord; for I have never eaten any thing that is common or unclean.

This vision which God had given to Peter not only changed Peter's life, but radically changed the direction for the whole body of Christ. It was by this vision that God opened the door wide for the Gentiles to come flooding into the kingdom. Please do not think for a moment that I am encouraging people to seek for visions or supernatural experiences, we do not seek supernatural manifestations or experiences, but we seek the face of God, and as God sees fit, he speaks to us in what ever way he so chooses.

When God does visit us with a vision or other divinely inspired visitations, we must never promote or exalt these experiences above the word of God. For example back in 1975 the spirit of God took me to hell for over 2 1/2 hours, and yet I very rarely ever speak about this experience. You can have a true visitation of God, but we need to make sure that we are promoting nobody but Jesus Christ.

Your hunger for God has a great influence upon the the divine visitations God will give you. The greater your hunger, the greater your visitations. I have discovered this reality with over 40 years of ministry. When I begin to truly press into God with all my heart just to get to know God, he begins to reveal himself in much greater ways to me. When I talk about seeking to know God, I am not speaking about seeking to have supernatural visitations.

James 4:8 Draw nigh to God, and he will draw nigh to you. Cleanse your hands, ye sinners; and purify your hearts, ye double minded.

I'm so glad for the visions that the Lord has granted onto me. God has used visions to save my life, to give me specific directions, to reveal to me wonderful divine truths and revelations. God also uses visions to activate and increase our faith in order to complete the mission he has for us in this life. When you get baptized in the Holy Ghost, and you begin to be led by the spirit, divine visitations will come, and increase.

Joel 2:28 And it shall come to pass afterward, that I will pour out my spirit upon all flesh; and your sons and your daughters shall prophesy, your old men shall dream dreams, your young men shall see visions:

CHAPTER SIX

#11 DREAMS

The **11th Way** in which God will speak to us is by supernatural and divine dreams. With in the Scriptures it speaks about dreams over 87 times. What is a dream? Webster (Webster's Third New International Dictionary) describes a dream in this way, "1a: a series of thoughts, images, or emotions occurring during sleep. . . . having ideas or images in the mind while asleep". So, dreams are thoughts and images occurring during sleep.

In Scripture, a dream is not only called a "dream", but also "a vision of the night" (Job 33:15), "thoughts upon my bed" (Daniel 4:5), "visions of my head" (Daniel 4:5; 7:15), "visions of his head upon his bed" (Daniel 7:1), and "night visions" (Daniel 7:7, 13). Now granted, the above references out of Daniel are in reference to dreams given miraculously by God, but even when the Word speaks of a "normal" type of a dream, it is still called a "night vision" (Isaiah 29:7-8). In fact, Job 33:15 clearly describes a dream as "a vision of the night". Scriptures also defines dreams as **"night visions"**.

Dreams are used of God to speak to people to a much greater extent than we probably understand or relize. The book of Job shares with us a powerful Scripture dealing with this subject.

Job 33:14 For God speaketh once, yea twice, yet man perceiveth it not.15 In a dream, in a vision of the night, when deep sleep falleth upon men, in slumberings upon the bed;16 Then he openeth the ears of men, and sealeth their instruction,

According to scientific research the average person experiences approximately 10 dreams every night. Those who have researched the subject say that the last 20 minutes before you go to bed, determines to a great extent what you will be dreaming about all night long. On average most people dream about two hours every night. You and I will have over 2200 dreams in a typical year. Now it is obvious that a lot of these dreams people are experiencing are **not** from the Lord, and yet you would be amazed at how many of these dreams are coming from God. What you are meditating, watching, and thinking about through the day has a powerful impact upon what you will dream about at night. For instance if you worry a lot, you will have dreams pertaining to what you're worrying about, and what you do, and say, that which you meditate upon will be the foremost thought in your mind. Your mind is like an incubator, and what ever you allow your thought life to become impregnated with, will cause you will to give birth in the area of images and dreams.

Are we responsible for our dreams? Clearly, Job gives us an example where his dreams tormented him (Job 7:13-15). If our hearts have the power to influence what we dream, then to some extent we are responsible for what we dream. The dreams we experience will be to a great extent based upon our lifestyle, daily meditations, and purpose for living.

Proverbs 23:7 For as he thinketh in his heart, so is he: Eat and drink, saith he to thee; but his heart is not with thee.

We are also responsible for how we respond to the situations we find ourselves in,whether while we are awake, or while we are asleep. If we lust after something or someone in our dreams, we are still responsible before God. If we carry out an ungodly act in a dream, we are responsible before God for this act. It is not the devil that caused me to react in a sinful way in the dream. Even if the devil did influence us to do some thing wrong (awake or asleep), we are still responsible before God for our actions. Amazingly on the flip side of the coin, we can also be blessed because of our response in a dream. Solomon the son of David is a perfect example of this.

1 Kings 3:5 In Gibeon the Lord appeared to Solomon in a dream by night: and God said, Ask what I shall give thee.6 And Solomon said, Thou hast shewed unto thy servant David my father great mercy, according as he walked before thee in truth, and in righteousness, and in uprightness of heart with thee; and thou hast kept for him this great kindness, that thou hast given him a son to sit on his throne, as it is this day.............10 And the speech pleased the Lord, that Solomon had asked this thing.11 And God said unto him, Because thou hast asked this thing, and hast not asked for thyself long life; neither hast asked riches for thyself, nor hast asked the life of thine enemies; but hast asked for thyself understanding to discern judgment;

Now there are such things as demonic dreams. The enemy many times will attack us in the night when we seem to be the most vulnerable. Yet thank the Lord we are not completely defenseless in these moments if we have a heart after God, and have filled our hearts with the word of God. Let me share one such experience with you.

*Demonic power tried to kill me

Here I was as a 21-year-old kid on-fire for God! I knew in my heart I was stirring things up in the satanic realm and the demonic world would try to find a way to destroy me. I did not have any fear in my heart because I had discovered the truth that "greater is He that is in me, than he that is in the world!"

Now I had a very realistic experience one night as I was sleeping. I saw this dark, faceless demon come running down the long hallway of the house I was staying in. It was just a tiny house that had actually been a chicken house converted into a small house with a guest quarters. I shared this house with an evangelist and his wife. I slept all the way down on the other side of this long narrow building. I'm not complaining (faith never grumbles or gripes). I could handle it even if it was not heated or air conditioned. The particular night, I saw in a very tangible dream this demonic spirit come running down this long hallway through the door and into my bedroom. When it came into my bedroom, it immediately jumped on top of me and began choking me. I could not physically breathe at that moment. Panic and fear overwhelmed me! Then I heard the voice of God speak to my heart, telling me to be at peace.

The Lord's presence came flooding in upon me at that very moment. I cried out to Jesus with a whisper and rebuked this demon that was choking me, in the name of Jesus. At this point I was fully awake by this time. As this dark image continued choking me, I saw a gigantic hand come down through the ceiling of my room. It grabbed this faceless, dark demonic power around the neck and ripped it off me. This gigantic hand shook it like a cat would a mouse and threw it out of the room. God's presence overwhelmed me as I was sitting up in my bed crying and weeping with joy and praising God! This experience was not just my imagination running wild, but it was literal and real!

God wants to open our eyes, guide and lead us to give us instruction through dreams. Like I said this doesn't mean every dream is of the Lord. That's why we must look at the dreams we have experienced through Christ and through the word of God. There are many examples of God giving men warnings and instructions by the use of dreams. God gave a message to King Abimelech about Abraham's wife:

But God came to Abimelech in a dream one night and said to him, "You are as good as dead because of the woman you have taken; she is a married woman." Now Abimelech had not gone near her, so he said, "Lord, will you destroy an innocent nation? Did he not say to me, 'She is my sister,' and didn't she also say, 'He is my brother'? I have done this with a clear conscience and clean hands" (Gen. 20:3-5).

God also gave dramatic dreams to Nebuchadnezzar, Daniel, Joseph, Jacob, Solomon, every prophet of God, and every day people. I'm totally convinced that as our mind and are heart is fixed on Christ, dreams and visitations of the Lord will increase.

Isaiah 26:3 Thou wilt keep him in perfect peace, whose mind is stayed on thee: because he trusteth in thee.4 Trust ye in the Lord for ever: for in the Lord Jehovah is everlasting strength:

God has many times given me instructions, directions and important information by the means of dreams. In dreams I have seen people doing certain things, positive and negative which was very helpful in me making the right decisions. It is very important that we are close enough to the Lord, and know enough of the word of God to determine whether or not these dreams are really inspired by the Almighty or not. I have seen people make insane accusations based upon a dream that they had about somebody. There are also times that I could have prevented (even did at times) certain events from happening if I would've simply took to heart the dream that God gave me. I'm sorry to say that at times I have not, thereby experiencing tragedy.

We must learn how to live in the realm of faith, not only a faith that opens the door for God to speak to us, but also a faith that will cause us to hearken and obey. I have said from the time I gave my heart to Christ, I can hear the voice of God! I say this to myself all the time, I can hear the voice of God. So many believers make the mistake by saying: God never talks to me! They say: I'm so confused, I don't know what to do. When you contradict what the word of God says, it opens the door for your enemy the devil to send you confusing signals. Jesus boldly declared when he said:

John 10:27My sheep hear my voice, and I know them, and they follow me:

Dreams are a major way that God was speak to us by the prophets.

I the Lord will make myself known unto them(Prophets)in the vision and will speak unto him in a dream.

I experienced an amazing dream not too long ago. God used this dream in order to bring direction, and peace of mind to my heart. I know it was of the Lord because I was not in the natural thinking upon this particular subject. I have had many such like dreams through the years. Now how do we know if these dreams are of the Lord? First they will never be contradictory to the divine nature of Christ, his will, or his word. Time also will tell whether or not we have really heard from the Lord.

*Bye-Bye Obama, Bye-Bye Obama, Bye-Bye Obama!

I had an amazing dream NOVEMBER 13, 2014. In this amazingly vivid dream my wife and I were in a very large outdoor meeting. A Minister I know was just finishing his message. A holy hush fell upon this large gathering of thousands of believers. As we were all waiting upon God for what was to happen next, my wife Kathleen who is at my side, stood to her feet, got out of our aisle and went to the front of the gathering. She stood behind the podium and began to speak in a wonderful heavenly language (this is a spiritual gift called diversity of tongues). In the midst of her speaking in this tongues scattered throughout the tongues were the words Bye-Bye Obama, Bye-Bye Obama, Bye-Bye Obama. On three different occasions she would stop speaking in tongues and say: Bye-Bye Obama, Bye-Bye Obama, Bye-Bye Obama.

To be honest in this dream I became extremely intimidated with what my wife was doing, because I knew that I was going to have to give the interpretation. When she finished with this tongues, immediately I sensed a very strong quickening of my spirit. A divine boldness came upon me and I stood to my feet. I stepped out of the row of people I was in and went up front. My wife had stepped aside, and I boldly stepped behind the pulpit and began to give the interpretation. As I gave this interpretation my physical, and voice inflections matched that which my wife had spoken as she was flowing in the gift of the diversity of tongues. At the exact same place in her tongues were she had said Bye-Bye Obama, Bye-Bye Obama, Bye-Bye Obama I spoke the exact same thing.

I watched myself give this interpretation in this dream, and I was amazed at what I heard the the spirit of the Lord saying to his people. I cannot exactly give you word for word everything that was spoken, but the meaning was that Obama was leaving. I am not speaking about him being impeached, but that he will be leaving at the end of 2 years, is my understanding from the interpretation of the tongues. Many conservatives, well-known people, believers and even so-called profits have been saying that Obama would declare martial law and stay in office longer than normal. If you did a search on Google about Obama, and martial law, you would see thousands of post. Even well-known people like Dr. Ben Carson believes that this might be the case. Dr. Ben Carson is a very well-known black neurosurgeon, who has repeatedly stated that he believes there is a chance that the 2016 elections may not be held at all. Many believe that widespread anarchy gripping the country could be reason enough for the Obama administration to announce the implementation of martial law and the suspension of some, if not all, of Americans' constitutionally protected rights — including the right to vote and hold national elections. People's hearts are being filled with fear that Obama is going to orchestrate some type of disaster in order to stay in power. As a result of this divine dream I had, I no longer fear this.

In the mist of this interpretation I heard the Lord say that Obama was like a Nebuchadnezzar that had God had used to bring judgment to America. That everything that was shaken and going to be shaken was in order to separate those who truly love Christ, from those who did not. That the division that was and is happening in our nation right now was simply the revealing of people's hearts. That now those who put their trust in God, and those who put their trust In Man has been revealed. That from here on out our nation will never be the same, but that this dividing between light and darkness will grow ever wider. The revealing and manifestation of this spiritual war and division has begun.

Daniel 12:10 Many shall be purified, and made white, and tried; but the wicked shall do wickedly: and none of the wicked shall understand; but the wise shall understand.

Now there are many dreams that are conditional in their fulfillment. Let us just take a moment to look at a couple of these conditional dreams. We know for instance in the book of Kings chapter 3 when God appeared to Solomon in a dream, there were warnings and instructions. God also revealed conditions for blessings or judgment.

1 Kings 3:5 In Gibeon the Lord appeared to Solomon in a dream by night: and God said, Ask what I shall give thee...........13 And I have also given thee that which thou hast not asked, both riches, and honour: so that there shall not be any among the kings like unto thee all thy days.14 And if thou wilt walk in my ways, to keep my statutes and my commandments, as thy father David did walk, then I will lengthen thy days.15 And Solomon awoke; and, behold, it was a dream. And he came to Jerusalem, and stood before the ark of the covenant of the Lord, and offered up burnt offerings, and offered peace offerings, and made a feast to all his servants.

God delights in giving us directions and guidance, actually without divine inspiration and guidance, men would be completely and utterly destroyed. We are likened onto sheep throughout the Scriptures. Sheep are some of the dumbest animals that have ever lived. Sheep are so stupid that they cannot even be trained or used in carnivals, fairs or circuses for any kind of entertainment act.

Jeremiah 23:28 The prophet that hath a dream, let him tell a dream; and he that hath my word, let him speak my word faithfully. What is the chaff to the wheat? saith the Lord.

We have to really use much divine wisdom because there are many who will give or declare false dreams of their own making. Most times these false dreams that so-called prophets give are always light and fluffy. Very seldom are they ever substantial or hard-hitting. Divinely inspired dreams are usually life-changing, transforming, hard-hitting realities. Jeremiah lived in a day when there were many false prophets giving many false dreams. These prophecies and dreams never called people to repentance. They always contradicted what God was saying to Jeremiah pertaining to coming judgment and destruction.

Jeremiah 23:25 I have heard what the prophets said, that prophesy lies in my name, saying, I have dreamed, I have dreamed.

Jeremiah 27:9 Therefore hearken not ye to your prophets, nor to your diviners, nor to your dreamers, nor to your enchanters, nor to your sorcerers, which speak unto you, saying, Ye shall not serve the king of Babylon:

Jeremiah 29:8 For thus saith the Lord of hosts, the God of Israel; Let not your prophets and your diviners, that be in the midst of you, deceive you, neither hearken to your dreams which ye cause to be dreamed.

Personally I have discovered that there are different levels of dreams. First there are divine dreams, that feel exactly like a dream. Then there are dreams that are so real that it literally physically feels like it is happening. I have experienced many of the first type, in which it had that natural dreamlike quality, and yet I have experienced through the years approximately about a dozen of the other type. Dreams that were so vibrant, so real, so authentic to where I could smell, feel, hear and experience with such clarity to where it seemed to be truly happening to me.

The very first thing I try to do after I have a visitation of the Lord, is to write down what I experienced. If you receive a dream, it is very important that you do not tell it all over the place. There is Scripture that deals with this in the book of Proverbs:

Proverbs 29:11 A fool uttereth all his mind: but a wise man keepeth it in till afterwards.

I would suggest that you do not even go to anyone you think is spiritual asking them what they think your dream means. The very first thing that you need to do is go before the Lord, asking him for understanding. Once you asked the Lord, you simply wait on him.

Be ready to write down that which he Quickens to your heart pertaining to the dream or the vision. Whenever I have a visitation along this line, God always begins to reveal to me what he was saying by Scripture. It's very important that you do not lean to the understanding of your own mind.

Proverbs 3:5 Trust in the Lord with all thine heart; and lean not unto thine own understanding.6 In all thy ways acknowledge him, and he shall direct thy paths.

Once you asked the Lord to reveal to you what he is saying to you, simply begin to thank him and praise him for the answer. From that moment forward you thank him for giving you understanding. No matter how long it takes for the Lord to speak to you pertaining to that which you experienced, just keep resting in him. I guarantee the divine download of understanding will come from the Lord. Do not seek the understanding, simply seek the Lord.

The spirit of God many times will speak to you in a dream, giving you specific directions of what to do, where to go, what to say. When Joseph discovered that Mary was pregnant with the child, he was very upset, and in a dream the Lord visited him, revealing to him the truth. There are three specific times that God spoke to the husband of Mary, Joseph through dreams in order to protect Mary and the Christ child.

Matthew 1:20 But while he thought on these things, behold, the angel of the Lord appeared unto him in a dream, saying, Joseph, thou son of David, fear not to take unto thee Mary thy wife: for that which is conceived in her is of the Holy Ghost. Matthew 2:19 But when Herod was dead, behold, an angel of the Lord appeareth in a dream to Joseph in Egypt.20 Saying, Arise, and take the young child and his mother, and go into the land of Israel: for they are dead which sought the young child's life.

Amazing Dream - Creation Held Together by a Divine Song!

I had an amazing dream. It's very hard to describe in human terms. I was sleeping peacefully when, at about three o'clock in the morning, I was suddenly smack dab in the middle of heaven, close to the throne of God. It was so real and tangible; it literally felt as if I was in heaven physically. God gave me eyes to see all of existence. It was as if I was omnipresent. All of creation lay before me. My mind and emotions, and all five of my senses perceived all things. I embraced everything at one time.

It was the most amazing experience you could imagine. It was so beautiful and magnificent that it is beyond precise description. It could be likened to being in the eye of a storm with everything spinning around you. With this supernatural, imparted ability I could perceive the spiritual and angelic. I saw angels of all types and ranks. I saw and felt the nature and the physical realms. I saw the planets, moons, stars, solar systems, and the whole universe. I saw animal life, plant life, oceans, seas, lakes,and rivers. I even saw the microscopic molecular realm. God supernaturally expanded my capacity mentally and emotionally to perceive all things. If it had not happened to me personally, I would be skeptical myself of someone saying these things.

In the midst of this experience I began to be overtaken by an absolute sense of incredible harmony. It was a unity and oneness of a mind-boggling proportion. It resonated through my whole being. I could feel it in my bones, flesh, emotions, and mind. My heart resonated with His harmony. My whole being was engulfed in this unbelievable symphony. All creation, the universe, and spiritual realm was in complete and total harmony and unity. Instantly I perceived everything was at one with God. Not one molecule, not one atom or proton was out of sync with God. As I was looking at creation, suddenly I perceived an invisible force permeating and saturating all of it. God literally gave me eyes to see this invisible force. I could see it moving, flowing, and penetrating everything. With this ability to see, He also gave me spiritual understanding. I realized at that moment that it was this incredible invisible force which was causing all things to exist and flow and move as one living, breathing creation.

What I am sharing with you was a progressive revelation unfolding before me like a flower blossoming. In the midst of this experience my ears opened, and I heard the most incredible music, a breathtaking song. This invisible force was literally a song that was being sung. Instantly I perceived that it was this music, this song, which was holding all of creation together. This song was permeating every animate and inanimate thing together. Not only was it holding everything together but also everything was singing along with it. It was the most incredible music and song you could ever imagine. Actually it is beyond comprehension or human ability to describe this song and what it was doing. All of creation was being upheld and kept together by this song. I could see it and feel it. It was inside of me. I was a part of it. No maestro, psalmist, no Beethoven or Mozart could ever produce such a majestic masterpiece.

As I watched and listened, I was overwhelmed with the reality that it was this song that was causing everything to be in harmony and unity. It was this song causing everything to live, move, exist, and have being. During this experience a curiosity took a hold of me. I began to wonder, where is this music, this song, coming from?

I began to look high and low, trying to discover where this song had originated. I finally looked behind me, and on a higher elevation I saw God sitting upon His throne. I did not see the clarity of God's form or face. He was covered in a glistening mist, somewhat like fog. But as I looked upon His form, it was as if my eyes zoomed in on His mouth. I was looking intently at the mouth of God. Out of His mouth was coming this amazing, beautiful, awesome song.

This song that God was singing was holding everything together and in perfect harmony. God the Father was making everything one with Himself through this song, this music coming out of His mouth. I literally could see, feel, and experience the song coming out of God's mouth. In my heart I said to the Father, "Father, how long will You sing this song?" And He spoke to me in my heart, "Throughout eternity, My voice will never cease to sing. My voice will never cease to be heard." I could see letters streaming from God's mouth. Words were coming forth from His mouth. They were swimming in a river of transparent life, like fish swimming in a river. These words seemed to be alive. They were spreading throughout the entire universe, causing everything to exist and to be in harmony. They were permeating all of creation, visible and invisible, spiritual and natural.

I knew in my heart that this was the Word of God, the divinely inspired Scriptures. The Word was swimming as if in an invisible transparent river. I knew that this river was a living, quickening force. I knew that it was this river which was causing the Word of God to be alive. The Word of God was being carried forth by this river. I said to the Father, "Father, what is this river that the Word is flowing, swimming, and living in?" And He said to my heart, "It is the Holy Ghost!"

I was stunned into silence. After a while I repeated my question. Once again He said to me, "It is the Holy Ghost. It is the breath of My mouth coming from the voice of My lips. And this voice is My Son, Jesus Christ. My voice is My Son, Jesus Christ. And out of His voice comes the Holy Ghost and My Word." Further He said to me, "My Word would not sustain, heal, deliver, or bring life unless it is quickened and made alive by My Spirit." Then the Father confirmed this to me by quoting the Scripture where Jesus said, "My Words are Spirit, and they are life." (See John 6:63.) The Father spoke to me again and said, "You can quote, memorize, and declare the whole Bible, but it will be dead and lifeless until you yield, surrender, move, flow, and come into complete harmony with the Word of God and the Holy Ghost."

This I believe, to some extent, reveals God's eternal purpose for you and I: to be in complete oneness and harmony with God, the Father, the Son, and the Holy Ghost!

One dream can change the whole perspective of your life.

It can open your eyes to truths and realities that you could never obtained by worldly knowledge or wisdom. Another amazing dream I experienced.

Dream about A fishing boat, mutiny & restoration!

Usually at least once a month I have a significant dream. I realize that many people have dreams, and that many of them are just simply from their own imaginations. My dreams are way different. In many of my dreams I have seen what has happened, what is happening, and what is about to happen. God has giving me amazing directions, instructions, corrections and warnings by dreams for over 40 years.

Now in this particular dream I was the captain of a large fishing vessel in the Bering Sea, up in Alaska. I do have some familiarity with this because in my younger years I had fished and worked on fishing boats in Alaska and off the coast of the state of Washington and Oregon. Now this boat that I was captain of was painted pure white. It was a large gill net boat with huge dragnet catapults and equipment. There was a large crew of men working everywhere as we were getting ready to go out to sea.

In this dream as we were out catching fish all of a sudden two men who I had hired led a mutiny against me. Somehow I survived this mutiny, being able to bring the vessel back to the docks of the port where we were stationed. In this dream I not only fired the two mutineers, but I let everybody else aboard the ship go. In the next part of this dream I perceived that decades had come and gone. Here I was still on the ship, but no longer was it painted white and beautiful. No longer did it have a large crew of fishermen. No longer was it a hub of activity and excitement. The ship itself had grown dark and moldy. Here I was with a mop bucket, and a mop in my hand.

I was washing the deck back and forth with this mop. I was all by myself, mopping the moldy deck, of a dysfunctional fishing vessel, with no crew. In this dream I was complaining to the Lord, and feeling sorry for myself. As I was mopping the deck of the large fishing vessel complaining, I heard the audible voice of God speak out of heaven to me. He said this to me: it's your fault! I stopped mopping, looking up to heaven and saying: what Lord? He repeated to me once again: it's your fault! I said to the Lord: what do you mean? Then the Lord said to my heart, you're the one who let everybody go! I never told you to do that.

He said: you overreacted. You did not need to get rid of the whole crew, only those who were causing the problems. In the midst of this reality great sorrow and repentance filled my heart. Then the Lord spoke a wonderful promise to me.He told me: I am about to restore all that the enemy has stolen from you, plus more. You are about to reap an amazing harvest. Get your boat ready, your new crew members are coming. Get the vessel ready for I am about to fill it to overflowing with fish. Then the dream was over!

#12 ANGELIC VISITATIONS

You know when I think about subjects of the Bible that are extremely important, I cannot think of a subject more important then hearing, hearkening, and obeying the voice of God. This is exactly how man got in to trouble when they did not listen to God, and the directions he gave them. The enemy came along, entering into a snake, he lied to the woman, and she was deceived by him.

2 Corinthians 11:3 But I fear, lest by any means, as the serpent beguiled Eve through his subtilty, so your minds should be corrupted from the simplicity that is in Christ.

Adam listened to his wife, and God said to Adam: because have hearkened to the voice of your wife, not listening to my voice, you are cursed! When somebody contradicts the known will and voice of God, we must close our ears to them, for they will only bring us to a place of death. It so utterly important that we hear God's voice and obey him. We are talking eternal consequences, life or death, heaven or hell. As God's sheep we hear the voice of our shepherd. but our major problem is that we do not listen and obey the voice of the Lord the way we should. Honestly what we love, is what we listen and respond to. What we love is what controls and directs our thoughts, they possess our life. We must be very careful what we give ourselves to. We need to love Jesus, love the Father, we need to love the voice of the Holy Ghost.

The **12th way** that God will speak to us is through angelic visitations. Over 280 times from Genesis to Revelation it talks about angelic visitations. A lot of the prophets of old had angelic visitations. We will look at some of those angelic visitations, then I want to share with you some of the **angelic visitations that I**

personally have experienced. You should purchase one of my books called: **The Chronicles of Micah**. In this book I go to great lengths to show how the angelic and demonic world operate. This book is a fiction, and yet it is the reality of my first three months as a Christian.

Now in all reality the Bible only talks about three angels by name. Their names are **Lucifer, Michael,** and **Gabriel.** No other time in all of the writings in the Bible are we ever told the name of the Angels. Yet you'll see angels manifesting themselves in dreams, in visions, and in the flesh and blood world, from Genesis to Revelation. The Scripture actually says that at times we will be entertaining angels unaware.

Hebrews 13:2 Be not forgetful to entertain strangers: for thereby some have entertained angels unawares.

I heard of a story of two women who were headed to to the Brownsville revival meetings in Florida in the 1990s. That as they were driving along on a major highway, they had an angelic visitation. There was a young man hitchhiking along the highway. Normally these ladies would not have picked up a stranger, but the spirit of God quickened it to their hearts to pick up this young man. As they were driving along with this young man, who was sitting in the back seat listening to the two ladies talking. They were talking about what God was doing at the Brownsville Assembly of God church. Out of the blue this young man leaned forward, with his head between the two women, and he said these words to the woman who was driving: The Lord's return is very near! Then this young man sat back in the car seat.

When he said that, both ladies attest to the fact that the hair on the back of their necks stood up. The lady who was driving looked in the rear-view mirror and to her shock and amazement the young man was gone. He had simply vanished from out of their car. They pulled off the highway and began to weep and cry. The next thing they knew someone was knocking on their window. Here it was a policeman. They rolled down the window to speak to this police officer. He saw that they both were crying, asking the ladies what was wrong? The ladies told him the story. The policeman seem to be very upset, telling them that was the third time he had heard of this happening in the last couple weeks.

Revelation 12:7 And there was war in heaven: Michael and his angels fought against the dragon; and the dragon fought and his angels,8 And prevailed not; neither was their place found any more in heaven.

Michael and his angels defeated the the enemy. Thus they were cast to the earth. So we have disembodied spirits, evil angels, that are now called devils and demons who are running loose on this earth. There is a spiritual conflict that is taking place all around us. Angels and demons respond according to that which we speak, and do with our lives. The heavenly holy angelic beings **hearken to the voice of God's word**. The demonic spirits are doing everything they can to get us to not hear God's voice, and are enticing us to disobey the voice of God even when we hear it. We understand according to the Scriptures that every human being is given a guardian angel at the moment of conception. Jesus revealed this when he said:

Matthew 18:10 Take heed that ye despise not one of these little ones; for I say unto you, That in heaven their angels do always behold the face of my Father which is in heaven.

Amazingly after your born again, when you have surrendered your heart to Christ, and for those who love the Lord, the Bible clearly says and literally implies that God gives you more than one angelic being. *Psalm 91:11 For he shall give his angels charge over thee, to keep thee in all thy ways.* At the same time the Scripture very clearly warns us, and instructs us not to exalt these angelic beings. They are simply sent to minister to those who shall be the heirs of salvation.

Colossians 2:18 Let no man beguile you of your reward in a voluntary humility and worshipping of angels, intruding into those things which he hath not seen, vainly puffed up by his fleshly mind,

Another reality is that we do not tell angels what to do. Believe me when I say that I know quite a number of people (even some of my close friends) who do this, but you and I do not have the authority to do this. There are a lot of people in the body of Christ at this time teaching this doctrine, yet the Scripture is very clear in its teaching that we do not have this authority. There is no example in the Bible of a human being telling an Angel what to do. I have gone through the whole Bible and I could not find not one place where anybody ever told angels what to do. Jesus Christ is our greatest example, and he never did it once in his whole earthly ministry. The reality is that even when Jesus was headed to the cross he did not say that he could tell the angels what to do.

Matthew 26:53 Thinkest thou that I cannot now pray to my Father, and he shall presently give me more than twelve legions of angels?

Well exactly then how do angels minister to those who are the heirs of salvation? It's very clear that they respond according to our obedience to God, and the speaking of the word.

Psalm 103:20 Bless the Lord, ye his angels, that excel in strength, that do his commandments, hearkening unto the voice of his word.

But brother Mike we were taught that we had to put the angels around about us. We were taught that we had to send angels before us and behind us, above us, and beneath us. I know, I had done the same thing before I discovered this reality, but in all reality that would be like us asking God to never leave us or forsake us every time we woke up in the morning, or were going somewhere. I hear people all the time say Lord be with us, this is not necessary because he said:

Hebrews 13:5 Let your conversation be without covetousness; and be content with such things as ye have: for he hath said, I will never leave thee, nor forsake thee.

The angels of God are around about them who love and fear the Lord. This is an amazing beautiful truth that we need to embrace. Now I can talk to the Father and ask him for more angelic help, but even Jesus did not do this in his greatest trial and test. I'm not saying the Holy Spirit would not ever quickened this request in your heart. I can say: Lord I thank you that your angels are around about me.

This particular information is taken from:
GotQuestions.gov http://www.gotquestions.org/angels-male-female.html

Question: "Are angels male or female?"

Answer: There is no doubt that every reference to angels in the Scriptures is in the masculine gender. The Greek word for "angel" in the New Testament, angelos, is in the masculine form. In fact, a feminine form of angelos does not exist. There are three genders in grammar—masculine (he, him, his), feminine (she, her, hers), and neuter (it, its). Angels are never referred to in any gender other than masculine. In the many appearances of angels in the Bible, never is an angel referred to as "she" or "it." Furthermore, when angels appeared, they were always dressed as human males (Genesis 18:2, 16; Ezekiel 9:2). No angel ever appears in Scripture dressed as a female.

The only named angels in the Bible—Michael, Gabriel, Lucifer—had male names and all are referred to in the masculine. "Michael and his angels" (Revelation 12:7); "Mary was greatly troubled at his [Gabriel's] words" (Luke 1:29); "Oh, Lucifer, son of the morning" (Isaiah 14:12). Other references to angels are always in the masculine gender. In Judges 6:21, the angel holds a staff in "his" hand. Zechariah asks an angel a question and reports that "he" answered (Zechariah 1:19). The angels in Revelation are all spoken of as "he" and their possessions as "his" (Revelation 10:1, 5; 14:19; 16:2, 4, 17; 19:17; 20:1).

Some people point to Zechariah 5:9 as an example of female angels. That verse says, "Then I looked up—and there before me were two women, with the wind in their wings! They had wings like those of a stork, and they lifted up the basket between heaven and earth." The problem is that the "women" in this prophetic vision are not called angels. They are called nashiym ("women"), as is the woman in the basket representing wickedness in verses 7 and 8. By contrast, the angel that Zechariah was speaking to is called a malak, a completely different word meaning "angel" or "messenger." The fact that the women have wings in Zechariah's vision might suggest angels to our minds, but we must be careful about going beyond what the text actually says. A vision does not necessarily depict actual beings or objects—consider the huge flying scroll Zechariah sees earlier in the same chapter (Zechariah 5:1–2).

The confusion about genderless angels comes from a misreading of Matthew 22:30, which states that there will be no marriage in heaven because we "will be like the angels in heaven." The fact that there will be no marriage has led some to believe that angels are "sexless" or genderless because (the thinking goes) the purpose of gender is procreation and, if there is to be no marriage and no procreation, there is no need for gender. But this is a leap that cannot be proven from the text. The fact that there is no marriage does not necessarily mean there is no gender. The many references to angels as males contradict the idea of genderless angels. Angels do not marry, but we can't make the leap from "no marriage" to "no gender."

God will use angelic visitations to speak to us, giving us direction and guidance. In the old covenant we see many examples of this. For example an angel of the Lord called to Abraham out of heaven.

Genesis 22:11 And the angel of the Lord called unto him out of heaven, and said, Abraham, Abraham: and he said, Here am I.

Angels appeared to lot and his family in order to rescue them from the coming destruction.

Genesis 19:15 And when the morning arose, then the angels hastened Lot, saying, Arise, take thy wife, and thy two daughters, which are here; lest thou be consumed in the iniquity of the city.

An angel spoke to Jacob in a dream. He also experienced a heavenly vision where he saw the angels ascending and descending to the earth on a ladder.

Genesis 31:11 And the angel of God spake unto me in a dream, saying, Jacob: And I said, Here am I.

Genesis 28:12 And he dreamed, and behold a ladder set up on the earth, and the top of it reached to heaven: and behold the angels of God ascending and descending on it.

Time would fail me to talk of every example in the Bible in which God used angels to speak, lead, guide, protect, and provide for his people by angelic beings. Daniel talks about angels over and over. Remember that angels came and shut the mouths of the lions when he was thrown into the lions den. I truly wonder how many times God has protected us with his angels. I could personally write a book on my own experiences with the angelic host. So many times God has used angelic beings to protect me and my family, to guide me and give me directions.

God does and can use angelic beings to give to us divine revelations also. In the book of Zechariah the prophet is communicating with angels, in which it is clarified as such 19 times. These angels are teaching and instructing Zechariah. *Zechariah 1:9 Then said I, O my lord, what are these? And the angel that talked with me said unto me, I will shew thee what these be.*

Now as we come into the New Testament all of a sudden angels come exploding upon the scene in even a more dramatic way. Over 170 times in the New Testament alone angelic beings are manifested. In the Old Testament it speaks about angelic visitations over 100 times. In the gospel of Matthew it speaks about angelic visitations 19 times. We discover that angels are very important in God's plan for man, for instance the angel Gabriel came and spoke to Mary pertaining to her giving birth to the only begotten son of God. This same angel appeared to Daniel twice in the Old Testament. Please do not think for a moment that I am suggesting that we seek for an angelic visitation. We should never seek for a supernatural visitation, because this opens the door to deceiving spirits that will manifest themselves to us. We simply set our heart upon the Lord, seeking his face with everything within us. God in his timing will manifest himself in whatever way he so chooses.

When Jesus had completed his temptations in the wilderness, God sent an angelic being to minister to him. Now because God is not a respecter of people, what he did for Jesus he will do for us in our times of deepest need.

Matthew 4:11 Then the devil leaveth him, and, behold, angels came and ministered unto him.

There was an angelic visitation when Jesus was in the garden of Gethsemane on the night he was betrayed, sweating as it was great drops of blood, as he prayed Father let my will be done!

Luke 22:42 Saying, Father, if thou be willing, remove this cup from me: nevertheless not my will, but thine, be done.43 And there appeared an angel unto him from heaven, strengthening him.44 And being in an agony he prayed more earnestly: and his sweat was as it were great drops of blood falling down to the ground.

When you get to the book of Acts it really gets interesting because in the book of acts the angels of the Lord appear to the disciples on many different occasions. Over **20 times it talks about angels in the book of Acts.** Remember when the disciples were taken to prison, and locked up, God sent forth an angel to deliver them.

Acts 5:19 But the angel of the Lord by night opened the prison doors, and brought them forth, and said,

Peter the apostle experienced an angelic visitation when he was also in prison. The angel actually had to kick him to wake him up.

Acts 12:7 And, behold, the angel of the Lord came upon him, and a light shined in the prison: and he smote Peter on the side, and raised him up, saying, Arise up quickly. And his chains fell off from his hands.:8 And the angel said unto him, Gird thyself, and bind on thy sandals. And so he did. And he saith unto him, Cast thy garment about thee, and follow me.

The Scripture reveals that Moses received the law of the Lord by the hand of an angel. Time would fail us to go to every one of these amazing experiences. We do not need to seek for an angelic visitation, but we should anticipate and expect them. When an angel does manifest himself to us he will never exalt himself. I question many visitations that people say they've had when it comes to angelic beings, in many of these experiences you'll discover angels that are exalting themselves. When ever an angel exalts himself (itself)you know they are not of God. Even the Holy Ghost does not exalt himself, though he is a part of the Trinity. The Holy Ghost came to exalt Jesus Christ, and to reveal the perfect will of the father. I'm telling you if an angel exalts it self, you know it is not of God. The Scripture even declares that the enemy will appear to us as an angel of light.

2 Corinthians 11:14 And no marvel; for Satan himself is transformed into an angel of light.

The Bible says when Christ comes back, he will be coming with his mighty angels in flaming fire. It also declares that he will send forth his angels to separate the wicked from the righteous. He will use the angels to gather together his people from the four corners of the earth.

When we finally get to the book of Revelation, which is a revelation of Jesus Christ, angelic beings are revealed to us without number. Over and over the book of Revelation talks about angelic visitations and angelic visitation. In the final conclusion at the end of the ages God begins to use amazing angels to fulfill his divine purpose. In the book of Revelation angels are spoken of 71 times.

QUESTION: What are the types of angels in the Bible?

When we talk about angels we need to keep in mind that there are two distinct classes of angels -- Holy and evil. For this search we are mainly focusing on the Holy angels. There are different types of Holy angels. Personally I believe that there are many different types of angels. just like there are many types of birds, types of fish.Let us start with the highest order of Angels revealed in the Bible, which includes:

#1 Arch-angels or chief angels who seem to be in direct contact with God the Father in the sun. (Colossians 1:15-18; 1 Thessalonians 4:16; Jude 9).

Michael is one of the chief princes, the prince of Israel (Daniel 10:13, 21; 11:1; 12:1; 1 Thessalonians 4:16; Jude 9; Revelation 12:7-9).

Gabriel stands before God and delivers important messages (Daniel 8:16-19; 9:20-23; 10:8-11:1; Luke 1:19, 26).

#2 Cherubim are known for their power and beauty (Genesis 3:24; Ezekiel 1:5-28; 28:12, 13, 17; 8:1-4; 10:1-22).

#3 Seraphim perform priestly duties (Isaiah 6:1-7).

#4 Living creatures are mentioned in Revelation, worshiping God (Revelation 4:6-5:14; 6:1-8; 7:11; 14:3, 9-11; 15:7; 19:4).

#5 Common angels are heavenly spirit beings (Matthew 1:20-29; 2:13-19; 28:2-5; 1 Kings 1:11-38; 2:9-21; Acts 5:19; 8:26; 10:3; 12:7-23).

#6 Guardian angels are given charge over us lest we stub our toes (Psalm 91:12).

#7 Ministering angels are like the one who cooked a hot meal for Elijah when he was running away from an angry Jezebel (1 Kings 19:5-7.

#8 Avenging angels are the ones that carry out God's judgment upon mankind for their wicked deeds (Genesis 19:1-29).

#9 Death angels bring a type of judgment upon a people who persecute innocent groups (Exodus 12: 23; Revelation 6:8).

Angels can travel at inconceivable speeds (Ezekiel 1; Revelation 8:13; 9:1). Faithful angels of the Lord were tested and tried at the time that Lucifer rebelled, which caused great disaster in heaven, leading one third of the angelic host astray. (1 Timothy 5:21; Job 4:1-8). The angels test man by unknowingly appearing at times to see how individuals treat strangers (Hebrews 13:2). God has used and is using the Bride of Christ to reveal his ultimate purpose to the angelic beings. [the Church] (Ephesians 3:10; 1 Corinthians 4:9). (from:http://www.allaboutgod.com/types-of-angels-faq.htm)

I've had a number of amazing experience with angels. In some of these experiences I literally saw them, and even spoke with them. At other times they were there protecting me, but I did not see them, yet I knew they were there because of the supernatural things that transpired. I remember one time as a young man, before I was even born again, when an angel saved my life. I want you to know that the stories I'm sharing are not exaggerated in the least. I take seriously the Scripture that says: liars will have their place in the lake of fire.

An Angel and a 12 Gauge Shotgun (1969)

When I was approximately 13 years old, I went through a special program on gun safety for teenagers. If you completed this course, the state of Wisconsin would grant young teenagers the right to hunt alone. That meant that I could go out into the woods with a rifle without parental guidance. Of course, going to a special training class for gun safety does not necessarily produce maturity, which was one thing that I was seriously lacking at the time.

One early morning, my father and I got up early to go hunting. There was a layer of snow on the ground and it was quite cold. Because of this, I dressed with extra layers of clothes in order to stay warm. When we finally got to the land where we were going to go hunting, my father positioned me in the woods right next to an open field with scrub brush and small trees. He then pointed out to me where he was going to go and hunt.

He told me that I needed to stay put no matter what, until he came back to get me. He informed me that because he knew where I was at that time, if he heard me shoot, then he would come running. This particular morning he had given me his old 12 gauge shotgun, loaded with deer slugs.

All that morning I stood very still where my father had placed me, scanning the horizon looking for deer. As the day progressed, the temperature began to rise. Before the day had progressed very far, the snow that had been on the ground had melted away. It was going from one extreme to another. It was very cold in the morning when we first went out, but now it was getting quite warm. Of course I had too many clothes on for this type of weather which was making me quite miserable. I was just too hot. I had on my hunting jacket, a hunter's hat, my orange vest, winter boots and insulated pants. Plus, I had no water with me or anything else to keep me cool.

It's hard to believe the next thing that I did. It was extremely stupid. There must have been divine angelic protection and deliverance even though I did not know Christ at the time nor was I right with God. Thank the Lord for His mercy, long-suffering, kindness and goodness towards sinners!

My dad's old 12 gauge shotgun was actually too large and heavy for me. I had been holding it all that morning which was hurting my arms. So what did I do? I sat the stock of the rifle down into the brush next to me. The barrel was aimed towards the heavens. Unbeknownst to me was the fact that there was a small briar patch at my feet that I had stuck the stock of my gun into.

I stood there for quite a while just looking around for possible deer. As time went on, I began to get tired of standing. The next thing that I did was even more stupid than the first. I decided to lean on the barrel of the gun. I mean, I literally took the barrel of the gun and put it under my armpit. The barrel of the gun was aimed in the pit of my arm. If it were to go off, the deer slug would pass up through my chest and out through my head. I would be a headless corpse. I put all of my weight on this gun barrel because I had grown extremely tired of standing.

Now, the next thing that I want to share with you is extremely amazing. There was absolutely no wind on this particular day. The gun stock was stuck in the briar patch with a branch that was inserted into the trigger guard. Of course, I did not know at the time that a branch was pushing up against the trigger which, if fired, would have taken off my chest and my head, killing me instantly. I would have gone immediately to hell because I did not know Christ.

So, as I'm leaning on the top of the barrel of the 12 gauge, I literally felt someone behind me flip the hat off the top of my head. I mean it literally felt like somebody took their finger and knocked that hat right off my head from the back to the front. Remember, there was no wind blowing whatsoever. The instant that my hat was knocked off my head, I leaned forward to get it as it was falling towards the ground. There was no wind blowing as I stated earlier. There is no reason why my hat should have fallen off. The second that I leaned forward, the barrel of this 12 gauge shotgun was no longer under my armpit. It was just inches away from my body behind my back. As soon as the barrel of the gun was out from underneath my armpit, the twig that was in the trigger guard pulled the trigger. I heard and felt a loud BANG!!!

The gun had gone off on its own. I stood there trembling and shaking knowing that it was a miracle that I was still alive. That 12 gauge deer slug would have taken my head off. God had rescued my sorry soul. I am absolutely convinced that the Lord had sent an angel or even my own guardian angel to rescue me. I believe that this angel took his little finger and flipped my hat off my head knowing that the trigger of my gun was going to be squeezed at any moment by a small branch. A little bit later my dad came by. I never did tell him or anyone else what had happened that day. Beyond any shadow of doubt I know that I would be dead if God had not rescued me.

The Angel's Catcher Mitt

We were pastoring one church in Gettysburg, Pennsylvania and another one in Chambersburg, Pennsylvania. My wife was about seven months pregnant with our second son, Daniel, when the event I'm telling you about took place. (I have three sons. From the first day that we were married I always said to my wife, "Mike and his three sons.") We were out one day doing house visitation with some of our parishioners. This really sounds stupid, but it's true. My wife, my son Michael, and myself were all on a Honda 450. Of course, I was in the front of the motorcycle driving. Michael ,who was two years old, was in the middle. Close behind him was Daniel and Kathee. (Danny was still in a protective bubble called a womb).Thank God there was a sissy bar behind Kathee. We had been visiting a family from the church near Roxbury.

We were now headed home on 997, or Black Gap Road. The sun was setting, and it was glaring in my eyes. I was looking for a shortcut that I knew about. This shortcut was a dirt road. (I'm notorious for my shortcuts). As I was going along, I finally saw it to my right. It was dark, so I could not see everything. I slowed up a little bit, and then turned off onto the path. I was probably doing about forty-five miles an hour. The speed limit through this area was fifty-five, and I usually always try to stay at the upper end, endeavoring to keep the law. However, when I turned off on this shortcut, I discovered to my horror and dismay that this was not the road I was looking for. It actually was a very shallow area that was long and narrow created for semi trucks to pull over on. Now right in front of us were three major obstacles: a heavy duty steel guard rail, a large pile of big rocks, and a large wooden light pole. All of these obstacles were only about twenty feet in front of us. I knew instantly there was no way I could ever stop. Even if I would have laid the motorcycle over on its side we would still slam into all of these items at forty-five to fifty miles an hour.

It was clear that we were going to hit the rocks, guard rail, and telephone pole. I did not even have time to put on my brakes. I just cried out to Jesus. (What I'm about to tell you will sound insane, but this is what truly happened.) At that very moment, it felt like two large hands pressed against us on both sides, left and right. We were still heading for the rocks, but then we instantly stopped. It literally felt like we had either run into a big, invisible, fluffy pillow, or a very soft baseball catcher's glove. There was nothing visible in front of us to stop us. We simply ran into some invisible force.

When we had stopped, we simply fell over on our right side. We fell over onto the gravel and rocks, but we really did not fall *onto* them. I know this sounds really far-fetched and strange. But it was like we fell unto another pillow! We fell into something soft between us and the ground. Here we are laying in the dirt and gravel and an overwhelming peace was upon us. There were no skid marks in the dirt. I looked at my wife, and she looked at me. What a miracle! Little Michael wasn't even crying. Then my wife informed me that just before we got to this area she had seen two pillars of fire, one to the left of us, and one to the right.

Kathee's Interjection:

Right before the accident I remember going through a little town which had no lights, but I saw two pillars of fire, one right to our left, and one right to our right. The pillars were like brilliant, white laser lights shooting towards the heavens. I realized at that moment that they were to angels of God! I began crying and praising God while on the back of that motorcycle, thanking him for His protection and goodness.I was still praising God when I noticed that we had turned off onto a dead end alley, and we were going to crash, however, I had the peace of God. Everything happened so quickly that I knew God was indeed with us!

An Angel Took Me to Heaven

One night I was all alone in deep prayer in my military barracks. I had been walking around with my hands in the air praying, singing,and talking to the Lord. Suddenly, my room was filled with an overwhelming presence of the Lord. It was so real that I fell to my knees and tears began to flow freely from my eyes.

I found myself lying flat upon my face totally caught up in this overwhelming Holy presence. My face was buried into the floor. I was weeping, crying, and praying. All of a sudden the room I was in was filled with an intense bright light.

I lifted my head to see what in the world was going on. There in front of me was a white brilliant portal. It was like an opening into another world. It was not square like a regular door opening. This doorway was circular on the top like an archway. The light coming from this portal was so bright and brilliant that I could not really even look at it.

I was completely petrified and did not know what to do. It felt as if I was frozen to the floor and unable even to move a muscle. A holy fear gripped my whole body. I could see that someone was walking toward me through this tunnel of light. Out of this glorious light stepped a large figure of a man. This was no ordinary man. He was about seven feet tall with a broad chest and shoulders but a slender waist. His flesh blazed like the burning of an arch welder, and he had dark hair. His face did not seem to have ever been shaved. In other words, there was no stubble on his face. He had the stature of a body builder only more solid and almost unearthly. He wore a glistening, brilliant, white gown with a slightly transparent belt around his waist that glowed of silver. I was not able to move or talk in his presence. When this angelic being finally spoke to me his voice seemed to fill the whole room.

The angel commanded me to stand upon my feet. To be honest with you I was shaking uncontrollably in the fear of the Lord. This angel stepped forward, leaned down, and took me by the hand. He lifted me to my feet. The way he lifted me up I must have been as light as a feather in his hands. It was as if he rippled with unlimited strength. I was like a little child in his hand. I knew in my heart that he could easily kill me without any effort. This angelic being took me into heaven. You can read about that experience in my book : "Horrors of Hell, Splendors of Heaven"

This was my first experience in a tangible way with an angel. From that time up to now I have been protected, provided through and helped by these amazing messengers of God.

CHAPTER SEVEN

#13 SIGNS & WONDERS

The **13th Way** in which God leads and guides is by signs and wonders. There are many examples of this from Genesis to Revelation. Christ used signs and wonders as a declaration of who he was. He told doubting Thomas:

John 14:10 Believest thou not that I am in the Father, and the Father in me? the words that I speak unto you I speak not of myself: but the Father that dwelleth in me, he doeth the works. 11 Believe me that I am in the Father, and the Father in me: or else believe me for the very works' sake.

When Jesus turned water to wine, it was the beginning of many miracles that he would perform throughout his earthly ministry before his sufferings, death, and resurrection. All of these signs and wonders were performed in order to bring people to the Father. When he opened the eyes of the blind, cleansed the 10 lepers, cast out devils and demons, this was God speaking to the multitudes and to all of humanity declaring who Jesus was. When Jesus raised Lazarus from the dead, the Pharisees were filled with great fear because they knew this had the power to persuade men and women to follow him. Jesus also made this bold statement that the works he was performing was not him, but his Father doing it through him.

John 10:25 Jesus answered them, I told you, and ye believed not: the works that I do in my Father's name, they bear witness of me.

John 10:32 Jesus answered them, Many good works have I

shewed you from my Father; for which of those works do ye stone me?

John 10:37 If I do not the works of my Father, believe me not.

John 10:38 But if I do, though ye believe not me, believe the works: that ye may know, and believe, that the Father is in me, and I in him.

He said it's my father that is doing these things, I'm only doing what my father tells me to do, and what I see my Father do. There's a place in the spirit when we can hear by your spirits, and see the will of the Father, and thereby we become one with the Father. You and I already have heard the voice of the Father, or otherwise we could never have come to repentance and salvation.

John 6:44 No man can come to me, except the Father which hath sent me draw him: and I will raise him up at the last day.

We really need to get in tune with God in his word. Our hearts cry needs to be: **Thy will be done on earth, as it is in heaven**. We have an enemy the devil who will come to distract us, and lead us astray. He is obsessed with getting us out of the will of God. It is only when he gets us out of Gods will that he can truly steal, kill and destroy our lives, and those we love. He wants to harden our hearts to the reality of sin so that we cannot hear, or respond to the voice of our heavenly Father. If he can cause our hearts to become hardened by the deceitfulness of sin, then when God speaks to us, Gods voice will bounce off of us like a rubber ball bounces off of a concrete wall. God is speaking to us 24 / 7 and I am convinced that we have simply taught ourselves or trained ourselves to ignore his voice. We have allowed fleshly sins to harden our hearts to where we just don't hear or won't listen to God.

Whenever Jesus said verily verily in the Gospels, he was trying to make a very important statement. Verily verily means truly truly. He was saying you guys listen up to what I'm about to say, because what I'm about to tell you will change your life, it will transform you! We need to understand that it is of the utmost importance that we are led and guided by God. The world we live in is a very dangerous place, and the enemy has set traps for us along every step of the way.

John 5:19 Then answered Jesus and said unto them, Verily, verily, I say unto you, The Son can do nothing of himself, but what he seeth the Father do: for what things soever he doeth, these also doeth the Son likewise.

God wants us to become so sensitive to him that he can even lead and guide us by his eyes.

Psalm 32:8 I will instruct thee and teach thee in the way which thou shalt go: I will guide thee with mine eye.

He has also promised to guide us continually, and provide for us along the way.

Isaiah 58:11 And the Lord shall guide thee continually, and satisfy thy soul in drought, and make fat thy bones: and thou shalt be like a watered garden, and like a spring of water, whose waters fail not.

When you begin to listen to the voice of God, it brings you to life and life more abundantly! In **John 10:10** Jesus reveals to us that he came to give us life, and life more abundantly. The whole context of John chapter 10 is the fact he is our shepherd and we are his sheep.

In *John 14:6 Jesus saith unto him, I am the way, the truth, and the life: no man cometh unto the Father, but by me.*

Let us also look at *John 10:37 If I do not the works of my Father, believe me not.*

The works he's talking about of course's are **signs, wonders and miracles.** God absolutely speaks to people through signs, wonders and miracles. You might say: pastor Mike that was in the earthly ministry of Jesus, but I will quote to you *Hebrews 13:8 Jesus Christ the same yesterday, and to day, and for ever.* To illustrate this we can say that **every time somebody gets healed** it is God speaking. God is declaring to us, **I am the healer, I am the Lord that healeth thee.** Jesus is saying: when I turned the water into wine, that's my Father talking to you. When I walked upon the water, that was the Father talking to you. God *confirms his word with signs and wonders following,* so the sign and the wonders is the evidence the Father is speaking to us!

God gave the **early church mighty signs, wonders and miracles to convince the world that Jesus Christ is the only way to the Father.** He uses the miraculous to say: I am God alone, and Jesus is my son. Every miracle that has ever happened in your life is God revealing himself to you. When God touches you physically by healing your sick body, which according to the Scriptures is a miracle, is God speaking to you. Healing is a sign from God, and it is God saying: I'm real, I'm here, I am who I said I am!

Acts 10:38 How God anointed Jesus of Nazareth with the Holy Ghost and with power: who went about doing good, and healing all that were oppressed of the devil; for God was with him.

God told Moses: go tell the children of Israel that *I am that I am.* Through mighty signs and wonders God revealed himself to not just the descendants of Abraham, but to the Egyptians and the whole world. I love how God operates, he comes exploding into the midst humanity with such wonderful feats of the miraculous that it becomes impossible for them to deny that he exist.

Jesus came to manifest his Father to the world with incredible signs, wonders and miracles. Actually when you and I received Christ, and were born again, we became a sign and a wonder to those who know us, our community and the world. We are the evidence of the reality of God to this generation. Just the fact that when you stand around people who are cussing and swearing, and you are not participating, it will bring conviction upon them. They begin to ask you why you're not like them? And you boldly declare and proclaim your love for Christ, and what he is done for you. This is a miracle right before their eyes, the transformation of the human heart, a sign and wonder to the unbeliever.

1 Peter 2:12 Having your conversation honest among the Gentiles: that, whereas they speak against you as evildoers, they may by your good works, which they shall behold, glorify God in the day of visitation.

I have written a book called: **"How Faith Comes 28 Ways"**. One major way in which faith comes to a person's life is by seeing mighty signs, wonders and miracles. It is when God performs the supernatural before the eyes of the people.

John 4:48 Then said Jesus unto him, Except ye see signs and wonders, ye will not believe.

John 10:38 But if I do, though ye believe not me, believe the works: that ye may know, and believe, that the Father is in me, and I in him.

In the last 40 years I have seen God do many wonderful miracles for people in order to bring them to a place of salvation. People I have been close to, and even strangers. God loves to reveal himself to the human race, for it is his desire that all men repent, and come to the saving knowledge of Jesus Christ.

My Mom's Hip Miraculously Healed

I was visiting my parent's home in Wisconsin. One day when I came home, my mother asked me to help her get her hip back into place where it belonged. For some reason her right hip would pop out of place which was extremely painful and difficult for her. When this happened she would lay on the floor and grab onto something heavy and solid like the china hutch or the dining room table leg. Next, she would have one of us four boys grab her right ankle and pull with all our might with a heavy jerk until her hip would go back into place. She was just a little lady, so when we pulled her leg it would pull her whole body off the floor.

I told my mother I would help her. She laid down on her back on the dining room floor and grabbed the dining room table leg. I knelt down on my knees and took a hold of her right ankle with both hands. She was waiting for me to jerk her leg with a powerful pull but Instead of pulling like I normally would, I whispered: "In the name of Jesus Christ of Nazareth I command this hip to go back into place."

The minute I whispered this a wonderful miracle transpired. Her leg instantly shot straight out. She was very surprised asked with a shocked voice, "Michael, what did you just do to me?" I told her what I had done. Then I shared the reality of Jesus with her. As far as I know until she went home to be with the Lord, for the next 25 years she never had another problem with that hip popping out of its socket.

And these signs shall follow them that believe; In my name shall they cast out devils; they shall speak with new tongues; They shall take up serpents; and if they drink any deadly thing, it shall not hurt them; they shall lay hands on the sick, and they shall recover (Mark 16:17-18).

God did not do this for Mike Yeager, but he did it because he was wanting to speak to my moms heart. He was wanting to tell my mom: I'm real, I'm here, your son did not do this, I did this!

God Heals an Antagonistic Mafia Man's Eyes!

I have a house where I take in and keep single men. Some of these men come from real rough backgrounds. I had one such gentleman that I was renting to who was quite large and intimidating. I would try to share Christ with him whenever the opportunity arrived, but he was so liberal in his thinking that it did not seem to be having any impact upon him. Everything I believe that is wrong, he proclaimed was right. And everything that I believe is right, he would argue against.

He informed me that in his past he had worked for the Mafia, and at one time he was what they called a THUMPER! I asked him what he meant by a thump-er? He said that he had never physically murdered anyone, but that they would send him to rough up people, you know thump them! I have no doubt at all that what he told me was true.

One day as I was at the house where I keep these men, I saw him standing in the main front room. He seemed quite upset and distressed. I asked him what was wrong. He informed me that he had just come from the doctors because he had been having terrible problems with his eyes. After the Doctor had conducted all of the test they came back with a very disturbing report. They informed him that he had an eye disease (long medical term) that was going to cause him to go blind.

At that moment the spirit of God rose up with in me, and I proclaimed boldly that in the name of Jesus Christ he was not going to go blind. I told him: close your eyes! He said what? I said: close your eyes! He shut his eyes, and I took my two thumbs and laid them forcefully over his two eyelids. I declared: in the name of Jesus Christ you lying spirit of infirmity, come out of these eyes right now! Be healed in Jesus name! I then removed my thumbs from his eyelids, he looked at me with questioning eyes. I said to him: it's done! He said what? I said it is done. You are healed in the name of Jesus. He said: really? I said: yes Christ has made you whole. It seemed for a minute that tears formed in his eyes as I turned around and walked away.

Approximately a week later he showed up at our thrift store that we manage. He walked into the store asking for Pastor Mike. They informed him that I was not there. Tears were rolling down his face, and they asked him what they could do for him. He told them with great joy and excitement that he had gone back to the doctors, and that his eyes were completely healed. He started hugging the people that where they're running the store. This large ex-Mafia thump-er gave his heart to Jesus Christ that day, and became a part of the church I pastor.

There has been times where I was preaching, and the Reality

of God was so real it literally felt like there was a hand on my shoulder. I'm telling you I could literally feel a and on my shoulder, even slightly squeezing it as I was preaching the word of God. I believe it was God speaking to me saying: you're going in the right direction, your preaching the truth. Why in the world would we think that God cannot do these things. He spoke everything into existence with in six days. Surely the Lord God of heaven and earth can manifest himself with physical signs and wonders in order to speak to us.

Divine Manifestation of Frankincense & Myrrh

We were having a woman's conference in our main sanctuary. In this particular gathering something wonderful and supernatural happened when all of a sudden a divine and wonderful fragrance of frankincense and myrrh came rushing into the service. The subject of the conference was on offering up our lives as a sweet fragrance in the nostrils of God. My wife and I had gone all the way to Lancaster in order to purchase the original incense (frankincense and myrrh) that the high priest used to burn in the holy of holies. The ladies who were putting on the conference had wanted this incense to burn at just the right moment in the meeting.

I was in the back with the audio and video people, waiting to light the incense when we were instructed to. Sister Joanna (daughter of Jack Coe) was ministering up front at the time. This special incense was sitting in a brass basin which we had bought, and was designed specifically for the burning of this incense. Everything was prepared for this event, with the matches sitting next to the basin. As sister Joanna was ministering something amazing and wonderful took place. All of a sudden the sanctuary began to be filled with the fragrance of the incense. I mean the smell of this fragrance was so strong that Sister Joanna up front literally stopped preaching. She looked back at me with what looked to be a look of consternation. You could tell in her facial expressions that she was wondering what in the world I was doing. Why in the world would Pastor Mike light the incense before I told him to? She had specifically told me to wait until she gave me the signal to light it.

The fragrance was growing stronger and stronger as it flooded the sanctuary. She finally said over the PA system: Pastor Mike I told you to wait until I specifically told you to light the incense. At that moment I picked up the bowl of incense in my hand, lifting it for all to see. I said: Sister Joanna I did not light the incense. The fragrance that you are smelling is not coming from this bowl of incense. Before we had begun this meeting, we had burned a little bit of the incense to see what it smelled like. Here we were smelling that exact same fragrance which had flooded our sanctuary. I was standing there with the basin full of incense unlit.

Myself and some of the personnel took a walk through the building, and out side to try to discover where this strong heavenly smell of frankincense and myrrh was coming from. We came back, reporting that we could not find the source of it.

As the realization that this was all a divine manifestation of Gods presence, the women began to excitedly praise and worship the Lord. There were tears flowing down many cheeks at that moment. We were all overcome with a very strong sense of God's presence and holiness. From that moment forward that woman's conference entered into a much deeper realm of the spirit. God was in the house.

As the realization that this was all divine manifestation, the women began to excitedly praise and worship the Lord. There were tears flowing down many cheeks at that moment. We were all overcome with a very strong sense of God's presence and holiness. From that moment forward that woman's conference entered into a much deeper realm of the spirit. God was in the house. Remember that God **Confirms His Word with Signs Following.**

Mark 16:20 And they went forth, and preached every where, the Lord working with them, and confirming the word with signs following. Amen.

Jesus said: *He That Believeth on Me, the Works that I Do, he will do also!* The Miracles, Signs and Wonders that I Do Shall He Do Also. Now we can talk about God's divine nature, divine character, and divine attributes, which are all wonderful, powerful and amazing truths, and yet God knew that it would take signs, wonders and miracles to wake men up to the reality of who HE is. These amazing manifestations to some extent I believe Is God shouting at the Human Race the reality of who he is.

When **Noah Built the Ark** ,that Was an amazing Wonder to behold. It Was one of the greatest Wonders of the then known world. I do not doubt for one instant that every human being in the world came by and saw Noah's Ark. I believe that 100% of the human race knew exactly what Noah was doing, plus every one of them knew that the animals had begun to gather to come on board this amazing vessel. Noah was a preacher of righteousness who proclaim God's coming judgment because of man's wickedness. These multitudes of humanity came to gawk at the Ark that he had built, and listen to him as he was calling them by the voice of God to repent, and to believe the gospel. None of those who died in the flood had any excuse not to repent. God had revealed himself to them by the miraculous construction of Noah's Ark, and the gathering together of the animals to that one place.

What does God have to do to get us to listen? There are times in history when God will speak to us in a very profound and amazing way, especially when major judgment or disaster is coming. I believe that God is speaking very profoundly to this generation through the little nation of Israel. It seems like all of the nations of the world have risen up against this very small country. Even many of the leaders of our own nation have turned their back on this country, and yet God is using them to declare, that they are his people, and none of you will be able to destroy them. I am using them to verify that everything I said in my book is real.

Isaiah 8:18Behold, I and the children whom the Lord hath given me are for signs and for wonders in Israel from the Lord of hosts, which dwelleth in mount Zion.

There is another way that God speaks to people and to nations. It is something that we do not want to a knowledge in this modern day church age. God talks to us through divine and natural disasters. There has been an acceleration of natural disasters in the last 20 to 30 years. If you study the statistics there actually quite frightening. I'm talking about earthquakes, tsunamis, floods, droughts, volcanic eruptions, and the list could go on and on. In previous generations world leaders acknowledge that this was the judgment of God because of the wickedness of man. Now people with wicked ambitions are declaring its global warming, and other such foolish notions. Instead of falling on their knees and repenting, they're using these terrible situations to fill their pockets with money and to gain more power and more influence over humanity.

Luke 21:25 And there shall be signs in the sun, and in the moon, and in the stars; and upon the earth distress of nations, with perplexity; the sea and the waves roaring;

It is by divine signs and wonders that God reveals to people who he is, it is also that which he uses to declare his approval upon our lives.

Acts 2:22 Ye men of Israel, hear these words; Jesus of Nazareth, a man approved of God among you by miracles and wonders and signs, which God did by him in the midst of you, as ye yourselves also know:

By mighty signs and wonders God causes humanity to stop and listen, it causes people to begin to realize that there is a God in heaven.

Acts 2:43 And fear came upon every soul: and many wonders and signs were done by the apostles.

Through the years I have seen God radically transform and change people's lives as the spirit of the Lord began to move in the mist of our meetings. God began to manifest his wonderful presence by mighty signs and wonders that everyone had to stop and consider.

Bones Supernaturally Snapping, Popping into Place

One night as I was ministering at a service, there was an older lady standing in front of me in the prayer line who I had never seen before. I knew immediately by the spirit that she had a major bone disease. I informed her of such, and told her the spirit of the Lord told me he was going to touch her and make her whole. At the time I was not thinking with my rational mind, I was just flowing in the Holy Ghost. By the spirit of the Lord I also told her that she should not be alarmed, because her bones would begin to snap and pop into place after I prayed for her. The bones in her body would literally begin to go back to where they belonged supernaturally when I finished praying.

I laid my hands on her in the name of Jesus Christ and spoke to the spirit of infirmity, commanding it to come out of her immediately in the Name of Jesus Christ of Nazereth. The spirit of God touched her in such a mighty way that she began to slightly twist and turn as she crumpled to the floor under the power of the Holy Ghost. We all stood there amazed as we heard and saw her body begin to come back in alignment. You could literally hear the bones popping in her body as the spirit of Christ adjusted and healed her bone structure. We continued to minister to others as she lay on the floor having a divine chiropractor working on her.

She came back approximately a week later sharing with us the wonderful news that she was completely healed. All the signs of the bone disease (she gave us the technical term but I do not remember) were completely gone, and eradicated. Thank you father God for the wonderful works you do in the name of Your Son, Jesus Christ of Nazareth! God Is What Was Concerned about Her Soul and He Said I'm Going to Show You I'm Real I'm Going to Show You I Remember

The Church I Pastor Is a Sign and a Wonder

The Church I pastor is an Amazing Sign and Wonder to the Community. We started the church back in about 1983. Now I told the Lord there's three things I did not ever want to do, I said Lord I never want to be a pastor, let me be an evangelist. He has had me pastor for almost 40 years, ever since 1977. Then I said: okay Lord, please just let me not have to live in Pennsylvania, and yet God has had me in Pennsylvania being a pastor. Then I said okay Lord, just please, please don't ever have me live or pastor in the Gettysburg Pennsylvania area. Well here I am, a pastor in Gettysburg Pennsylvania since 1983. I strongly suggest you never tell the Lord what you don't want to do.

From the very beginning of being a pastor in Gettysburg it has been extremely challenging. Especially if you are not going to compromise, dilute,or water-down the true gospel with a feel good message. If you are a people pleasing, fun and games kinda pastor, granted you can probably get a large crowd, but if you tell everybody that comes through the doors that in order to make it to heaven, you have to be living a godly and holy life, it's a miracle if anybody shows up at all.

Granted, I have made a lot of mistakes as a pastor, and you can read about it in my book: **"I Need God Because I'm Stupid"**. The honest truth is also that I have done a lot of things right, with many being healed, delivered and set free. Most of the community actually believe that we are an occult because we believe that God still does what he did back 2000 years ago.

Our church is a sign and wonder because we are still here. We have no large financial backers or supporters. We have never gone after people in order for them to give to us financially. God supernaturally and divinely provides for us all the time when it looks like we are gone, God does a miracle once again. We just had to do an insurance appraisal on our facility for our bank. It came in at just under $4 million for replacement cost, including the value of the property. I am simply bragging and boasting on what Jesus Christ has done.

Some time ago I Went down to a Motorcycle Rally in Gettysburg, located at the Harley-Davidson dealer ship. At this rally there was a Christian Booth Set up giving out free literature. My Wife and I Began to Talk to the people who were in this booth. We started Sharing Christ, and the marvelous miracles we have seen him do, and I was sharing, he asked me what church I belong to? I told them I was the pastor at Jesus is Lord ministries international. They acted completely surprised, with one of the men saying: you're still there? I heard that you guys were closed up a long time ago. I started laughing basically telling him that our demise has been extremely exaggerated. I told him nope, we are still going strong, reaching out by radio, TV, Internet, the writing of books, and in any other way that God makes available.

Sometimes I think we are a little bit like Israel who seems to be such a pain in the worlds neck. The world absolutely hates the Jews, but can't seem to get rid of them no matter how they connive, or what they do. God still has a plan and a purpose for their existence. Israel is a sign and wonder, a divine miracle of the evidence of the reality of God. The world looks at them and says: how in the world can they survive? I believe that the church I pastor is the same. You cannot point to any man-made, natural reasons why we are still in existence. It is all supernatural and divine, as a sign and a wonder, a miracle that God is real. While many other churches have shut down, compromised, or just given up, we are still standing strong in Jesus Christ.

#14 PEACE & JOY

The **14th Way** I would like to share with you on how God leads and guides us is through peace and joy. There are many scriptures that deal with this particular way in which God speaks to his people. In all of these many different faceted ways in which God leads and guides us there will always be the peace and the joy of the Lord in the midst of them.

Isaiah 55:11 So shall my word be that goeth forth out of my mouth: it shall not return unto me void, but it shall accomplish that which I please, and it shall prosper in the thing whereto I sent it.

God sends his word, and if we will accept and embrace his word then notice something wonderful takes place within our hearts and our lives.

Isaiah 55:12 For ye shall go out with joy, and be led forth with peace: the mountains and the hills shall break forth before you into singing, and all the trees of the field shall clap their hands.

The spirit of the Lord will literally lead and guide us with peace and joy. This is such a wonderful way to know whether or not your in the will of God. Whenever we are tormented, upset, miserable, or confused, then something is wrong. We need to stop, and seek the face of the Lord once again. Every time I have ignored this warning, this red light on the dashboard of my life, I get in trouble. Now we understand that we must live and move by faith, that if there is anything we do that is not of faith, then we are in some aspect of our life out of the will of God. Faith will always be walking hand-in-hand with peace and joy.

1 Peter 1:8 Whom having not seen, ye love; in whom, though now ye see him not, yet believing, ye rejoice with joy unspeakable and full of glory:

I am telling you that when faith is operating it brings joy, it brings peace and rest. The subject of peace is spoken of over 400 times in the Bible, and not the peace that the world understands. This is a supernatural divine peace that will pass all natural understanding. This is not a peace that comes from drinking alcohol, popping pills, listening to music, taking long walks through the woods. I did not realize that everything in this world that produces some type of natural peace is completely artificial and fake compared the supernatural divine peace of God which we are talking about. People spend millions of dollars trying to find peace and fulfillment in this life. To some extent this is what people call R & R, when they go to the Bahamas, lay back on the beach, cross there ankles and drink a glass of ice cold lemonade, soaking in the sunshine. People think and believe this is ultimate peace and fulfillment. In truth this is nothing but fleshly and worldly temporary satisfaction. This is not the peace that passes all understanding that the Bible talks about.

Philippians 4:7 And the peace of God, which passeth all understanding, shall keep your hearts and minds through Christ Jesus.

Committing Suicide, then Something Supernatural Happened!

God is wanting to lead and guide us with peace and joy. This is a divine inner manifestation of God's presence. It is not based on your feelings, circumstances, or situation. I remember a good friend of mine sharing how he first experience this amazing peace and joy. He shared with me how that he was all wrapped up in drugs, alcohol, women and wild living. He had just come home from a wild night on the town , and he was standing on the deck of his back porch at 11 in the morning. He stood on the outside deck contemplating suicide because he was so stinking miserable. He hated his life and everything about it.

As he was standing there, he finally cried out to God, surrendering his life to Jesus Christ. As he gave his heart to Jesus, something wonderful and amazing happened. It seemed like all of nature was singing at once he told me as he looked out over the valley behind his house, and it was like all of nature was singing to him. The peace of God overwhelmed him from head to toe,even to the ends of his fingertips he told me. The sky was bluer then he had ever seen it. The grass was greener, the trees were greener and more full of life, the flowers were more beautiful and brilliant than he had ever seen them. Christ had come into his heart and completely changed every perception that he had ever had.

One minute he is so tormented that he just wants to die, and the next minute he is so full of life, love, joy and peace that he felt like he had died and gone to heaven. This is the wonderful and marvelous experience of the new birth. When you totally surrender your heart, your mind and your life to Jesus Christ.

He did not realize it at the time, but this was the peace that passes all understanding, the peace that makes you feel like everything is going to be all right no matter what is happening.

My Mom on Her Death bed

My mom died in December of the year 2000. Thank God that I had the opportunity to lead her to Christ back in 1979. My sister Debbie was there that night when my mother passed on. She filled me in with all of the information of what exactly transpired. You see my mom had asthma as far back as I can remember, and actually I was born with lung problems myself. I still remember as a young boy looking out from behind an oxygen tent laying in the hospital in a bed. When at the age of 19 years old I was gloriously born again, and I discovered that by the stripes of Jesus Christ I am healed, and at that time in my life I received healing for my lung condition. Than God for over 40 years I have never had another problem with my lungs.

My mom was only 66 years old when this terrible incident happened. She went to the doctor for a regular checkup pertaining to her asthma. The Dr. informed her that he was going to change her prescription, the only problem is that he did not tell her that she needed to begin to transition from one medicine to another very slowly. This new medication for asthma was much stronger, and it turns out it was quite a bit more dangerous than her previous prescription.

Because she did know better she stopped using her old medication, replacing it with the new medication immediately. My sister lived with her in the same house at the time this happened. The next thing you know she is telling my sister Debbie that for some reason she feels like she just can't get her breath. What she did realize is that it was not that she could not breathe, but that the medicine was causing her heart to spasm. Approximately one day later at night while my sister was sleeping, she thought she heard something that did not sound right. Here it was my mom calling out to my sister Debbie over and over for help, but she could not catch enough breath to cry out loud enough for my sister to hear her. When Debbie finally woke up she immediately perceived that something was wrong, she jumped up out of her bed and ran for my mom's bedroom.

She found my mom very close to death because of the heart clamping shut because of the medicine. Immediately my sister called for the ambulance to come and get her. While my sister and mom were waiting for the ambulance, they had an opportunity to talk. She told my sister Debbie not to worry, and that everything was going to be okay. Debbie said that there was absolutely no fear in my mother's voice, no worry, no anxiety whatsoever. That there seemed to be this tangible and overwhelming peace that had come upon her as she laid there just barely alive. As they took my mother away, she squeezed my sisters hand with a gentle reassurance that she was okay. She passed on to be with the Lord that night with the peace of God possessing her mind and her soul.

FALSE PROPHETS

Their are false prophets that tell people peace, peace, when in all reality there is nothing but coming destruction and judgment because of sin. It is like a man telling you that everything is going to be okay, when it in all reality is not going to be okay. False preachers are telling people all the time that they are right with God, and that God loves them no matter what they do. They put these poor souls into a very dangerous and precarious position because instead of seeking the Lord, these people who have been told that everything is okay, simply believe this lie. If somebody would've told them the truth, they could've been crying out to God for his mercy and his forgiveness.

A false prophets will keep you out of the will of God, by letting you believe that you can do what ever you want, live however you want, act however you want, and the blood of Jesus Christ covers all of your sins, even the ones that you are living in and committing. They will tell you that you are okay the way you are.

Do not listen to the words of the prophets who prophesy to you ...They speak a vision of their own heart, Not from the mouth of the Lord. They continually say to those who despise Me, 'The Lord has said, 'You shall have PEACE'; And to everyone who walks according to the dictates of his own heart, they say, 'No evil shall come upon you.' " Jeremiah 23:16-17

Heaven sent prophets will warn people when they are out of the will of God. All of the true prophets of God from the beginning of time have warned people of coming judgment if they did not repent,and get right with God. Elijah warned the people, Ezekiel warned the people, Isaiah warned the people, John the Baptist warned the people. If you study the epistles you will discover that every New Testament apostles, prophet and minister warned the people. They came to exhort the people to live in holiness, righteousness and obedience. When we are operating in the will of God, by faith, the peace of God will rule and reign in our hearts. We are exhorted throughout the New Testament to be led by the peace of God.

Philippians 4:6 Be careful for nothing; but in every thing by prayer and supplication with thanksgiving let your requests be made known unto God. 7 And the peace of God, which passeth all understanding, shall keep your hearts and minds through Christ Jesus.

The Scripture declares that the peace of God, the tranquility, the harmony, the unity of God which passes all of mans natural understanding will keep my heart and mind in Christ Jesus. This peace is a divine and supernatural protective shield wrapped around our minds from the fiery darts of the enemy.

I discovered through the years that when I get into difficult situations God enables me and empowers me, giving me entanglements according to my position within the body of Christ. One thing that I have discovered which is very important is the peace of God in my heart and my mind, in my dealings with people and circumstances. When dealing with people outwardly many times it looks like everything is okay with them, and with their spiritual walk, but God knows their true spiritual condition and what is going on in their lives. Many times through the years I will be speaking to someone who seems to be okay, but on the inside it is like someone is scraping their fingernails against a chalkboard. I am not speaking about judging anyone's heart, or being fault finding or critical. There's many people who think they are operating in the spirit of discernment, but in all reality they are operating in a spirit of assumption and self-righteousness. When you are truly moving in the spirit of compassion and love, the Lord will begin to reveal things to you in order to help others. Many times also the Lord will speak to you about somebody in order to protect yourself and your loved ones. I wish I could say that I have always been obedient to that spiritual perception, but I haven't. Every time I have missed God, it has brought bad results. When the peace and the joy of the Lord is not operating in your heart, you need to stop and asked the Father what is happening?

I Brought a Fox into the Hen house (1997)

They say stupid is as stupid does. I guess this is a simple explanation of decisions I have made at times. Whenever you lose the peace of God, you need to have enough wisdom to stop and ask the Father what is happening. In this particular situation I'm going to share with you, I did not apply this truth. The church I was a pastor of was growing so fast that I decided that I need to hire more personnel. There was a man who used to work for us in our radio station, who also had been a pastor, who I thought would fit the bill perfectly. My wife strongly encouraged me not to hire him, but I did not listen to her, if the truth be made known, I did not even pray about it. I decided to hire him based upon the fact that he seemed to be really good with people, and was such a natural salesman, where I was kind of rough and blunt. I have an apostolic call on my life, and do not operate as most pastors do, therefore many people misunderstand me. Through the years people have told me that they did not think that my calling was as a pastor. They could not recognize nor spiritually discern the difference between a pastor and an apostolic gift.

I used people's complaining and crumbling as my excuse to hire this man, to have him fill in the gaps of my so called short-comings. I complained, "Lord, you know that I'm not really a pastor, I am apostolic and people just do not comprehend the difference." My whining swung the doors wide open, allowing the enemy to really begin to work. Yes, against my better judgment, and my wife's warnings, with no peace in my heart about hiring him, I hired him.

Eventually, it came out that this brother who my wife told me (in no uncertain terms) not to hire as an assistant pastor was meeting privately with my deacons and was stirring the pot. I had hired him in part because of his social charm but that was now coming back and kicking me in the head. He was going to the deacon's homes and spending personal time with each one of them. A warning siren was going off in my heart. I confronted him, notifying him of his inappropriate conduct and informing him that he needed to stop. But, of course, he did not. After he left, I discovered that he had been spreading all kinds of fabrications about me. One such example is that when he would visit the sick per my request; when he did, if he did, he would tell them that I commanded him not to visit them. Instead, he would tell them, "I came to see you anyway because of the great love that I have for you." Often times, we have an Absalom in our midst and we are completely clueless about it.

Before I knew what was happening, there was a full-fledged rebellion going on in the church. My world began to fall apart. The elders I had with me at the time stood faithful and strong. (Of course, I'm only sharing with you the tip of the iceberg.) The seven deacons had given themselves over to a wrong spirit. Those we follow will direct our course. We had better be very cautious who we choose to follow. Of course, I hold myself accountable for my own poor decisions. I was being deceived, which allowed a spirit of deception to hover over our church. This so-called brother tried to take over the church. Praise God, the Lord Himself interceded and the man failed. He took the deacons, their wives and other members of the congregation and went down the road about 18 miles where they started a new church that did not last very long. Most of the people who followed this particular man ended up experiencing tragic circumstances. My heart still reaches out to them. I pray for complete restoration and healing! This so-called brother ended up in prison and is still in prison at the writing of this book. He never did come back and repent. But, of course, that's between him and God. Just keep your hearts sweet, loving and forgiving even as Christ forgave us.

The important reality is that we are living in very dangerous times. There are many deceivers and false prophets who have entered into the body of Christ. We truly need to be led by the spirit of God in every decision we make. In all of our associations with people, we have to really become sensitive to what the spirit of the Lord is saying. I am not talking about having a critical or faultfinding attitude, or being paranoid, but being sensitive to the Holy Spirit. Jesus warned us: the thief cometh not but for to steal, to kill, and to destroy. When the peace and the joy of the Lord is not manifested, we need to stop and ask: Father what is going on?

You might ask: pastor Mike how will I know that God is speaking to me when it comes to peace and joy? I want to use the word feeling, but it's way more than a feeling, or a sensation that comes from your heart. There are times when I'll see something in my spirit, I perceive something, or I do not have peace, but I just keep my mouth shut, simply waiting upon the Lord. It might be to 2 weeks or 3 weeks of simply being quiet before the Lord. There is a Scripture that has helped me many times in these situations.

Proverbs 29:11 A fool uttereth all his mind: but a wise man keepeth it in till afterwards.

There is another Scripture that I really love, In which we all need to get revelation on.

Ecclesiastes 2:14 The wise man's eyes are in his head; but the fool walketh in darkness:

Many times people have tried to keep important information from me as the pastor. They said to themselves: we really do not want to bother the pastor with this problem, or this situation, but yet without them telling me I knew by the spirit of God what was going on. Sometimes I cannot put my finger on it, but if I simply wait on the Lord long enough, it will manifest even as the Bible says that everything that is done in secret will be made manifest.

John 14:27 Peace I leave with you, my peace I give unto you: not as the world giveth, give I unto you. Let not your heart be troubled, neither let it be afraid.

I have discovered that many people in the body of Christ are extremely tormented, confused, discouraged and even bitter. Brothers and sisters this should not be within the body of Christ. Realize that when you are in any of these conditions that you are to some extent out of the will of God. Now there's many different ways in which you can be out of the will of God, and without even knowing it. For instance Job was a righteous man, and yet he was absolutely out of the will of God in his attitude, his words, in how he perceived what was happening to him, and his family. He sincerely thought it was God that was causing all of this destruction, death and disaster. He was making such foolish statements, to where he stated that it would have been better if he had never been born. He had completely lost all of his peace and all of his joy, and actually before he was even attacked by the devil, he was tormented by fear. Whenever you do not have peace and joy, you need to STOP and ask God what is going on.

John 14:27Peace I leave with you, my peace I give unto you: not as the world giveth, give I unto you. Let not your heart be troubled, neither let it be afraid.

1 John 4:18 There is no fear in love; but perfect love casteth out fear: because fear hath torment. He that feareth is not made perfect in love.

Many believers have absolutely no peace, and no joy in their lives whatsoever. You will see many believers spending all of their money, and time on useless vein pursuits trying to find satisfaction and fulfillment. Real peace and joy only comes from Christ, and being in the middle of his will. When Job finally had a visitation from God, seeing the error of his ways, repenting, peace and joy came flooding in to his heart and his soul like a mighty River, and Prosperity once again overtook him.

Job 42:5 I have heard of thee by the hearing of the ear: but now mine eye seeth thee.6 Wherefore I abhor myself, and repent in dust and ashes.....10 And the Lord turned the captivity of Job, when he prayed for his friends: also the Lord gave Job twice as much as he had before.

More than 1 in 5 Americans now (2008) takes at least one drug to treat a psychological disorder. These drugs rang from antidepressants like Prozac, to anti-anxiety drugs like Xanax. Americans are taking a "startling" amount of mental-health related medications, according to a big new study by Medco Health Solutions. Depression is absolutely rampant among the young and the old. Most of the alcoholism and drug use today is based upon the fact that people are tormented. They are trying to find some way of escaping from their torment. The Scripture says: *there is a way which seems right onto man, but the end thereof is death.* Drugs and alcohol, materialism and vain amusements, will not bring the ultimate peace and joy that people so desire to possess.

Psalm 16:11 Thou wilt shew me the path of life: in thy presence is fulness of joy; at thy right hand there are pleasures for evermore.

This is a major **KEY: when you lose your peace, don't ignore it, but stop and find out why you lost it.** I am not suggesting that you lean to the understanding of your mind, but you simply get before the Lord, asking him what's wrong? You need to start speaking and meditating upon the truths of God's word, quoting Scriptures to yourself dealing with the subject that you need victory in. I guarantee that in the mist of this, the Lord will start speaking to you. You should be ready to hear from God by having a writing pad at your side, paper and pen in hand, expecting God to speak to you. You should do a quick scan over all of your relationships with all of the different people you know, and all of the recent decisions you have made, or are about to make. The spirit of the Lord will cause you to see what is wrong, and It will almost seem like you are trying to put a square block into a round hole.

Gang Leader Kept Trying to Stab Me to Death

After being born again for a while, I perceived in my heart that I needed to reach out and witness to the gang I used to run with right outside of Chicago. We were not a gang in the sense that we had a name or any entrance rituals that we had to go through. We were just a group of young men who were constantly involved in corruption, drinking, fighting, using drugs, stripping cars, and doing other things to horrible that I will not mention. One day, I was sitting in a car between the two instigators of most of our shenanigans, Gary and Claire. Both of these men were very large and quite muscular. I had fervently shared Christ with them and the others to let them know how much God had changed me. They sat around drinking, using dope, and cussing while I shared the good news with them. I explained I was on a heavenly high that drugs and the world could never take them to. Most of them just stared at me, not knowing how to respond. They all had known the old Mike Yeager. The crazy and ungodly stuff that I had done. They had seen me many times whacked out on drugs and alcohol. Now here I was a brand-new creation in Christ preaching Jesus with a deep and overwhelming zeal.

Now Gary who was one of the main leaders was different in many negative ways than the other guys. He was like a stick of dynamite ready to explode at any moment. He had been up to the big house already and spent some time behind the bars of justice. He never did like me, but now there was an unspoken, seething hatred for me under the surface, which eventually exploded. We were coming out of Racine, Illinois, as Gary was driving the car we were in. Claire was sitting against the door on the right side in the front seat, with me in the middle. At that moment I did not realize why they had put me in the middle, but it became very obvious. Before I knew it, Gary reached up and grabbed a large knife from the dashboard of the car. I believe the vehicle was an old Impala that had the old-style steel dashboard. The heating and air conditioning were controlled by sliders in the dash. The knife had been shoved down into one of the slots. He pulled the knife out of the dashboard with his right hand, jabbed it high up into the air, and drove it down toward me very fast, trying to stab me in the gut with this knife. I saw him reach for the knife, and at that very moment I entered into the realm of the Spirit when time seemes to come to a standstill. This has happened to me on numerous occasions in such dangerous situations.

When I enter this realm, time slows down while my speed or movement seems to increase. You could argue whether I speed up or time slows down. I really can't say, though; it just happens. The knife came down toward my guts in slow motion, and I saw my hands reaching up towards the knife and grabbing Gary's wrist to prevent him from stabbing me through the gut. I could not prevent the knife from coming down, but I was able to cause it to plunge into the seat instead. His thrust had been so powerful that the knife literally pierced all the way down through the Springfield car seat. He immediately pulled it out of the car seat and tried to stab me again. He continued to try to stab me as he was driving down the road. Every time he tried to stab me, I was able to divert the stab just fractions of an inch away from my privates and for my legs.

During this entire event the peace of God was upon me in an overwhelming way. I was not shaking or breathing hard in the least; neither was my heart beating fast. It sounds unbelievable, I know, but it felt as if I were in heaven. The presence and the peace of God was upon me in a powerful supernatural way. I know this might sound extremely strange and weird, but I was actually kind of enjoying myself as I was watching God deliver me from this madman. During this entire time it was like a slow-motion review of a movie. Up and down the knife came as he kept on trying to kill me. This large muscular man was not able to kill a small 5'8" skinny guy. I just love how God does the supernatural miracles. There was not one thing in my life in which that I knew I was out of God's will. I believe if I had been out of the will of God most likely Gary would've succeeded in murdering me. He kept on trying to kill me until up ahead of us a police car came out from a side road. Gary's car window was open and when he saw the policeman he threw the knife out the window.

Gary continued to drive down the road without ever saying a word about what had just happened. In this whole situation Claire who I had thought was a friend of mine, did not in any way try to help me. No one said a word as we drove down the road, but the peace of God was upon me like I have the invisible blanket.

Thou wilt keep him in perfect peace, whose mind is stayed on thee: because he trusteth in thee. Trust ye in the LORD for ever: for in the LORD JEHOVAH is everlasting strength (Isaiah 26:3-4).

The Green light, Red light syndrome!

Dealing with the subject of how God leads and guides us there is a principal I call: **The green light, red light syndrome.** We all know very well what a signal light is. Whether you drive or you don't, you have seen them over and over since you were a child. The signal lights may seem insignificant, and maybe at times even and annoyance, but yet they are extremely important. Many people have died because they did not heed, or pay attention to the signal lights that they were approaching. When you come up to a green light, it means keep on going., but if you come up to a red light it means you better stop. Red lights are so important that they use yellow lights in order to warn you about the up and coming Red light! God will give us yellow lights, before the red lights ever appear.

If you are like most people, when you're not very far from the signal light, and all of a sudden it turns yellow, you put on the gas to try to speed up, and make it through before the yellow light turns to red. We might be able to get away with this when it comes to a natural signal light, but you will never get away with it when it comes to spiritual realities.

Did Jesus Make Us Free from Red Lights?

I acknowledge that this sounds like a really stupid question, but let's just stop for a moment, and apply this question to what we are being told by many today in the pulpit. What if I would teach that because of the sufferings and agonies of Jesus, we are now free forever from the red lights at intersections. (and all other driving laws) That we can basically choose to ignore the red lights and not even blink at the yellow warning lights, because Jesus took care of all the red lights.

It's only when you're a sinner that you have to be concerned about the red lights, but if you will confess Jesus as Lord, then you too can be free from the red lights. What if I taught that all of the major accidents, deaths, tragedies, and destruction that happen on the Highway of life (because we are ignoring the red lights)............. well, that is just the devil! Of course silly.......... God loves you no matter how many red lights you ignore, because that is exactly why Jesus suffered, it is for you could drive your vehicle with no rules or regulations. (If you listen to anybody who says there's rules and regulations it equals legalism) Why don't you know my poor simpleton ----- this is why Jesus died for you! You are now free, free, free to drive without any rules, laws, or restrictions, and if somebody mistakenly sends you a traffic ticket, just tear them up, because don't you know: Jesus paid for all of those traffic tickets, past, present and future. Now you can drive any way you want, and all of those other poor suckers who are obeying the signal lights, they are living in bondage and legalism. Happy driving!

PS: If you believe this bizarre philosophy then the next time I see you coming, I will be heading in the other direction as far away from you as I can get. You may not know what, but you are a major catastrophe going somewhere to happen! **By the way God has traffic cameras on you every time you run a red light!**

Drama Queen Christianity

If you are going be led and guided by the spirit of God, then you must never become a drama queen, and if you are a drama queen, then you need to repent, and stop it. What is a drama queen? Someone who turns something minor, and unimportant into a major deal, or someone who blows things way out of proportion. These are people who are highly sensitive to their needs, their problems, and there difficulties. They will take molehills and turned them into these gigantic and overwhelming mountains. This is the opposite of having a spirit of faith, but it is a spirit of unbelief. Unbelief always exalts the world, the flesh, and the devil, every sickness, disease and problem. God cannot lead us, or guide us when we are drama queens.

Through the years I have known many drama queens as a pastor. I literally had a woman who left our church one time because she said I did not shake her hand. I can honestly say that I do not remember not shaking her hand. In all reality the Lord has put his amazing love in my heart for people, and yet I had to acknowledge a long time ago that I am not called to be the remedy or solution to people's problems. I do not desire to be anybody's hero, because there is only one hero, and his name is Jesus Christ. I know many Christians that the minute they have a problem, a pain in their body,or some situation, they run to the experts. Well, I agree run to the expert, and His name is Jesus Christ, the great physician, the provider, the deliverer, the answer and solution to every problem.

Isaiah 26:3 Thou wilt keep him in perfect peace, whose mind is stayed on thee: because he trusteth in thee.4 Trust ye in the Lord for ever: for in the Lord Jehovah is everlasting strength:

Here is a major key to God leading and guiding us reveal to us in a powerful and wonderful Scripture.

Psalm 119:165 Great peace have they which love thy law: and nothing shall offend them.

In order for God to lead us and guide us, we have to love his word. This is one of my wife's favorite Scriptures to quote to me. Whenever I get offended, upset or aggravated she reminds me that if I really truly love God's word, I will have great peace, and that nothing will offend me. Nobody and nothing in this world should rob me of the peace and the joy that Christ has given to me if I love the word of God, and I am meditating in it day and night.. You might say that peace and joy is the divine GPS that leads and guides me where ever I need to go. If we would really do an in-depth study on the life of Christ, we would be amazed, because he never was never bitter, hateful, or ungodly in any way, form, or fashion. Jesus Christ was always sweet, in the sense that the divine nature of the Father was manifested in every part of his being.

Here is a wonderful example the peace and the joy of the Lord. God has given to us tongues that have an amazing ability to taste what is bitter and what is sweet. If you put a spoonful of honey in your mouth, instantly your mouth is filled with nothing but sweetness. If you take a mouthful of lemon concentrate, your mouth is instantly filled with nothing but bitterness. Sweet and bitter is so obvious to our human tongues that nobody has to teach us the difference. I believe that this is also true with our inner man when it comes to that which is sweet or bitter. Now we can deceive ourselves into thinking that we are sweet when we are really bitter, ugly, mean and nasty people. The devil will also try to convince us that we are bitter, when we are really operating in the sweetness of Jesus. We need to really be sensitive to the spirit of God to discover if what is going on is sweet, or bitter. Do we have the joy and peace of the Lord ruling and reigning over our hearts? There is a Scripture that says that those who are peacemakers, shall be called the children of God. I have known quite a number of so-called Christians through the years who just love to stir up strife, division, and hate.

You will know when you are not trusting God because you will be fretting, upset, angry, or worried. The devil loves to manipulate us, to control us by our emotions, but when you have great peace, and when you have the joy of the Lord, it completely throws the enemy into confusion.

The communists were waiting to kill me

I have been in the Philippines multiple times. When I go, I work directly with a Filipino Bible college in the province of Samar. I have been told that this is one of the most poverty-stricken parts of the Philippines, and one of the most dangerous. Missionaries very rarely go there because of this. It is far away from all the modern conveniences of Manila. It is also inhabited by the New People's Army which is a Communist movement. The NPA are extremely dangerous. I have personally known Philippine pastors who I had preached with who have been killed by them.

When I was finishing up on one of my missionary journeys there, the Spirit of God quickened my heart to ask them where the most dangerous place to go to in that area was. They told me it was an island called Laoang. They said that two American missionaries had gone into Laoang, and did not come out alive. The NPA had slit their throats. As they were telling me this story, the Spirit of the Lord quickened giving me a amazing peace within my heart, telling me that I needed to go and take this place for Jesus. I told them the next time I come back, I needed to go to that island and preach the gospel. They asked me if I was serious. I said absolutely! I told them I would give them the money that they needed to make the flyers and posters to spread the word that we were coming.

About six months later, I arrived back in the Philippines with one of the men from my church who is now a pastor in the Phoenix, Arizona area. When we arrived in the province of Samar, the brethren informed us that the Communists were aware of us coming and were going to be waiting for us. I did not ask them to explain to me what they meant. I absolutely had no fear in my heart. It is hard to explain to people what it is like when you are operating in a gift of faith. It is not normal faith. It is faith that makes you know that in Christ you cannot be defeated. In the operation of this faith there is always overwhelming peace. It is the peace of God that passes all understanding. The minute you lose your peace, you need to stop and asked the Father what is wrong. This is a major way in which God leads and guides us is by his peace.

Isaiah 55:12 For ye shall go out with joy, and be led forth with peace: the mountains and the hills shall break forth before you into singing, and all the trees of the field shall clap their hands.

In order to get to this island we were going to have to take canoes. We took the road that ran through Catarman. The main bridge was out going to Laoang, so we had to take an alternative route to get over a large river. We stayed on this road until it ran into the Philippine ocean. From there we took two large canoes. Each canoe had an outboard motor on the back of them. We would have to traverse on the ocean almost a mile to reach Laoang.

I was in the first canoe up front at the very tip of the vessel. There is great excitement and peace in my heart to see what God was about to do. I had great expectations of God manifesting himself on this island that had shut off the gospel for many years. I knew that God was going to have to perform miracles to keep us alive, and yet there was absolutely no fear within my heart, nothing but overflowing peace. As we were coming closer to the island, I could see that there were men lined up along the beach. There was no fear in my heart. There is approximately 30 men who were standing there waiting with guns and machetes in their hands.

The Filipino brothers who were navigating the canoes kept the engines of the canoes running fast enough so the canoes would drive themselves up a little bit onto the dry shore. As we approached the shore I stood up to my feet, getting ready to leave out of this canoe towards these communist. It had to be the spirit of God within me, because no sane man would lead to his death. I almost out at that moment like that picture of George Washington as he crossed the Delaware River. The minute we hit the beach, I was up and out of the canoe. The Communists were standing there waiting to kill us. The Spirit of God, the gift of faith, the peace of God was possessing me as I began to walk towards them very rapidly. I headed right for the center of this crowd gun and machete wielding communist. As I reached them, it was like the Lord splitting the Red Sea. They separated from left to right and allowed our team of men to walk right through the midst of them.

That night we held a crusade right in the middle of the village. As our worship team was singing, the Communists and pagan religious people were marching through our meeting. We simply ignored them and kept on with the meeting. There seemed to be a very large crowd that night, probably because they wanted to see a white man. It was very seldom when Americans or Europeans came into this area. The tourists flock to Manila and Mindanao. It had been 10 years since anybody had dared come to this island to preach Christianity. The last missionaries they had murdered. Now here I was about to preach the gospel of Jesus Christ that saves, heals and delivers just like it did in the days when Jesus walked in his earthly ministry.

After the singing it was my opportunity to preach. It literally felt like the spirit of God was flowing through me like a mighty river of electricity and power. I preached under the unction of the Holy Ghost, to a great extent not thinking at all what to say, but letting the spirit have his way. When I was done preaching, there was barely enough light to make out the crowd in front of us. They had lit some torches around the meeting area, trying to bring as much light as possible. Because I could not get down into the crowd to pray for them, I had to speak the word of healing over them. I began to command their bodies to be healed in the name of Jesus Christ of Nazareth. Every time I would speak something in the name of Jesus, the interpreter would copy me in their language.

Miracles began to happen. One old lady who had been blind in one eye could now see. A little boy who had been deaf could now hear. It was too dark out for us to tell how many miracles happened that night, but to this day I have been told there is a thriving church there because of this meeting. The precious brothers we worked with had arranged for us to be put into a two-story house. We would be on the second floor, while they were going to be on the first floor. I know why they did this! They were going to make the Communists have to kill them before they would let the NPA get to us. These were the kind of men that would give their lives without hesitation for the sake of the gospel.

It was really late by the time we went to bed. They gave my friend and I some type of straw mats to lie on. We threw these mats on the wooden floor, and tried to go to sleep. During the night we could hear the Communists outside making a racket. The communist had surrounded our house with groups of men, had started little bonfires around the house where we were staying. As I went to sleep, I saw two large angels like pillars of fire in a dream with swords drawn standing over the top of the house we were in. When we woke up in the morning, it was very peaceful. And the Communists were gone.

CHAPTER EIGHT

#15 PEOPLE

The **15th Way** that God will lead and guide us is found in the book of Acts 9:10. There was found a certain disciple by the name of Ananias whom the Lord spoke to in a vision.

Acts 9:11 And the Lord said unto him, Arise, and go into the street which is called Straight, and enquire in the house of Judas for one called Saul, of Tarsus: for, behold, he prayeth,12 And hath seen in a vision a man named Ananias coming in, and putting his hand on him, that he might receive his sight.

Ananias obeyed and went, entering into the house, and putting his hands on Paul saying: brother Saul the Lord even Jesus that appeared unto you in the way, has sent me that you may receive your sight, and be filled with the Holy Ghost. Immediately there fell from his eyes as had been like that of scales, and he received his sight. He arose and was water baptized. Now God used Ananias to bring healing and salvation to the apostle Paul. God used Ananias to bring healing and salvation to the apostle Paul. This is the **15th Way** that God leads and guides us. God will speak to us by speaking through people. He also speaks to us by people who are under the inspiration of the Holy Spirit. God has spoken to me many times as I have read books that people were inspired to write.

Acts 1:8 But ye shall receive power, after that the Holy Ghost is come upon you: and ye shall be witnesses unto me both in Jerusalem, and in all Judaea, and in Samaria, and unto the uttermost part of the earth.

We are called to be witnesses, to speak the truth, and to give counsel to people as God directs us by his word and by his spirit.

Proverbs 27:17Iron sharpeneth iron; so a man sharpeneth the countenance of his friend.

God speaks to us through people, and I'm not just referring to Christian people. How do we know if it is really God speaking through that person? It will always be in line with the word and the divine character, and nature of Jesus Christ. The Lord rescued me once from a terrible temptation by the mouth of a man who wanted nothing to do with God.

The devil had me like a Fly in a Spiders Web!

Jesus said, "The Prince of this world comes, and he can find nothing in me." I'm sorry to say that this is not the experience of any Christian in this world. There are many things within our hearts, emotions and minds that are so deeply buried that we do not even realize that they are there until we are put through the flames of trials and temptation. The enemy of our soul is constantly trying to find ways to destroy us, always probing our defenses. There is a doctrine out there that declares that once one is born again, the carnal nature with its lusts and sinful desires is dead. Oh, how I wish that this were true because that would make life so easy! However, scripture declares otherwise as well as my own personal experience in my Christian walk. Evil desires often just lie there dormant, like a seed in the soil, waiting to spring forth. The bible school that I went to taught that philosophy. I believe that the results would be shocking if one would follow up on the lives of the various graduates from this faith-based bible school. Many of them have returned to the ways of the world since they lacked a solid foundation in the entire Word of God.

Too often, Christians chase one tangent after another, failing to digest the entire Word of God. Their diets are limited and they become spiritually malnourished, never achieving maturity in the things of God. Even when I was at this world-famous faith school, the founder of this movement stood up with tears in his eyes talking about the blatant sin that was going on among the students.

Okay, back to my embarrassing story that I really do not want to share with you, but maybe it could help to rescue your life. Before I had met my wife, I had been dating my childhood sweetheart who was my next-door neighbor. I'm ashamed to say that I had a relationship with her before I knew Christ. Mentally and emotionally, she had captured my heart at a time when neither of us were born again. Actually, I discovered years later that she had not been faithful while I was in the Navy, but that is neither here nor there. We had planned on getting married once I finished my tour in the Navy but three months before the end of my military enlistment, I had a supernatural encounter with Jesus Christ. I was gloriously born again and delivered from all of my disgustingly wicked habits and corrupt lifestyle. I enthusiastically wrote my wife to be what God had gloriously done for me. It wasn't long before I received her response: a dear John letter basically telling me to hit the road, Jack. She wanted nothing to do with my me or my relationship with Christ. That was the best thing that could have happened to me because it liberated me to go all the way for God. Unbeknownst to me, I never did fully let her go in my heart.

Over 20 years had passed with me being married to my precious wife Kathleen, the mother of our five children. We were going through a rather rough time in our lives; hence, my thoughts began to stray back to my "first love". I never spoke of my past transgressions with any glee or excitement in front of my children or my wife. I knew that could be used against them. So, if I ever shared with them what I had been through, including the fact that I had known a woman before I knew their mother, it was always with tears in my eyes. This is a major tool the devil can use against our children. Be very careful when you talk about the good old times because, as you very well know, they probably really weren't such great times after all.

Despite this, I began to wonder what ever happened to my old girlfriend. I did a little bit of investigation and discovered that she had been divorced and was now single. I should have immediately taken authority and cast down those thoughts, but our hearts are so easily led astray. I began to think about her more and more frequently. Suddenly, an idea came into my stupid, silly head which I should've known was of the devil, but I was deceived. I thought about going back to my hometown and looking her up. Of course, during this time, there was no internet that would give me access to this information. I knew in my heart that I should not be thinking like this but, hey, it was just an innocent thought. I was not planning on anything that would be wrong anyway, I just simply wanted to see how she was doing and to talk to her.

What a lie from the pit of hell! The Scriptures clearly tell us that we are extremely weak and easily led astray. This is why the minute an evil thought arises, we must immediately submit to the Lordship of Jesus Christ, resist the devil and he will flee from us. But this was not my case. I got it into my stupid head that I was going to go back to Hometown, Wisconsin and look up my old girlfriend. I went to my wife telling her that I was really missing my family back home and that I would like to take a ride out there to see some of my old friends and immediate family. She did not think for a moment that something else was going on in my heart. This is exactly how the devil sets us up. I was a little bit surprised with her response because she actually thought that it was a good idea.

Now that the idea had really taken root in my mind, I began to make plans. There was only one problem; I didn't know where she was now living and the only one who could tell me was her immediate family. At one time, her older brother was my best friend but he had completely rejected me since I had given my heart to Jesus and became a minister of the gospel.

I decided that before I went out to Wisconsin, I needed to find out where she was. I certainly didn't want to go on a wild goose chase. Believe me, at the time I had no intentions of doing anything evil, but I was like a moth that had been led to the flame. A fly caught in a spider's web. I had kept her older brother's telephone number with me through the years because they had a tool and die shop in no where town, Wisconsin. I finally decided to make the move, calling the telephone number to their business. Her older brother answered the phone. I spoke up that it was me, his old buddy. I carried on a conversation with him for a while, catching up on the lives of past acquaintances in the area, asking how they were all doing. I was maneuver the conversation to spring my question in a very crafty, sly and subtle way. I finally got around to it and came right out and asked him, Hey, Bro, how is your younger sister doing, naming her by name, and asking where she now lived?

His response really surprised me because out of his mouth came nothing but cuss words, telling me in no uncertain terms that what his sister was doing, where she was at, and what was happening in her life was none of my blankety-blank business. Wow, he really laid it on me, but I can truly say: THANK GOD HE DID!

He knew I was married, pastor-ed a church and had children. This man did not know God, and did not want to know God, but when I asked about his sister, such indignation rose up inside of him that he literally would have torn my head off if I would have been in the same room with him. Now, this may not sound like it was God, but it was God using him to rescue my poor bacon out of the fire.

After his rant, the light of heaven came flooding into my mind and my heart at that very moment I saw that the devil had set me up. There is zero doubt that if I would had gone to Wisconsin, I would have been devoured spiritually. I might have lost my precious wife, my children, my ministry and possibly even my salvation. I was like a fly in a spiders web, in which case I would have been consumed like so many others whom the devil lead astray on to the path of destruction. Thank you **Lord Jesus**, for humbling me, even by using a notorious sinner to rescue me from a spiritual guillotine.

God spoke through another man by the name of Ananias who was a deceitful and a conniving man, who was the high priest of the Jewish religion. This Ananias said by the spirit of the Lord:

John 11:50 Nor consider that it is expedient for us, that one man should die for the people, and that the whole nation perish not.51 And this spake he not of himself: but being high priest that year, he prophesied that Jesus should die for that nation;

The Bible says: *Proverbs 1:5 A wise man will hear, and will increase learning; and a man of understanding shall attain unto wise counsels:*

Proverbs 11:14 Where no counsel is, the people fall: but in the multitude of counsellors there is safety.

God used a fleshly, worldly backhoe operator

We need to understand that God can use anybody he so chooses, in order to speak a word to us or others. Of course we have to discern if what they're saying is inspired by the spirit of God, or is it simply the flesh speaking to us. Here's a good illustration: I had a man who attended the church that I pastor who was a bit of a stinker. Now this particular brother in the Lord was a backhoe operator who had his own backhoe, and did small excavating jobs in our community. When we were getting ready to build our church facility (back in 1985), he came to me saying that he knew someone who could help us strip the topsoil from our property in order to get it ready for the new building. This brother never informed me of the value of the topsoil that they would be stripping.

Being totally ignorant on this particular subject, I agreed to let them come in and excavate the property. I was paying these men by the hour to prepare the land for the building. In the midst of their stripping the land with a backhoe and a bulldozer, they were hauling load after load of wonderful rich black topsoil off of the land as fast as possible. This went on for probably a week, when one of the brothers from the church who had some knowledge of the value of topsoil, asked me what they were doing with the topsoil? I told him that I didn't know. This brother in Christ informed me that this topsoil was like gold, and it was worth a lot of money.

Here this brother was from our church, and his partner ripping off the topsoil from us. No, I did not take them to court, or prosecute them, but I did send them a cease and desist letter. I also informed them that they were no longer allowed to be working on the church's property, or to take anymore topsoil. The brother who was a backhoe operator continued to attend our fellowship in spite of this situation. To be honest my opinion of him had sunk pretty low.

One week I had a seminar on how the laity can minister to people one-on-one. This particular brother attended all of these services, which at the end of the training I gave people an opportunity to minister to those who wanted prayer. This man was in no condition in my opinion to minister to anybody, not only because he had a part of ripping off the church, but because he still had some very filthy habits. I invited the people who had been taught and trained to come and minister to those who were standing up on the prayer line. This particular brother came to minister to somebody, and I was about to stop him, yet the Lord spoke to my heart very strongly, telling me to stand behind him, to be quite, and to listen. The Lord told me that he was gonna teach me something out of this man ministering to this other man. I stood behind this brother, and listened to him as he was speaking to the man he was ministering to.

I'm telling you what God began to speak through this carnal and fleshly brother absolutely blew me away. He literally got right to the point, telling this person exactly what he needed to hear. I told the Lord in my heart: Father this is amazing, how can a man be so carnal, fleshly and yet speak such words of wisdom? Because, he told me: it is me speaking through him. If I speak through a donkey, cannot I speak through a worldly and fleshly man. I think a lot of times we as ministers or pastors think that we are the ones who have to minister to the people. That we are the only ones with enough wisdom, and understanding to help people the way they need to be helped. We are completely and absolutely wrong in this assumption,because nobody is the answer but God himself, and he can speak through anybody, or anything as he so wishes. You see I had a spirit of pride, which I need to be delivered from, and God used this stinker, this sneaky, fleshly backhoe operator to humble me. I repented to the Father for thinking too highly of myself.

God will speak to us through the people he so chooses. Many times he chooses to use the foolish to confound the wise. There are so many Scriptures dealing with this particular subject, for instance let us look at the following the Scripture.

2 Peter 1:21 For the prophecy came not in old time by the will of man: but holy men of God spake as they were moved by the Holy Ghost.

Ephesians 4:10 He that descended is the same also that ascended up far above all heavens, that he might fill all things.)11 And he gave some, apostles; and some, prophets; and some, evangelists; and some, pastors and teachers;12 For the perfecting of the saints, for the work of the ministry, for the edifying of the body of Christ:

Exalting Jesus Christ & Not the Anointing

Some people try to use one particular Scripture discovered in the first epistle of John to create a philosophy which is not biblical. They are completely taking this one Scripture completely out of context, and not rightly interpreting it or discerning its meaning.

1 John 2:27 But the anointing which ye have received of him abideth in you, and ye need not that any man teach you: but as the same anointing teacheth you of all things, and is truth, and is no lie, and even as it hath taught you, ye shall abide in him.

Of course the word **Christ** means anointed, and based upon this reality we can say that Jesus Christ is the one who is anointed, and that Jesus Christ lives in us. God has not anointed me, but the living word which is Jesus Christ living inside of me. That is why Jesus said it was expedient for him to leave, for he could come back and live in us. Once he had paid the ultimate price for our redemption, entered into us, and then the Father could send the promise of the spirit. Many people brag and boast about the anointing that is upon their lives when they simply do not realize that the anointing is upon the word, which is Jesus Christ. Based upon this reality we give to Jesus Christ all of the praise, the glory, and the honor that is due unto his holy and wonderful name. This is why Peter spoke this amazing statement in the book of acts when he said:

Acts 10:38 How God anointed Jesus of Nazareth with the Holy Ghost and with power: who went about doing good, and healing all that were oppressed of the devil; for God was with him.

Jesus Christ is the one who raises the dead, heals the sick, cleanses the lepers, and cast out devils. In the gospel of Luke and the book of Isaiah when it talks about whom the spirit of the Lord would rest upon, it is referring to Jesus Christ, who is the living word of God.

Luke 4:17 And there was delivered unto him the book of the prophet Esaias. And when he had opened the book, he found the place where it was written,18 The Spirit of the Lord is upon me, because he hath anointed me to preach the gospel to the poor; he hath sent me to heal the brokenhearted, to preach deliverance to the captives, and recovering of sight to the blind, to set at liberty them that are bruised,19 To preach the acceptable year of the Lord.

You might say: pastor Mike the Bible tells us to heal the sick, cleanse the lepers, raise the dead, cast out devils, freely we have received, freely give. Yes, I am not denying that we go forth and do mighty wonderful deeds, but how? We do it in the wonderful and powerful name of Jesus Christ. Who is it who really is causing all of these miracles to happen? Is it us, or is it Jesus Christ? I Proclaim Boldly and Strongly: it is Jesus Christ who is doing the miracles, by the power of the Holy Spirit, working through us.

There is no room for us to gloat or walk about like peacocks, bragging and talking about how wonderful we are, with our amazing anointing. It is Jesus Christ who is doing the miracles as we simply obey the leading of the spirit and the word of God.

2 Corinthians 4:7 But we have this treasure in earthen vessels, that the excellency of the power may be of God, and not of us.

GOD Said: You Better Not Lie, or You'll Die to!

One day I picked up a book by a well-known author. This book had come highly recommended by one of my favorite preachers at that time. The topic was about angelic visitations. This was something I was interested in, because of my many experiences with the supernatural. I began to read this book, and noticed immediately that there were experiences he said he had, which did not seem to line up with the Scriptures. I did not want to judge his heart, but we do have the responsibility to examine everything in light of God's Word. If it does not line up with the word of God, then we must reject it, no matter who wrote it.

As I was pondering the stories in this book, the Spirit of the Lord spoke to my heart very strongly. It was as if He was standing right there next to me, speaking audibly. What He spoke to me was rather shocking! The Lord told me that the writer of this book would be dead in three months from a heart attack. I asked the Lord why He was telling me this. He said the stories in the man's book were exaggerated, and judgment was coming. The Lord warned me that day that if I were ever to do the same thing, judgment would come to me. I did not realize that the Lord would have me to be writing books, many them filled with my own personal experiences. Now I know why he spoke this to me, telling me that I better not exaggerate my experiences.

When the Spirit of the Lord spoke this to me, I turned and told my wife. I held the book up and said, in a very quiet whispering, trembling, wavering voice, "Honey, the man who wrote this book will be dead in three months from a heart attack." Plus, I told her why the Lord told me this. I wish I had been wrong. Exactly 3 months later, the man died from a heart attack. God can speak to us through the positive and the negative circumstances of life. We better take heed to what he is saying

One day Jesus asked his disciples who men said he was? Then he asked them who they thought he was? Peter speaking by the spirit of God said: you are the Christ, the son of the living God. When Peter responded to Jesus with this statement, Jesus said to him: blessed are you Simon bar Jonah, for flesh and blood has not revealed this to you, but my father which is in heaven. Then he declared that the gates of hell would not prevail against the church based upon the fact of who Jesus Christ is. Notice how the spirit of God spoke through Peter to reveal God's ultimate plan for his church. That we would walk in the Revelation knowledge of who Jesus Christ is.

There has been times when the spirit of the Lord spoke to my heart and told me that certain things were going to happen with certain people. In some of these situations I have shared with my immediate family what I heard the Lord say. They would say to me: dad let's pray that this does not happen. Now that is a wonderful thought, but I'm sorry to say God knows what's going to happen. There are times you can pray and believe God that it won't, but many times it was already established and settled. You see God knows the hearts of every man, our past, our present, and our future. For instance, Jesus knew that Judas would betray him for 30 pieces of silver. There is nothing that Jesus could do to stop Judas from doing this. Jesus also knew that Peter would deny him three times. Still Jesus said I have prayed for you, and when you are converted, strengthen your brethren. There is a place in the Holy Ghost where you can know what God is going to do before he ever does it. The Holy Ghost can actually show you the future.

Now I cannot stop you from speaking in the flesh, or speaking by the spirit. What is amazing is that everything that Jesus said was by the spirit. Many times we say things that do not need to be said. I have said things to my wife that I have never said. We need to learn to let God deal with certain situations instead of us sticking our nose into the mist of them. Hearing the voice of God is so important in every situation, because when we disobey his voice we get ourselves into terrible and avoidable predicaments, and then we have to cry out for God's mercy. There has been times when I wanted to leave my house dressed sloppy, but the Lord would reprove me, informing me that today I would run into somebody who needed to be ministered to, and if I was dressed sloppy they would not be able to receive what I had to say.

Some Preachers are filled with wisdom when they are in the pulpit, but are used of the devil in everyday living.

I had a well-known lady who spoke here one time at a women's conference. I invited her, because I had listened to some of her messages someone gave me, and they were powerful and wonderful. When she spoke at our conference, her messages were marvelous, filled with wisdom and revelation. Now after one of the meetings, all of the speakers, including myself and my wife went out to eat. Something extremely shocking and disheartening happened as we were sitting there around the table eating and listening to her speak.

As this lady began to open her mouth at the table what came out of her mouth was terrible. I never heard such garbage, gossip and complaining come out of one person's mouth in such a short period of time. In the pulpit as she ministered the word of God, truth and revelation came forth, but in her private life what came out of her mouth was terrible.

I ran into another similar situation a number of years ago. There was a young man that the Lord had me help, giving him the opportunity to speak for the first time in his life in the pulpit. I knew by the spirit of the Lord when I met him that he was called to preach and teach the word of God, even though I had never heard him. From the very moment he began to speak, everybody knew the spirit of the Lord was calling him to preach. There was only one major issue that I could see that would destroy every endeavor that he would ever strive to accomplish for Christ, it was the fact that he was extremely critical and faultfinding of almost everybody he knew. I constantly encouraged him not to be finding fault with others, to no avail. Even those he called his closest friends, and even relatives, behind their backs he would be constantly finding fault and speak negatively about them. Every time he would say something negative about a person, I would try to come back with something positive. Now this was a generational curse that was passed on from his mother, from his grandmother, and who knows how many other generations.

This young man had no concept of respecting those in authority because he had been raised from a child by those who had no respect for authority. For two years,(I still continue to pray) I prayed daily for him, and his family members that they would be delivered from this satanic attitude. While my wife and I were gone to another country, that spirit rose up in him, and he began to speak to the congregation evil and slanderous words about myself and my family. When we arrived back from our journey overseas, people who had been with us for years were now gone. I'm not speaking evil of this particular person, just the fact that we need to walk tenderly and softly before the Lord. We will be judged by the same judgment that we judge others with. We need to deal with these generational curses that are so deeply rooted in our mind and our heart, that without Christ we will never be delivered and set free from.

God can use us in such wonderful ways as we are ministering the word, by the Holy Spirit, and yet the enemy can use us in such devastating ways out of the pulpit. Balaam the prophet is such an amazing example of this. He prophesied underneath a powerful anointing by the spirit of of the Lord pertaining to the nation of Israel, but then he turns around and connives with the heathen kings in how to destroy Israel. The end of his life was very sad, for he was slayed by Joshua the prophet of God, who was over the armies of Israel. Yes, God can use us in wonderful ways, but if we do not deal with the satanic strongholds in our minds and our emotions, generational curses, the enemy will destroy us. How many good ministers have been destroyed not because they were not powerful preachers, or teachers, but because they had issues in their hearts that they would not deal with.

Ephesians 4:29 Let no corrupt communication proceed out of your mouth, but that which is good to the use of edifying, that it may minister grace unto the hearers.

James 4:11 Speak not evil one of another, brethren. He that speaketh evil of his brother, and judgeth his brother, speaketh evil of the law, and judgeth the law: but if thou judge the law, thou art not a doer of the law, but a judge.12 There is one lawgiver, who is able to save and to destroy: who art thou that judgest another?

Proverbs 27:9 Ointment and perfume rejoice the heart: so doth the sweetness of a man's friend by hearty counsel.

Opinions Are like Noses!

We need to really use wisdom when we begin to speak our own opinions, and everybody has an opinion. When people begin to share their opinions with you, it needs to be filtered through the word of God and the spirit of God. If you follow people's opinions, then you will go astray from what it is that God is wanting to do in and through your life. I have my own little quote that I came up with many years ago. **Opinions are like noses, people like to put them where they don't belong**.

If I followed every opinion that people have given to me in the last 40 years of ministry, I would not have survived even one month. As a pastor I have always told people that they need to hear from God directly, and not to ask my opinion. I have watched people followe the directions that people have given to them, causing them to experience complete and total destruction. I have heard people say: I wouldn't let my husband get away with that! I wouldn't let my wife get away with that! This is what I would do if he was my kid! It's amazing how many people are experts about things that they have absolutely no experience with. We need to seriously examine the fruit of these people who are giving us their opinion, which most times we did not even ask for. Do they really know what they're talking about? Have they really had to deal with these issues, and what is the end results of their decisions? Does it agree with the spirit, the nature, and the personality of God? What is so amazing to me is that these people will get offended because you do not follow their opinion. You will be hard-pressed for me to give you my opinion, because I will always try to direct you back to the word of God. I will always encourage you to hear from God your self.

Famous Preacher telling me to sell the church

I've been a pastor since 1977, and I have had more experiences than I can share when it comes to dealing with people and with ministers. The church that I pastor, which (I began in 1983) has a sanctuary that can seat 800 people. Now, if I really wanted to fill up this facility, I know exactly how to do it. You just simply give people what they want, and you can follow the same business model that the world does, and you will be so full that you will not have room enough to keep everybody. The only problem with this idea is that I would be completely out of the will of God. It would be a church filled with people who really are not hungry for Jesus, hungry for righteousness, hungry for obedience, hungry for holiness. I could easily write a book on how to fill up a church the wrong way, and actually this is not even necessary, all you have to do is look at the mega churches of the modern day church. Pastor Mike, if you could fill your church to overflowing, why don't you do it? I truly believe that I would lose my soul! We are not called of God to entertain people, tickle peoples ears, or make them feel like they're all right with God, when they are not. We are called of God to challenge them to give everything to Jesus Christ, to go all the way with God, to forsake this world, deny themselves, take up their cross, and follow Jesus.

You cannot believe how many times people come in to our church facility and begin to tell me how I need to do certain things in order to get the church to grow. I do not argue with these people, because they are operating within their own carnal reasoning. You see, I want a church that grows exactly the same way that the church grew in the book of ACTS. I simply want, hungry, thirst, and desperate people like they had in the early church. I do try to listen to what people have to say, but I'm listening very closely to see if God is speaking through them, or just flesh. Well back to the story that I was gonna share with you.

I had a very well-known minister who came to speak for me one time, actually he has spoken for us many times. He has a brother that is even way more well-known than he is. When he is standing in the pulpit, and the spirit of God is moving, almost every time he begins to declare by the spirit of God that our church will be filled with those who are hungry and desperate for Jesus. He says by the spirit of the Lord, that he sees them coming from the north, the South, the East, and the West. That we will have so many people coming that our biggest problem will be were to put them all. He is not the only one who has spoken this when he stood in our pulpit. More preachers than I can remember through the years have also prophesied this over our local church here in Gettysburg Pennsylvania.

Now readers here is the very strange part. After this man gets done preaching in our pulpit, usually when we go out to eat, or are having fellowship, he strongly encourages me to put the facility up for sale, and go somewhere where people can receive what I am preaching. He acknowledges that the spirit of the Lord, God's presence is powerful in my life, and why are you wasting your life in an area where people just do not want these truths? I do not argue with him because in the natural I would like to do exactly what he's telling me to do. There is only one major problem, God has called me to be here in this area, to this church, to this congregation. Why would this famous preacher stand in the pulpit you ask, and prophesy a mighty move of God, and then tell me to sell the facility? Because in the pulpit he is moving underneath the presence and the power of the Holy Spirit., but when he steps out of the pulpit he is operating in the flesh, being moved by what he sees, and not operating in the realm of faith. Many of the different guest speakers I have had in our church do the exact same thing. It's easy to talk faith, but it is a challenge to live by faith, staying in the perfect will of God for your life and your ministry. I have determined in my heart to obey the voice of God, no matter how it looks, I hope you do too.

Hearing the voice of God is the straight and narrow way.

You must train and discipline yourself to listen, and obey the voice of God, no matter what is happening around you. You need to know that the enemy of your soul wants to get you out of the will of God, and he will use the Vices and the pleasures of this world, which are addictive. Getting out of the will of God is addictive, and we must be broken and set free from these addictions. The enemy will use brothers and sisters in Christ who are full of strife and division, critical and fault finding in order to get us out of the will of the Father. This barrage of criticism should roll off our back like water off of the ducks back. Jesus never allowed himself to be moved by those who were moving and operating in the flesh. Many have been deceived into thinking that the spirit they are operating in is the spirit of God, but in all reality it's the spirit of the world. James and John, the sons of thunder are a good example of how easy it is for us to be deceived.

Luke 9:54 And when his disciples James and John saw this, they said, Lord, wilt thou that we command fire to come down from heaven, and consume them, even as Elias did?55 But he turned, and rebuked them, and said, Ye know not what manner of spirit ye are of.56 For the Son of man is not come to destroy men's lives, but to save them. And they went to another village.

When the devil begins to speak he will always take you out of the will of God, into strife and division, faultfinding and criticism, argumentativeness and nastiness. It could be lackadaisicalness and lukewarmness, easy believism and slothfulness. He always pushes a doctrine of I'm okay you're okay, everything is all right no matter how you are living. Our souls are in extreme danger if we listen to these voices that are not challenging us to live, follow, serve, obey, and go after God with all of our hearts.

Proverbs 6:16 These six things doth the Lord hate: yea, seven are an abomination unto him:17 A proud look, a lying tongue, and hands that shed innocent blood,18 An heart that deviseth wicked imaginations, feet that be swift in running to mischief,19 A false witness that speaketh lies, and he that soweth discord among brethren.

I am absolutely amazed at the different ways in which God was speak to his people. There is one time that God even spoke to me through a TV commercial.

Come Back to Jamaica

This is kind of a strange experience that I had in 1983. First let me start this story by saying that we do not have a TV in our house. My wife and I just simply decided that we did not need one, or want one. I was ministering at a local church when I mentioned the fact that we did not have a TV in our house, and did not want one or need one. A number of days later there was a knock at our house door, and here it was one of the older sisters from that particular meeting in which I had been ministering. She seemed so excited and happy. She said: the other night you stated that you did not have a TV, praise the Lord I had a brand-new black-and-white TV set at my house that I have never used, and I want to give it to you.

Bless this older sisters heart, she must have misunderstood what I was saying at the meeting. I did not want to offend her, so I put a smile on my face, and accepted her gift. It sat in its box for a while in the living room, in a corner, on the floor. One day as I walked past it, a thought came to my silly head that said: just plug it in for a moment, it won't hurt anything. I gave into this thought, taking it out of its box, and plugging it in. The reception wasn't very good at all, allowing me only to pick up 2 to 3 channels that were kind of foggy, so this TV just sat there, never really being used. One afternoon as I was busy working in the house, it came into my heart to turn on the TV, and Immediately there appeared on the screen a commercial that said: **Come back to Jamaica!**

As I watched this commercial something strange happened in my heart. I was so moved in my heart that I started weeping for the souls that were in Jamaica. I had never even thought about Jamaica, or prayed for Jamaica, or ever had a burden for Jamaica. Here I was now literally weeping over Jamaica. People who really do not have good understand of how God works would have immediately bought an airline ticket, jumped on a plane, and gone to Jamaica. It's important that we get before the Lord to find out exactly what he is saying before we run off and respond to these visitations.

I went before the Lord with a very seriously attitude and began to pray over Jamaica, knowing the Lord was speaking to me through this commercial. Yes, God can talk to you through a secular commercial. I did not sense in my heart that the Lord wanted me to go there at this time.(Eventually I did make a trip to Jamaica) Now every time I would see this commercial whether at my house, in a store, or somewhere else, I would literally begin to cry for Jamaica. From the moment I saw this commercial about Jamaica, I began to stand in the gap, interceding and pray for its people, for the nation, and for what God was wanting to do there. I knew the Lord was doing, or about to do something wonderful in Jamaica. Approximately three months went by with this burden in my heart, when one day this burden suddenly lifted off for me.

A short time later I received a newsletter from a well-known evangelist who had just come back from Jamaica, reporting that a tremendous move of God had taken place while he was there. The Lord spoke to my heart and said this to me: I placed a burden upon your heart for Jamaica in order that you would pray and intercede, to stand in the gap to prepare the way for these meetings. He also revealed to me that I was not the only one he had given this burden to. That there were many others during this time who were also praying for Jamaica. Those who had made the commercial about coming back to Jamaica had no idea that God would use this commercial to create a burden for the precious souls of that land.

Living in a cabin in the mountains is not God's will for you!

Ninety percent of the time when I give a prophetic word to someone in the spirit, I do not remember what I said. Sometimes I'm just so lost in the Holy Ghost, it is like I've entered into another world. God by his spirit, speaking through people will bring wonderful deliverance and healing to their lives. Now when some one is talking about moving up into the mountains, living in a cabin, and getting away from everybody on a permanent bases, you know that they are in the flesh. Jesus did not want us to be taken out of the world, but to be kept in the midst of it. God wants us to be witnesses, salt and light, ambassadors for the King of Kings and Lord of lords.

My earthly father thought it was the ultimate dream to live in a cabin away from everybody else. He wanted to be all alone, so he left my mother, breaking her heart, and then he completely closed the door on all of his children except for my younger brother one. Yes, he ended up living in a cabin all alone, but unbeknownst to him birds had built a nest in the chimney. There was enough airflow to keep the smoke out of the cabin room, yet not the carbon monoxide. He was 68 years old and in good health, but the carbon monoxide poisoning still got him. He allowed this satanic thought to take a hold of his mind that he didn't need anybody but this cabin. This desire to be all alone might have seemed wonderful to him, and yet is what the devil used to kill him. The enemy uses a lot of silly ideas to kill people.

The Holy Spirit wants to speak through us with prophetic words as we gather together with the body of Christ. This is in order to help, to bless, to minister, and to set the captives free. Yes, it is Jesus speaking, but it is us opening up our mouths and letting God say that which he desires to say through us. This will bring conviction, healing, help, and deliverance to others.

1 Corinthians 14:24 But if all prophesy, and there come in one that believeth not, or one unlearned, he is convinced of all, he is judged of all:25 And thus are the secrets of his heart made manifest; and so falling down on his face he will worship God, and report that God is in you of a truth.

God's giving you three months to get it together!

A number years ago I was speaking and preaching, when the spirit of prophecy moved upon me mightily. As I was looking out over the congregation the spirit of the Lord arrested my eyes upon an older gentleman. He was sitting over on the left-hand side of the sanctuary from where I was standing. I said this: there is a brother here right now whom the Lord has told me to tell you that you are wonderfully gifted and equipped to minister for the Lord. The Lord says that he has somewhat against you because you have ceased to minister for him. You are just sitting and warming the pews, and you have ceased to labor in the vineyard. This is a warning from the Lord for you. The spirit of the Lord says he's giving you three months in order to roll up your sleeves and get back to work for him. If you do not work for Christ, the Lord says he has no reason to keep you on this earth. If you will say in your heart today: I will once again go to work for God, then the Lord says: I will bless you and use you in a mighty way. Your latter days will be way more fruitful than your early days. (This man had been an active soul winner and worker in the harvest field for years)

If you do not go to work for me says the Lord: Then you will be dead in 3 months. I repeated this warning over the pulpit: if you do not get up and go to work for Christ once again, you will be dead in three months. I spoke this over the whole congregation, so no one knew exactly who I was speaking to, though I did. Now this older brother who has never once stayed after the service to speak to me, stayed this time. He came walking right up to the front of the church to where I was standing. This had to be the spirit of God arresting him, and speaking to him. With him walking up to me it was literally God confirming that I had heard correctly from the spirit of the Lord. I said this to the brother: you need to take heed to this word that I just spoke. I told him it was God speaking directly to him. I told him that if you do not get up and go to work for the Lord, there's no reason for him to keep you here in this earth. I implored him to do something for Christ, and that I was there to help them in whatever endeavor he felt in his heart he was to perform.

I wish I could tell you that this story has a good ending, but it does not. I kept on encouraging this brother to get up and do something for Jesus every time I seen him, but it seemed to simply go in one ear and out another. Exactly 3 months later when my wife and I were out on the West Coast on a business trip, I received a phone call from his daughter. She was weeping and crying, informing us that her dad had just out of the blue died. Please do not think for a moment that I'm saying he went to hell. I'm positive he went home to be with the Lord because he was a good godly saint of a man. For some reason though he was deceived into thinking that in his old age he could lay back and take it easy.

Dear brothers and sisters there is no such thing as retirement for those within the body of Christ. We must not retire, but we must re-fire. I have absolutely no plans on ever retiring on this side of heaven, which is the land of opportunity. If I am ever going to do something for Christ, I need to do it NOW while I still have time left on this earth. I truly believe that many believers are dying early because they are living for themselves, and not for Christ. We need to begin to become very sensitive and obedient to the voice of God. When the captain of the Lord of hosts gives us directions, we need to jump to it, and obey him.

#16 NATURE

The **16th Way** that God speaks is by nature! It very important that we hear the voice of God for our selves in every situation. Now we discover in the book of Genesis that after man committed sin, when Adam and his wife heard the voice of God, they ran from his voice. I am convinced that many people hear the voice of God, even more then we want to acknowledge, but they run away from Him. It's the same way that darkness runs away from the light, when the light is turned on. Flesh runs away from the truth because darkness cannot exist with light. The flesh cannot exist where the spirit of God is quickening. A major way that God speaks to us, and all of humanity is by that which God has created. As I was doing a research on this particular way in which God speaks, I ran into so much information that we could literally talk about God using nature to reveal himself to mankind for days on end. Just the first two chapters of the book of Romans clearly declares this.

Romans 1:17 For therein is the righteousness of God revealed from faith to faith: as it is written, The just shall live by faith.18 For the wrath of God is revealed from heaven against all ungodliness and unrighteousness of men, who hold the truth in unrighteousness;19 Because that which may be known of God is manifest in them; for God hath shewed it unto them.20 For the invisible things of him from the creation of the world are clearly seen, being understood by the things that are made, even his eternal power and Godhead; so that they are without excuse.

A powerful truth revealed to us in the book of Romans is that humanity is without excuse. Sinners are without excuse for rejecting Jesus Christ as the only way to the heavenly Father. God is speaking to them through the rising of the sun, he speaks to them through the blue skies, he speaks to them through the deep blue seas, he speaks to them through the flowers and the trees, the animals and the plants. Creation itself, the stars of heaven, the sun, the moon, the planets, the Galaxy and the Universe.

Romans 1:21 Because that, when they knew God, they glorified him not as God, neither were thankful; but became vain in their imaginations, and their foolish heart was darkened. 22 Professing themselves to be wise, they became fools,

It is so obvious that all of nature is in harmony, and that there was a master creator behind it all. You have to be willingly ignorant and purposely harden your heart in order to believe in evolution. Actually the British say evolution the right way, by calling it evilution! The devil just laughs at us in blatant will for ignorance, in that he does not even hide the reality of the deception he has exposed men to. Here's a good example, the Internet for instance is called the worldwide web, like a **spiders web.** Now think about this just for a moment, evolution is called Evil Lucian which is named after (Lucifer) who is evil! It is an in your face lie and mockery right from the pit of hell. Pastor Mike don't you believe everything evolved into what it is today? Absolutely not. My God is so amazingly powerful and big that he easily did it all in six days. How can you believe that? Because I Have Faith in God! Evolution is a horrendous lie propagated by the devil, to discredit the reality of who God is.

EVERY SINNER IS WITH OUT EXCUSE!

As a sinner, we were surrounded by the love of God, His goodness, provision, and blessings. I may not have recognized or even realized it. Whether I knew it or not, God was watching over us. He was protecting, helping, and reaching out to us, even though we were not serving Him or loving Him.

Nature, birds, animals, and all of creation display the unfathomable love of God. The shining sun, the green grass, the budding flowers, the blue gray waters of the sea, the light blue skies, the glowing moon, and the sparkling stars at night. They all declare God's awesome love for His creation. The beautiful fragrances that float upon the wind and the singing birds with their beautiful songs declare His love. God has blessed us and revealed Himself to us by His awesome creation according to Scriptures on God's goodness.

"Or despisest thou the riches of his goodness not knowing that the goodness of God leadeth thee to repentance?" (Rom. 2:4).

"That ye may be the children of your Father which is in heaven: for he maketh his sun to rise on the evil and on the good, and sendeth rain on the just and on the unjust" (Matt. 5:45).

For God is the Author, Creator, Maker, Architect and Master Designer of all of creation. God gave us the breath we are breathing, the clothes we are wearing, the food we are eating, the body we are living in; it all comes from God. He gave us all of the talents and abilities we have in order to put within our hands these possessions. All that we have that is good and beautiful, lovely and beneficial, comes from God. It is God's divine marriage proposal, a divine romance. For you see, God is calling, pleading, imploring, and asking us to follow Him into light everlasting.

"Behold, I stand at the door, and knock: if any man hear my voice, and open the door, I will come in to him, and will sup with him, and he with me" (Rev. 3:20).

Jesus paid the ultimate price for the hand of His bride. He bought us with every drop of His precious blood in His body. And He longs for us to follow Him down the wedding aisle to the throne of His Father, to be one with Him forever. You see, my friend, God is striving to lead us to a place of turning our backs upon our selfish lives, to crucify and mortify the corruptible and damnable seed of selfishness, which is the very nature of the devil and his fallen angels—the demonic horde. We must believe on the Lord Jesus Christ. We must walk in His divine nature of love so that we can be one with Him forever. His abundant goodness, His kindness, His patience, and the fact that He has suffered a long time waiting for you? Do you not grasp that His kindness is meant to cause you to turn away from selfishness?

All of creation will be our jury, and they will declare us guilty of the most perverse wickedness and corruption if we do not respond to God's love. To think that we would turn down such a wonderful and awesome gift from God is unfathomable. The reality is that Jesus is offering us to be made one with Himself simply by acknowledging our wickedness and by forsaking all in order to follow him. Yielding to the divine grace of His nature within us. While we have an opportunity, we need to respond to His unspeakable and amazing love.

Creation Declares there is a GOD!

The Law of Genesis says:

Genesis 1:21 And God created great whales, and every living creature that moveth, which the waters brought forth abundantly, after their kind, and every winged fowl after his kind: and God saw that it was good.:24 And God said, Let the earth bring forth the living creature after his kind, cattle, and creeping thing, and beast of the earth after his kind: and it was so.:25 And God made the beast of the earth after his kind, and cattle after their kind, and every thing that creepeth upon the earth after his kind: and God saw that it was good.

Botanists are scientists who study plants. Zoologists are those who study animals. Naturalists study animals, plants, humans, and nature. Herpetologists study reptiles and amphibians. Ichthyologists study fish. And Entomologists study insects and spiders.

Biologists today generally classify all living things into five kingdoms. Two of these are the familiar plant and animal kingdoms. The other three are comprised mainly of very small organisms, like bacteria, larger single- celled creatures, and fungi. The animal kingdom has by far the most species, well over a million. There are over four hundred thousand known plant species, most of which are flowering plants with seeds, such as trees, grasses, and the like. The latter comprise more than a quarter of a million different species. The other three kingdoms contain at least a few hundred thousand different life forms. The animal kingdom is divided into about thirty phyla. The nine largest phyla contain the majority of species. Indeed, one phyla, the arthropods, which includes insects and spiders, constitutes about 75 percent of all known animal species. More than nine hundred thousand arthropods have been described, and according to some estimates there may be more than five million more.

For all animals other than arthropods is about 250,000. The largest group (formally "class") within the phyla of arthropods and the most diverse class in all kingdoms, is insects. Over 750,000 have been described. Some suppose that there are perhaps as many as three million different species of insects in the world. Include butterflies and moths (more than one hundred thousand species), bees and wasps (more than twenty thousand species), and ants (about ten thousand species). With over thirty thousand known species, spiders, which are not insects, constitute one of the large families of other kinds of arthropods. Only two other phyla within the animal kingdom, the roundworms and the mollusks, are known to contain more than one hundred thousand species. All other phyla generally have far less.

I am sharing this scientific information with you to help expand your horizon that we might better understand who God really is. God is so creative and so full of life that there is no end to His creative ability. These are all natural things that we can discover with the human eye. What myriad of angels, angelic beings, and spiritual beings exist that we cannot see or perceive? Millions? Billions? Trillions? Who can say?

Romans 1:22 Professing themselves to be wise, they became fools,23 And changed the glory of the uncorruptible God into an image made like to corruptible man, and to birds, and fourfooted beasts, and creeping things.24 Wherefore God also gave them up to uncleanness through the lusts of their own hearts, to dishonour their own bodies between themselves:25 Who changed the truth of God into a lie, and worshipped and served the creature more than the Creator, who is blessed for ever. Amen.

Jesus taught many parables, approximately 57 parables. As

you begin to go over the parables you'll discover that many of them, actually most of them are pertaining to nature and how it is like unto the kingdom of God. In all reality it is not that Jesus chose to use nature as an illustration, but that nature was created as an illustration of how the kingdom of God works. Let us just for a moment take a look at some of these parables, the stories which Jesus used to share the principles of the kingdom of God with the multitudes. We have the parable of the sower, the parable of the wheat and the tares, the seed when it is planted how it grows, a parable of the mustard seed. Christ gives to us the parable of the leaven, the parable of the fish and the dragnet. We have the parable of the laborers in the vineyard, the parable of the fig tree, and the parable of the lost sheep.

These parables just go on, and on, and on. I know so-called Christians who tell me that they do not need to come to church because God speaks to them through nature. That they literally get more out of walking through the woods then when they are sitting in a pew, and hearing a preacher. In some instances I would agree with you, but God has given to us, (Christ himself) the apostle, Prophet, evangelist, pastor and teacher. He gave us these gifts because he knew that we would need these gifts in order to grow spiritually, and to become fruitful in the kingdom of God. Listen to what the multitudes said about Jesus, as they heard him teach and preach these truths.

Mark 6:2 And when the sabbath day was come, he began to teach in the synagogue: and many hearing him were astonished, saying, From whence hath this man these things? and what wisdom is this which is given unto him, that even such mighty works are wrought by his hands?

Up until Jesus spoke these truths their eyes were blind to what God was trying to say to them through nature, through the wheat, through the tares, through the fish, through all of these different and wonderful natural truths. All of these realities were locked up in nature, and needed someone anointed by the spirit of God to bring them to light. Creation is God speaking to us about God's invisible attributes and of his eternal power. It is God saying **hello,**

I'm here, I'm real, I made all things, how can you deny me. Do not tell me that God never talks to you. The lightning and the thunder is God speaking to us!

Job 37:5 God thundereth marvellously with his voice; great things doeth he, which we cannot comprehend.

Job 38:25 Who hath divided a watercourse for the overflowing of waters, or a way for the lightning of thunder;

Did you know that when God sends the **Heavy snow,** and it is Him speaking to us!

Job 37:5 God thundereth marvellously with his voice; great things doeth he, which we cannot comprehend.6 For he saith to the snow, Be thou on the earth; likewise to the small rain, and to the great rain of his strength.7 He sealeth up the hand of every man; that all men may know his work.

Pulpit Commentary
Verse 7. - He sealeth up the hand of every man. In the winter season, when the snow falls, and the heavy rains pour down (ver. 6), God "seeleth up the hand of every man;" i.e. puts an end to ordinary out-of-doors labour, and establishes a time of pause or rest (comp. Homer, 'Il.,' 17:549). He does this with the object that all men may know his work; i.e. that, during the time of their enforced idleness, men may have leisure for reflection, and may employ it in meditating upon him and his marvellous "work."

It is Gods dramatic way of saying, listen I'm here. What is amazing is that our American forefathers knew this. Whenever natural disasters would happen earthquakes, floods, hurricanes, they would call our nation to repentance and once again to seeking Gods mercy! Most of our modern-day leaders are completely ignorant of the reality of God, and it is an ignorance and arrogance of their own choosing.

Men have studied nature in order to advance technology like sonar from dolphins, radar from bats, spiders for weaving, even the spinning of cocoons from caterpillars. Much of our technology did not coming from the human brain, but it comes from nature. It all came from creation, and from the one who created it all. Nature itself reveals God's holiness, it reveals God's glory, it reveals God's righteousness. Nature is a major tool by which God speaks to us. It reveals to us certain standards of conduct. Just think about the laws of nature, the law of gravitation, the law of aerodynamics in how a bird flies. How about the law of seed time and harvest?

Ecclesiastes 3:1 To every thing there is a season, and a time to every purpose under the heaven:2 A time to be born, and a time to die; a time to plant, and a time to pluck up that which is planted.

These laws all have spiritual implications!

Galatians 6:7 Be not deceived; God is not mocked: for whatsoever a man soweth, that shall he also reap.

People say: what about those poor pygmies deep in the Amazons forest that have never heard the gospel? First nature itself teaches them that there is a God. Here is another reality that we need to look at, I am convinced that if they want to know the one true God, and they begin to cry out from their hearts, God will send them missionaries. If you do research on this particular subject, you'll discover story after story how God sent missionaries to those who were desperate to know him. I have read amazing stories of people who were led of God to go into the deepest and darkest parts of Africa in order to reach those who have never heard the gospel.

I read a thick book once about David Livingston (1813-1872) and Stanley. They were Explorers who went to Africa. Livingston's real purpose was to be a missionary for Jesus. His stories are just astounding in this out of print book that I read about their adventures! It was about 400 Pages long, and I could not put it down. You would have to read the book in order to understand all of the dangers, hardships and difficulties they went through to reach the natives. In one situation they had to walk four weeks none stop in order to make it through a swamp. They began the trip with over 200 men, but by the time they made it out to the other side of the swamp there was only a small handful of men left. They experienced quicksand, vaporous snakes, crocodiles, poisonous spiders and even cannibals that could not wait to eat them. Along the way they discovered tribes of people who were eager and willing to hear the gospel, where whole villages embrace the gospel of Jesus Christ, and were converted.

Matthew 24:14 And this gospel of the kingdom shall be preached in all the world for a witness unto all nations; and then shall the end come.

God has going out of his way to rescue people. *God wants all men to believe the gospel, and to repent everywhere, in order to be saved.* God uses nature to protect his people, to provide, to lead and guide, and he also has used the forces of nature to defeat the enemies of Israel. One of the most famous songs about how God uses nature is called "How Great Thou Art"

Lyrics to **"How Great Thou Art"** written by Carl Boberg

O Lord my God, When I in awesome wonder,
Consider all the worlds Thy Hands have made;
I see the stars, I hear the rolling thunder,
Thy power throughout the universe displayed.

When through the woods, and forest glades I wander,
And hear the birds sing sweetly in the trees.
When I look down, from lofty mountain grandeur
And see the brook, and feel the gentle breeze.

And when I think, that God, His Son not sparing;
Sent Him to die, I scarce can take it in;
That on the Cross, my burden gladly bearing,
He bled and died to take away my sin.

When Christ shall come, with shout of acclamation,
And take me home, what joy shall fill my heart.
Then I shall bow, in humble adoration,

And then proclaim: "My God, how great Thou art!"

Psalm 24:1The earth is the Lord's, and the fulness thereof; the world, and they that dwell therein.

Psalm 89:11 The heavens are thine, the earth also is thine: as for the world and the fulness thereof, thou hast founded them.

I remember as a young Christian when I was living up in Belleville, Pennsylvania (1978) I would go up behind the little house where I was living, where there was a large rock on the side of a hill that overlooked the Valley. I would go out there when the sun was about setting, and I would just sit on this rock. I would pray and cry out to God, meditating upon the word of God, looking across the horizon. I would watch the deer come and go, the rabbits, and the groundhog's would be playing in the fields. There would be all kinds of birds I would watch as they flew by or landed in the open valley before me. It was a divinely mystical and amazing experience as I watched nature. You could sense God revealing himself in the sunset, the blowing of a slight breeze, the animals playing. In the late fall I watched as the geese were flying south for the winter. I watched the changing of the season sitting on that rock as I was in prayer and meditation. There were times when I was up there with a strong wind blowing, and the snow was coming down from the heavens and drifting. In all of these experiences, I felt the presence of God, and knew that all of creation is in harmony with the tr i-unity of God. God created all of nature and all of the physical realm, that he is using it to reveal himself to us.

Colossians 1:16 For by him were all things created, that are in heaven, and that are in earth, visible and invisible, whether they be thrones, or dominions, or principalities, or powers: all things were created by him, and for him:

Revelation 4:11 Thou art worthy, O Lord, to receive glory and honour and power: for thou hast created all things, and for thy pleasure they are and were created.

He has given to us the ability to see, taste, hear, smell, touch and experience that which he has created. There are Scriptures after Scriptures that talk about God's dealings with man and nature. When God first created man he placed him in an amazing beautiful garden, called the garden of Eden. The first garden of Eden that God created is nothing compared to the amazing garden that God will prepare for his people at the end of the ages. Time will cease, and we will walk in the midst of God's beautiful amazing creation, with all of the amazing animals that he has created.

Psalm 104:20 Thou makest darkness, and it is night: wherein all the beasts of the forest do creep forth.21 The young lions roar after their prey, and seek their meat from God.22 The sun ariseth, they gather themselves together, and lay them down in their dens.

Men have knowingly and willingly hardened their hearts to the reality of God revealed to them in nature. They have closed their eyes, have plugged their ears, and hardened their hearts in order to ignore the reality of God, but they are without excuse. People who declare that they are atheist, were not born as atheist. They were born alive onto God, and at some point in their lives they chose to believe a lie, and turned their backs on the living God. They have convinced themselves that if they deny his existence, and ignore him, he will go away, and leave them alone. They are sadly and sorrily deceived. God will reclaim all that is his, that is rightfully his, for he is the author and maker of all existing things.

Psalm 139:7 Whither shall I go from thy spirit? or whither shall I flee from thy presence?8 If I ascend up into heaven, thou art there: if I make my bed in hell, behold, thou art there.9 If I take the wings of the morning, and dwell in the uttermost parts of the sea;

You cannot get away from God, for he is everywhere, and he is speaking to humanity nonstop by his creation. Even if you are physically blind, still your ears hear, your nose smells, your tongue tastes, that which is a clear declaration of who God is. Let us say for instance that you go to the grocery store. You decide to walk through the produce department, and there you see the salary, you see the cucumbers, you see the onions, and you see the tomatoes, then you look at the fruits, and see the grapefruit, the bananas, the oranges, the lemons, the strawberries, the peaches the cherries, and they are all declaring that there is a God in Heaven! God is so ingenious in his creation of so many different types of food, fruits, vegetables, animals, insects, birds, and fish. To deny the reality of God is to embrace utter foolishness and insanity, and it reveals the complete and total depravity of the heart. All of creation declares the reality of God, and I embrace this and revel in this reality. To think this amazing God has offered to sinful man eternal salvation, and to walk, to rule, and reign with him forever, it almost takes away my breath. Oh how marvelous and wonderful you are Lord in all of your majestic ways, and your ways are more than I could number or even imagine. Thank you wonderful Jesus.

Our taste buds declare that there is a God, and they alone will be more then sufficient to convict us **on the day of judgment. Our taste buds will stand up and say that we had no excuse not to follow and serve God.** We have tasted the wonderful taste of the pineapple, the wonderful experience of a banana, and we have tasted the wonderful varieties of a carrots and of salary. If evilution was true every thing would be nothing but blah, dead boring. There would be little if any flavor to the wide variety of plants, and yet there are so many flavors.

How can there be so many colors, colors that are so mystical in and by themselves. Just the fact that colors are frequencies is mind-boggling within itself. Every color is a declaration that there is a God who created all things. When we see a male peacock spreads his feathers, it is God saying: hello, I am, and I am calling out to you right now, how long are you going to ignore me. It is time to stop running away from God, it is time to stop ignoring him, for he is knocking upon the door of our hearts. He wants us to know him, to walk with him, to fellowship with him throughout eternity.

Revelation 3:20 Behold, I stand at the door, and knock: if any man hear my voice, and open the door, I will come in to him, and will sup with him, and he with me.

It is our responsibility to open up the door of our hearts, open up the door of our minds and lives to our creature. God will not bust down the doors of our live, even if it's for our salvation. We need to say: okay God here I am, I surrender, I submit, I yield, I will follow you all of the days of my life!

Psalms 23 is such a wonderful and powerful revelation that a shepherd boy (David) had of who God is. David saw himself as one of God sheep, and he saw Jesus as his shepherd, and he said:

The Lord is my shepherd, I shall not want. He maketh me to lie down in green pastures. He leadeth me beside the still waters. He restores my soul. He leadeth me in paths of righteousness for His namesake. Yeh though I walk through the valley of the shadow of death, I will fear no evil, for thou art with me. Thy rod and thy staff they comfort me. Thou prepares a table before me in the presence of mine enemies. You anointed my head with oil. My cup runs over. Surely goodness and mercy shall follow me all the days of my life, and I shall dwell in the house of the Lord forever!

A SHAKING of HEAVEN & EARTH is ABOUT to HAPPEN!

In this Dream I found myself standing outside of a small town on top of a grass covered hill. Other saints (some that I am familiar with) were gathered together there with me. (There were seven to a dozen of us). The stars were shining brightly from above. There was no moon this particular night. It was a beautiful warm summer evening. You could hear the night life all around us. The crickets and frogs were joined together in their song. As I was standing there with the gathering of these saints, I sensed in my heart that something astounding was about to happen in the heavens above us.

15 Then a spirit passed before my face; the hair of my flesh stood up: Job 4:15 (KJV)

Many times in my life I have had such experiences, Perceiving that God is about to do something right before it happens! I can testify that over and over through the years he is confirmed these dreams and visions. Those who are close to me can relate to others that which I told them by the spirit of God, which came to pass.

Now I perceived that the heavens were about to be shaken. I perceived in my heart that it was necessary for all of us to immediately get on our backs, and look into the heavens. When I shared this with those who were gathered together with me on the Hill, they all agreed and we immediately laid down on our backs. Within just a matter of minutes the heavens above us exploded into activity. It was as if a great battle was unfolding in the heavens. There was destruction happening throughout the sky as if it was in great travail and pain, and yet that there was a birthing, a coming forth of life and a new heaven.

Joel 2:30 And I will shew wonders in the heavens and in the earth, blood, and fire, and pillars of smoke.31 The sun shall be turned into darkness, and the moon into blood, before the great and the terrible day of the LORD come.32 And it shall come to pass, that whosoever shall call on the name of the LORD shall be delivered: for in mount Zion and in Jerusalem shall be deliverance, as the LORD hath said, and in the remnant whom the LORD shall call. (I believe we are entering into those days)

25 And there shall be signs in the sun, and in the moon, and in the stars; and upon the earth distress of nations, with perplexity; the sea and the waves roaring;26 Men's hearts failing them for fear, and for looking after those things which are coming on the earth: for the powers of heaven shall be shaken. Luke 21:25-26

29 Immediately after the tribulation of those days shall the sun be darkened, and the moon shall not give her light, and the stars shall fall from heaven, and the powers of the heavens shall be shaken: Matt 24:29

At the time of his dream I had not realized what was happening in the heavens with our Sun ,(Lunar and solar eclipses). If I understand correctly we will see things in the heavens that the scientists say will not be repeated for another 2000 years. That we are about to have massive solar flares. That these solar flares according to NASA will have the potential of destroying our whole grid system, sending us back into the dark ages.

What we watch unfold before us was mind boggling and dumbfounding, it was frightening and yet exhilarating. This event seemed to go on for hours, and jet as fast as it had begun, it was over with. All of us present on that hill slowly arose to our feet. We were so overwhelmed and dumbfounded with what we just saw that none of us spoken word, because we were utterly speechless. Our hearts were filled with complete wonder and amazement. I perceived that all of those who were present knew that God was revealing himself to the human race in a way he had not previously demonstrated. That God was doing something in the heavens and the earth that humanity had not yet seen or experienced.

TWO MAJOR EVENTS

#1 The Gathering of God's People! #2 The Return of Jesus Christ!

Major happenings in the heavens!

After this experience, this dream, I asked the Lord what it was that I was seeing? He informed me that this was the great migration. I asked him what he meant by that? He informed me that all of nature and creation is an illustration of his will, plans and purposes. That when we watch nature like the fish return to their spawning grounds, or flocks of birds fling south, or insects when they come bursting forth at certain seasons, that this is an illustration of what he is going to perform in the last days when he gathers together but alas great harvest, the great migration.

The beginning of this great migration will be revealed by terrible signs, sights and wonders in the heavens, and in order for there to be a great gathering of the saints there must first be an out pouring of God's divine fear upon all of humanity. If you ever study the revivals of the past you'll discover that all true revival begin with a revelation of the awesomeness of God. There will be only one of two responses from those who experienced the fear the Lord. Either they will come running to God as fast as they can, like the prodigal son coming back to his father, or they will run to the caves and the dens of the earth trying to hide themselves from God's wrath and anger.

We all dispersed from the hilltop slowly going our own separate ways. I found myself on a sidewalk beginning to enter into a small community where the streets were filled with people looking into the heavens. I could see great fear filling the faces all of those who were present. They were speaking back and forth to one another in whispers about what all of this could mean? I continued to walk down the sidewalk not speaking to anyone. The atmosphere was filled with a sense of great fear and anticipation.

I believe with all my heart that this visitation I had is a revelation of the great fear that is about to come upon the whole human race. First, I believe that the fear of the Lord will come back to the church, the body of Christ, the bride of Jesus, but there will be those in the church who instead of repenting will run away from God. They should be running to God, crying out for his mercy and help, but instead will be running away from him. If they would run to God, he will have mercy upon them, and embrace them in his loving arms. May we run to God as fast as we can in these last days.

CHAPTER NINE

#17 QUICKENING

Jesus said: *my words are spirit and they are life. It is the spirit that quickened, the flesh profits nothing.*

Remember that the 1st Adam was a living soul, and the 2nd Adam is a quickening spirit. The quickening of the Holy Ghost is when the word of God is made alive by the spirit of God. It is when the reality of Christ becomes more real to you than the natural world around us. Actually to a great extent this is what faith is, when God and his word becomes more real to you than the natural surroundings you find yourself in. Now I do not need to have a quickening to raise my hands, or to obey the every day instructions of God's word.

James 1:22 But be ye doers of the word, and not hearers only, deceiving your own selves.

There is a natural aspect of just doing what the bible says to do. When I 1st got born again I had never been around any one who raised their hands, or who danced before the Lord, or any one who shouted, or who laid on their face before the Lord. I simply read it in the Bible, and when I saw it in the Bible, I began to do that which I read.

1 Timothy 2:8 I will therefore that men pray every where, lifting up holy hands, without wrath and doubting.

These Scripture that had impacted my lifestyle were not quickened to me by the spirit, I just simply did what I read. Here's a good example: God commands us to forgive, and therefore we do it by faith. The Bible says if you do not forgive, you will not be forgiven. As we study the **17th Way** in which God will lead us and guide us, do not think, or believe that you have to be quickened by the spirit in order to do the basic things God's word instructs us to do. Actually as we do these simple basic things, the spirit of God will begin to Quicken us to do many other amazing things. I believe that every supernatural act that God has us perform is a supernatural quickening by his Holy Spirit. These quickening s can happen so quickly, so unexpectedly, that it will surprise you when it happens. You could have read a verse from the Bible for many years, then all of a sudden one day as you are reading it, it literally jumps right out of the Bible into your heart. Faith becomes alive in you, and now your excited, and full of joy and peace. **This is what we call a quickening of the Holy Spirit.**

Hebrews 4:12 For the word of God is quick, and powerful, and sharper than any twoedged sword, piercing even to the dividing asunder of soul and spirit, and of the joints and marrow, and is a discerner of the thoughts and intents of the heart.

The Holy Ghost will take the word and breathe life into it, causing the letter of the word to be turned into spirit. In order for the Holy Spirit to do this, we must be in complete agreement with the Bible. You do not need to understand the Scriptures in order to agree with them. Simply boldly declared to yourself, I agree with the Bible, no matter what it says. Every dream, vision, supernatural experience is a quickening of the Holy Ghost. This quickening is revealed to us in the book of Romans when God spoke to the heart of Abraham.

Romans 4:17 (As it is written, I have made thee a father of many nations,) before him whom he believed, even God, who quickeneth the dead, and calleth those things which be not as though they were.

God had to Quicken us in order for us to be born again, in order for us to be drawn to God.

John 6:44 No man can come to me, except the Father which hath sent me draw him: and I will raise him up at the last day.

The quickening of the Holy Ghost makes all the difference between victory and defeat. Now you could have heard the gospel for your whole life, and yet not be convicted or touched by the spirit of God in the least. The word of God was just sliding off of your back like water off of the back of a duck. Then all of a sudden one day out of the blue everything changed. The spirit of God quickened your heart in such a dramatic way that it felt like God was reaching into your chest and squeezing your heart. You fell under tremendous and overwhelming conviction, with everything inside of you crying out to be right with God. This is the quickening, convicting power of the Holy Spirit that will wonderfully change and transform you. This quickening is not just for the salvation of our souls, but it is a major way in which God will lead us, and guide us. Many times the messages that the Lord has me preach is because of the quickening of the Holy Ghost in my heart. God will Quicken certain Scriptures to my heart throughout the week as I get ready to minister my message on Sunday. This is the spirit of God leading and guiding me by his quickening. The spirit of God will Quicken your heart throughout the day, as you walk moment by moment.

A falling Lamp Pole would have killed my son!

This actually happened to my son Michael a number of years ago. If you ever visit our facilities, you will see in our parking lot a number of real tall metal street lights. We installed these street lights almost 25 years ago. Now, one day Michael, my oldest son was out in the parking lot with his back to one of these heavy steel street lights. He was just standing there minding his own business looking across the parking lot, when out of the blue there was a Divine quickening in his heart to take a step over to his right side. He told me: dad I wasn't even thinking, just in my heart I knew I had to step over to the right-hand side. Now at that very moment when he moved to his right side, something came whizzing past him very close to his left shoulder and arm. Then there was a loud crash of something hitting the ground.

Here in less than a second after Michael had moved that tall, heavy and large steel street light, fell over. It slammed down right next to him on to the parking lot. If he would not have moved exactly at that moment when he did, he would' have been slammed in the head by that heavy falling steel lamp. In all probability it would have killed him instantly on the spot. Thank God for the quickening of the Holy Spirit, and Michael's quick response to that quickening. Many people die early deaths because they do not hearken to the moving of the spirit. Just a matter of inches and seconds made all the difference in the world between life and death for my son Michael. I am convinced that when we get to Heaven we will talk to many of Gods people who will tell us that they died early deaths because they did not listen or respond to this quickening. When God puts a quickening in our hearts, we need to respond immediately, without thinking.

Amazing Overwhelming Conviction fell upon a Women

Kathleen and I had a burden for souls. We prayed about what to do and where to go. In order to reach sinners, we knew we had to go where they were. It was Quickened in our hearts to go to a town called Mount Union, which was about fifteen miles away. I knew we would have to believe for a bus, but so be it. We began to go door-to-door to the people in the low income housing projects in this town. They were basically African-American people. There were already two other churches running their buses through this area. We would simply go to each door, and knock on it. When a person opened up the door, we introduced ourselves and told them that if they had any needs, we would love to pray for them. We began to see wonderful results immediately. A miniature revival erupted in that community. People were getting saved and healed everywhere! They were also getting filled with the Holy Ghost.

One day I was out with another brother instead of my wife. As we were working our way down the street, I saw an African-American lady about five apartments ahead of us. She was hanging laundry out to dry on a clothesline behind her apartment. At that very moment, she looked up and saw us. Our eyes made contact for a brief second, and then she dropped her clothes and literally

literally ran into her house. I knew instantly that something strange was happening. We continue going door to door.

About 20 minutes later we arrived at her door. Her regular solid door was open, with just her screen door closed. I knocked on her door when a woman's voice yelled from upstairs. She told us to come on in. I did not want to just step into her house, being a total stranger, so I yelled through the screen door and asked her if she knew who we were. She yelled back down at us, "Yes she said: you're men of God." We stepped into her house not knowing exactly what to expect. She appeared at the top of the stairs with wet hair and a completely different set up close on.

The next thing we knew she came down the stairs to the bottom step. The minute she got to the bottom of the stairs, she literally fell to her knees weeping and crying. She asked us to lead her to Jesus Christ. I led her into the sinner's prayer and then I perceived she was ready for the Holy Ghost. So I prayed right then and there for her to be filled with the Holy Ghost. Immediately she began to speak in a brand-new heavenly language. We were awestruck on how God had moved upon this precious lady so fast. She later informed us what had happened. She said that when she saw us going door-to-door, she knew in her heart that she was not right with the Lord. An overwhelming conviction came upon her, and she knew that she was filthy and lost. She felt so dirty at that moment that she said she had to go in to her house, and go upstairs and take a quick shower. She felt as if she needed to put on clean clothes before we arrived. And put on some clean clothes. God was working so strongly in her that by the time we got to her house, she was ready to be saved and filled with the Holy Ghost. Thank God for the convicting and quickening power of the Holy Ghost.

We Must Understand This Spiritual Truth!

We need to learn how to be lead by the quickening of the Spirit of God. Everything that Jesus did was because he was quickened by the Spirit. The word of the Lord has to become alive on the inside of us. Most times the word is not quickened to us because we're not meditating upon the Word of God the way we should. Our mind and heart is like an incubator, or you might say like that of an oven. With an incubator, you have to put the fertilized eggs inside, and let the life within the eggs develop in that hot warm moist atmosphere. When the life inside of those eggs are mature and develop enough, they will break forth out of their shells into the visible physical world. You do not have to any thing to cause that life to come forth.

When you place a turkey, a ham, or a roast in the oven at the right temperature, in the proper amount of time, the aroma will begin to fill and flood the air. The time will come when you will know that the meat is completely and fully cooked, and only at that time will it be edible. It is exactly the same way with the word of God being meditated upon . The spirit of the living God will Quicken his word in your heart, and in your mind as you meditate hour after hour, day after day upon Gods truths. The life of Christ will come exploding out of you like the bursting forth of a chick coming out of its egg shell. Now, if we try to break open that chicken egg before the life inside is ready, it will die a horrifying and terrible death. If you try to partake of that Turkey, or eat that meat before it's fully cooked, you could end up dying from food poison.

Everything in its proper time. Meditating on the word of God is like putting the seed in the ground, and allowing it to germinate, sinking its roots deep into the rich soil. When it is ready, the life under the ground will come shooting forth to the surface. Even though the seed has been quickened in the ground, yet it still was not ready to produce fruit. People are trying to eat the fruit from a plant that is still not producing. We are living in a microwave, instantaneous society, they are under the deception that we can snap our fingers and have it instantly. There is a price to be paid for spiritual growth, and may God help us to understand this reality.

Psalm 119:11 Thy word have I hid in mine heart, that I might not sin against thee.

Psalm 39:3 My heart was hot within me, while I was musing the fire burned: then spake I with my tongue,

In the book of Psalms 119: David speaks about the quickening of God 11 times. This is a powerful chapter that reveals the reality of how God Quickens us with his word, and by his spirit. Without this quickening, we will find our selves in serious and overwhelming difficulties. Remember that Jesus Christ is the quickening spirit, where as the first Adam was simply a living soul. Christ desires to Quicken us by his spirit, and what is it that the spirit quickens? The word of God that we have hid in our hearts. I have experienced amazing miracles in my life, and it has always been connected to the meditating and memorizing of the word of God. As I speak, sing, and quote the word of God to myself, the Holy Spirit begins to Quicken Gods word to my heart. Let us look at some of the examples that David spoke about in Psalms 119. Realize that everything he said by the spirit of God absolutely was the truth.

Psalm 119:93 I will never forget thy precepts: for with them thou hast quickened me.

Psalm 119:154 Plead my cause, and deliver me: quicken me according to thy word.

Psalm 119:159 Consider how I love thy precepts: quicken me, O Lord, according to thy lovingkindness.

Understanding Righteousness & Grace

For us to truly live and move in the righteousness of God, we must be quickened by the spirit of God. The same spirit that raised Christ from the dead, wants to Quicken us in our mortal flesh. True biblical righteousness is a quickening of the spirit. Christ was made sin, that we might be made the righteousness of God in Christ Jesus. Many have misunderstood this particular verse, thinking that righteousness is simply a confession of faith, but oh how wrong they are. When Paul was talking about the grace of God, he was talking about the quickening of the Holy Ghost.

Grace is the divine life of Christ manifested in us, quickened by the Holy Ghost, because of the word of God hidden in our heart.

Psalm 119:40 Behold, I have longed after thy precepts: quicken me in thy righteousness.

The new birth is when the reality of Christ is quickened in your heart by the Holy Ghost. It is like that of an egg, that is fertilized. The minute that egg is fertilized, it is considered living. When a chicken lays eggs that are fertilized, they are considered as unhatched chickens. In order for these chicks to mature and to come breaking forth they must go through an incubation period of natural growth. When the reality of Christ was quickened in my heart, and I believed in him, I was born again. That life of Christ within me now needs to be developed and matured. The life that is in that chicken egg, and all that this baby chick needs is in the egg until it comes forth. All that we need as born again believers is found in Christ, and the living word. I believe the most amazing and wonderful gifts that God has given to us as his people are basically three realities.

#1 Jesus Christ! **#2** the Holy Ghost! **#3** The Word of God!

John 1:14 And the Word was made flesh, and dwelt among us, (and we beheld his glory, the glory as of the only begotten of the Father,) full of grace and truth.

When I wrote: Living in the Realm of the Miraculous

Back in 2011, I was ministering in a church in Wild-wood, New Jersey. In this particular meeting I began to share a number of my amazing experiences that I have had with the Lord since 1975. After the service, pastor Rob told me that people really love to hear the stories. At that moment it was dropped into my heart to go back to the hotel, and begin to write down all of the miracles that God had done in my life. Within two hours the Holy Spirit had brought back to my mind over 120 stories. I simply gave each story a title, with a brief description of the story at that time.

When my wife and I arrived back home in Pennsylvania, the Lord spoke to my heart, leading me to write a book about these experiences. This was so quickened to me by the spirit of God that literally within 2 1/2 weeks I wrote a 200 page book. Of course this did not include the editing and the printing of this book. As far as I know, there is no one in my family lineage who has ever even written a book, or even accomplished very much in the natural. My accomplishments are all by the quickening, energizing, power of the Holy Ghost, quickening the word in my heart. God by his spirit has so quickened me, that up to this moment I have memorized 10 books of the New Testament, and thousands of other Scriptures. Now, God is not a respecter of people, and he wants to manifest himself in the supernatural in a powerful way in all of our lives.

There are so many wonderful examples of God's quickening power in the old covenant, for instance when the spirit of God moved upon Samson in an amazing way, Quicken his mortal flesh, causing Samson to do that which in the natural he could never do, by performing incredible feats of strength. Every supernatural divine act of those we read about in the old covenant were performed by the quickening of the Holy Ghost. The spirit of the living God would come upon them, and quickened them to accomplish these feats. Now, we come into the New Testament, based on better and more powerful promises by the redemptive work of Christ. We have a right to partake of the quickening which Christ Jesus himself performs within our hearts and our lives on a moment by moment bases, that's why in Ephesians chapter 3 it makes this powerful statement:

Ephesians 3:20Now unto him that is able to do exceeding abundantly above all that we ask or think, according to the power that worketh in us,

Oh, brothers and sisters if only we could take a hold of this reality, that God by his quickening can empower us in ways we have not yet imagined. That God by his quickening spirit will lead and guide us in every affair of life. Now to what degree God Quickens us is determined by the amount of the word of God we have hid in our hearts.

Romans 8:11 But if the Spirit of him that raised up Jesus from the dead dwell in you, he that raised up Christ from the dead shall also quicken your mortal bodies by his Spirit that dwelleth in you.

The spirit of God can Quicken our mortal flesh to dance, or shout, sing, speak or run. The spirit of God will enable you to preach and proclaim the truth in the way that you never could in the flesh! There are so many wonderful examples of this from Genesis to Revelation. It tells us in the old covenant about the time that the prophet Elijah being quickened by the Holy Ghost, out ran the King and his horses.

1 Kings 18:45 And it came to pass in the mean while, that the heaven was black with clouds and wind, and there was a great rain. And Ahab rode, and went to Jezreel. 46 And the hand of the Lord was on Elijah; and he girded up his loins, and ran before Ahab to the entrance of Jezreel.

God calls us, he quickens us and enables by His word and Spirit. When God told Joshua and the Israelite's to go into the land of Canaan, he also quickened them by his word, and enable them to overcome all of the enemies. If you study the Scriptures very closely you'll also discover that David overcame the lion and the bear, Goliath and the other obstacles in his life because God quickened him by his Spirit. I am convinced that God quickened the heart of David to confront Goliath, and enabled him to overcome this giant.

Proverbs 3:5 Trust in the Lord with all thine heart; and lean not unto thine own understanding.6 In all thy ways acknowledge him, and he shall direct thy paths.

When God quickens us, we need to learn how to submit, and to operate tin that quickening.

James 4:7Submit yourselves therefore to God. Resist the devil, and he will flee from you.

*W*ho exactly is it that the devil does not have to flee from? From those who will not submit to God. Have I disobeyed the voice of God today? I am convinced that the more sensitive I become to God, and obey Him, the more God can quicken my heart, my flesh, and my mind!

Old Preacher with hot cup of Coffee

Kenneth E Hagin used to tell a true story about an old-time preacher, drinking coffee with a young minister. The story goes that this old preacher invited a young preacher to sit down and have a cup of coffee with him at his house. The old man poured himself a steaming hot cup of coffee, and then poured the young man a cup. This old preacher picked up his cup of coffee and began to drink it in a normal fashion. This young preacher followed the older preacher's example. Without thinking this young preacher took a big mouth full from his cup of coffee.

Instantly his mouth was severely burned by the coffee. He practically dropped the cup of coffee as the hot coffee blistered his lips, tongue and his mouth. Kenneth E Hagin went on to say that the reason why the older man could drink such hot steaming coffee was that through the years he had seared and callused his mouth by drinking hot coffee. Hagin used this as an example of what happens to the human heart when we begin to feed it that which is ungodly. When you allow things to come into your ear gait, your eye gait which is against the will of God, it will cause your heart to become so hard, that when God sends conviction, it will slide off your back like eggs in a Teflon pan.

Most modern-day believers have become so hard in their heart, that they are no longer convicted by watching immorality and perversion on TV, and in the Movies. Their hearts have become so hard by the deceitfulness of sin that it does not bother them to not gathered together with the body of Christ, or to not pray, or to not read their Bibles, or to no longer share Christ with lost people. You cannot believe how many believers I know that are living in sin with another person, and still believe they're going to heaven. We have come into a time of such extreme hardness of heart and insanity of the human soul that it boggles the human mind.

Now in order for God to soften our hearts there must be an attitude of repentance, and a desire to please the Lord. We must give ourselves to the word of God and prayer, separating ourselves from that which is immoral and against the will of the Father. We must cry out for God to once again convict us, and bring the fear God back into our lives. If we would do this, once again the Holy Ghost will begin to quickened God's word to our hearts, and we will begin to truly live as the sons and daughters of Almighty God.

When Christ came into my heart, he Quickened my mortal flesh, he broke the power of sin and set me free. The whole purpose of Christ coming was to take away the stony heart, and to give us a heart that is sensitive to the will of the Father.

Ezekiel 36:26 A new heart also will I give you, and a new spirit will I put within you: and I will take away the stony heart out of your flesh, and I will give you an heart of flesh.

It is important that we have a tender heart, soft heart, sensitive heart toward God. After you are born again, you can once again harden your heart by partaking of that which is against the divine nature and character of the Father. Even though we are born again, we do not lose the power of choice.

2 Peter 2:21 For it had been better for them not to have known the way of righteousness, than, after they have known it, to turn from the holy commandment delivered unto them.22 But it is happened unto them according to the true proverb, The dog is turned to his own vomit again; and the sow that was washed to her wallowing in the mire.

#18 CIRCUMSTANCES

The **18th Way** that God leads us and guides us is by Divine circumstances. I would say this is very touchy area that we need to approach it very cautious way. Realize that the enemy will always attack us with circumstances, and the apostle Paul talked about this when he wrote the Thessalonians.

1 Thessalonians 2:18 Wherefore we would have come unto you, even I Paul, once and again; but Satan hindered us.

Many times when the enemy attacks, and we cry out to God's for help and mercy, the Lord divinely intervenes. Now circumstances are not what I would call the typical way in which God leads and guides. **Yes, we acknowledge that all things work together for good, to them that love God, and that are called according to his purpose.** This is not the kind of circumstance that we are referring to in this particular teaching. It is very important that we discern the difference between#1 Divine circumstances,#2 the enemy interfering, #3 every day natural circumstances.

God Did Not Put You in the Hospital With a Medical Problem to Share Christ!

Through the years I have run into many believers who have believed flaky ideals based upon their circumstances. I think one of the most typical mistakes that people make is when they say that God allowed this sickness, or disease in order for them to reach people in the hospital for Christ. Please do not misunderstand what I'm saying here, yes you can share Christ if you're in the hospital with something wrong with you. What the devil meant for evil, God can turn for good as you share the gospel with those around you. In the last 40 years I have found myself many times in the hospital sharing Christ with those I could. The wonderful news is that I was not there because I was sick or had a disease. Let me just share one of these circumstances:

God Gave Him A Brand-new liver

One day I walked into a man's room who I did not know. The Holy Spirit drew me to this particular room as I was walking down the hospital hallway. I asked the man who was lying in the bed what his problem was. He told me that his liver was completely shot, and that he was dying. I perceived in my heart that it was because of alcoholism. I told him that I would like to pray for him, and asked if that was possible. He agreed to my request. I laid my hands on him, commanding in the name of Jesus Christ for the spirit of infirmity to come out. And then I spoke into him a brand-new liver, in the name of Jesus Christ of Nazareth! I do not speak loud. I do not have to because I know my Authority in Christ, when I am submitted to the authority of Christ! I do not pray real long prayers, or even dozens of scriptures. The Word is already in my heart!

Now believe me when I tell you that if I wanted to pray real long prayers in those situations I easily could. I could stand over the person and quote whole books of the Bible by memory. When you are moving in the realm of faith none of these things are really necessary. Many times I think people are simply trying to work up faith. If you study the life of Jesus and his ministry he never spent a long time praying or speaking over people. The long hours of prayer, and speaking the word was done in private, when he was up on the mountain, or alone in the wilderness. When I was done praying I simply said goodbye, and out the door I went. I went to go see another sick person who was in the hospital. It was three years later when I found out what happened on that particular day.

One day one of the members of my congregation was down on the streets of Gettysburg witnessing to those he met. He ran into this particular gentleman who was dying because of a bad liver.

This particular man said: I know who your pastor is! The parishioner asked: how do you know my pastor? He said: three years ago I was dying with a bad liver, and your pastor walked in to my hospital room. He laid his hands on me, commanding me to be healed, and to have a brand-new liver, and God did give me a brand-new liver!

In order to discover whether or not the circumstances that we find our self in is of God we need to see if it contradicts the divine nature and character of God. For instance, if a man or a woman is married, God is not going to send them another mate. It is absolutely unbelievable the bizarre things I hear people say. Many times God gets blamed for things which is not of his doing at all. I have known quite a number of people who have claimed that certain events they experienced were of the Lord when they simply were not. Most of these people will not change their minds even though you show them within God's word they are wrong.

Proverbs 16:18 Pride goeth before destruction, and an haughty spirit before a fall.

The Leaning Chimney

One time I was with this gentleman who was a rather large fellow, and who was significantly older than me. This brother really believed that he was super spiritual. I was walking with him through his neighborhood by his side one day. Out of the blue he stops, he looks up, and points at a chimney on a house that was leaning over precariously. This brick chimney was in bad condition and must have had a crumbling foundation, and was about ready to fall over. Now this reality seemed to escape this spiritual brothers understanding. He pointed to this faulty falling chimney and said that God was speaking to him by this chimney. I asked him: what is God saying to you about it? He told me that by that leaning chimney, God was revealing to him that he was leaning into Christ. Dear brothers and sisters a chimney that is about to fall over is not God telling us that we are leaning into him. Too many people are walking in the flesh, claiming that they are in the spiritual. Later on this man caused major problems in the church he was attending.

Hebrews 5:13 For every one that useth milk is unskilful in the word of righteousness: for he is a babe.14 But strong meat belongeth to them that are of full age, even those who by reason of use have their senses exercised to discern both good and evil.

So many times I hear believers say: I just feel this or that. Now, may be what you are feeling is of God, but maybe it's not! We need to make sure that we are not so quick to proclaim that what we are feeling is of the Lord. The reality of the fact is that there are times when God will use your five senses in order to give you direction, and yet most times our feelings are fickle. What we need to realize is that if God is speaking to us by our feelings it will never contradict the character and the nature of Christ. If what you feel is completely against the word of God, the will of God, the nature of God, the character of God, then it is not of God. If what you are feeling is encouraging you to do that which Christ would not do, you know it's the flesh and the devil. I have discovered that behind almost all deception is pride, selfish ambitions, human reasoning, wrong teaching or even demonic fear. I'm talking about being led by circumstances. Yes, there are times when God will speak to us by our feelings and emotions, but it is something you really have to check, double check, and triple check.

The Alcan Freeway Washed out

In May of 1975, my sister asked me to drive her car up to Anchorage Alaska. I had just been discharged from the Navy, and she was stationed in New Mexico in the Air Force. She had received her new orders to relocate to the Air Force Base in Anchorage, Alaska. In my heart I really felt like I was supposed to go back to Wisconsin, to share Christ with the gang of men that I used to run with before I was born again. Now, I felt like I was between a rock and a hard place, because I was committed to driving her 1973 red Maverick up the Alcan Freeway! I had just driven the Alcan the year before right at the onset of winter. From Anchorage to Mukwonag Wisconsin was 3,500 miles long. (At that time I was only eighteen years old and not yet saved. I cover that experience in another book.)

I experienced heavy rains as I headed up through Canada on the dirt road which took me to Fairbanks. The farther I adventured, the worse it got. Some people were adventuring on taking the roles that logging trucks drove, but my sister's car was not designed for such rough terrain. I spoke to one family that had a large passenger van who had endeavored to do this. Numerous times they had to cross rivers and streams, hoping and praying they would make it a cross.

I had to face the fact that I could not make it up to Anchorage Alaska with my sister's car. I had to stop and turn around. The flooding was so bad that year that they maintenance crew could not give any reasonable dates when the bridges and the road to Alaska would be opened once again for public traffic. The only other option I had was to drive my sister's car back to Mukwonago, Wisconsin where my parents lived.

Looking back, I now realize that God was in this event, in order that I would share Christ with the men that I used to do drugs, alcohol and other gang related activities with. The spirit of God strongly convicted me, saying I told you to go back to Wisconsin. I had from the beginning felt like I was supposed to go to Wisconsin, but because of my commitment to my sister, I had not listen to my heart. God has a wonderful way of divinely intervening when it is necessary for his plan to be fulfilled. It kinda reminds me of Jonah taking the ship so that he could ignore going to Nineveh. God spoke to me through this circumstance.

Revelation 3:8 I know thy works: behold, I have set before thee an open door, and no man can shut it: for thou hast a little strength, and hast kept my word, and hast not denied my name.

Multilevel Marketing Madness

So many times God's people are deceived by circumstances that look favorable for them in order to make big money. I know one Spirit filled older couple who are very close to us, who told us that they had been suckered into over nine different multilevel marketing programs through the years. They informed us that they had never made any money, not even one time through these multilevel marketing schemes. People are sincere and excited about the business that they are launching off into being completely convinced that it is God who sent this opportunity to them to make all of this amazing money. They want you to be a part of this wonderful money making opportunity to make money for the kingdom. They're completely convinced that this is God leading them and guiding them, not realizing it's simply the lust of their flesh. They want you to be a part of what they're involved in, because first of all they need your participation in order to build their team. Then they need you to build your team in order to get a residue of your sales, to make them successful.

Through the years many people have tried to get me involved in these kind of businesses. Thank God that 95% of the time they have not been able to sucker me in. Now in about 2005 I fell for one of these schemes, hook, line, and sinker. Not only did I fall for it, but I got my wife involved, my oldest son, members of our church, and other friends. Yes, like a dummy I was led like a sheep to the slaughter, and yes, we all lost our shirts. Please do not misunderstand me, I'm not saying that people cannot make a living off of some of these different endeavors. It's basically that you have to pour your whole life into trying to make them work. My purpose in life is to not get caught up in making money, but in trying to win souls for Christ, and to see the captive set free. I find most people that get wrapped up in these schemes, are not looking truly at seeing people saved, but they are looking for potential new representatives. Without really wanting to, or ever acknowledging it, they see a dollar sign written on every persons face.

We need to go to the word of God in every circumstance, in every situation. We need to ask ourselves if we could truly see Jesus involved in this circumstance. We need to rightly discern whether or not this circumstance is directed of God, or simply the devil trying to set us up. Through godly spiritual exercise we will come to the place of knowing whether something is of God or not.

It's like that of the developing of physical natural muscles. You might not be able to one hundred push-ups when you first begin. You might have to start with only 3 to 5 push-ups, but as you progress through the years you will begin to increase your natural physical strength. It is the same with developing spiritual discernment in every circumstance of whether this is the Lord or not.

Philippians 2:12 Wherefore, my beloved, as ye have always obeyed, not as in my presence only, but now much more in my absence, work out your own salvation with fear and trembling.

Jonah is a tremendous book where God used circumstances to get Jonah where he wanted him to be. Jonah did not want to go to Nineveh, because he wanted the people of Nineveh to be destroyed. If you study history you'll discover that the people in Nineveh were really wicked and ungodly people who done terrible things to the decedents of Abraham. Jonah decides he is going to run from the call of God. He purchases the tickets to get on a boat that is taking him in the opposite direction of Tarsus. There is a storm that arises, and this is not a storm caused by the devil. **God raised up this storm! Why would God raise up a storm?** Because God had a plan to use Jonah to bring repentance to the people of Nineveh.

I am convinced that many of the storms of life that we experience is simply God trying to stop us, and get our attention. If you would go back and study the history of America, you would discover that many of our governmental leaders knew that when disasters came, it was because our nation was out of the will of God. They would call our nation to days of national repentance and prayer. Now we have come to a time that the leaders are spiritually ignorant. Instead of calling our nation to repentance and prayer, we are blaming many of these natural disasters upon global warming or some other type of nonsense.

You might say, brother Mike are you sure it's not the devil bringing destruction? Let me respond with a question of my own, did we open the door for the enemy to come in because we are out

of the will of God? Jonah opened the door for destruction because
he was purposely running away from God. Can you believe that we
have believers trying to bind the devil, even though they are out of
the will of God. I strongly suggest that the first thing we do is
submit to God, then resist the devil, and he will flee from us. What
is amazing to me is that even the heathen on this ship knew that
something was wrong. They began to inquire of their gods who
was on board the ship who was out of Gods will. The lots fell to
Jonah. They asked him what in the world he had done to anger the
God of Israel? He informed them of his rebellion, and what the
solution to his rebellion was. He told them that they were going to
have to throw him off of the ship. Even in this incredible situation,
God had prepared a way for his will to be done.

***Jonah 1:17 Now the Lord had prepared a great fish to swallow
up Jonah. And Jonah was in the belly of the fish three days and
three nights.***

For three days Jonah was in the belly of this fish. Amazingly
God use this circumstance to reveal what he was going to do with
his son in his death and his resurrection. The soul of Christ was in
the pit of hell for three days, and His body was in the tomb for thre
days!

***Matthew 12:40 For as Jonas was three days and three nights in
the whale's belly; so shall the Son of man be three days and three
nights in the heart of the earth.***

After three days God has this gigantic fish spit Jonah up on the
shores of Nineveh. Jonah shows up in Nineveh bleached white
from head to toe with seaweed and fish slime covering his body. I
am sure that he smelled like stinking rotting fish. God uses the
circumstances to bring Complete and utter fear to the people of
Nineveh. After Jonah preaches through out the city of Nineveh he
sits down in the hot sun, waiting for God to pour out his judgment
upon the wicked people. In the mist of his waiting, God creates
another amazing circumstance. He causes a gourd to grow up
overnight over the top of Jonah in order to shade him from the heat
of the sun. Jonah sits back, and enjoys this wonderful circumstance

arranged by God, anticipating the soon coming destruction of the wicked people of Nineveh.

Now, to Jonah's dissatisfaction, the Lord destroys this plant, causing it to wither up. Jonah grumbles and gripes about the destruction of the plant, when God speaks up, and says this to him:

Jonah 3:10 Then said the Lord, Thou hast had pity on the gourd, for the which thou hast not laboured, neither madest it grow; which came up in a night, and perished in a night:11 And should not I spare Nineveh, that great city, wherein are more than sixscore thousand persons that cannot discern between their right hand and their left hand; and also much cattle?

Again we see God speaking to men through the lack of rain when Elijah cried out to God to seal up the Heavens! It did not rain on the earth for the next three and half years. God was using a circumstance in order to speak to the human race.

God Enabled Me Beat a Chess Champion

This is about a friend of mine who to a great extent was an agnostic, if not an atheist. This particular friend of mine was a local champion chess player where I grew up. Before I was born again he could easily beat me at almost every game of chess. I had not played chess with him since I had left for the Navy back in 1973. Now, here it was 1975, and he was filled with more pride than ever, believing that he had advanced a long way in the game of chess. He had made it an absolute priority in his life to be the best. Well after I was born again, I kept trying to tell this arrogant friend of mine about Jesus Christ. He simply did not want to hear anything about the Lord. Now he was really biting at the bit to play chess with me again in order to make me look like a fool. He had to realize that something supernatural had happened in my life in the last three years because the terrible speech impediment that I had my whole life was not completely gone. When I had been baptized in the Holy Ghost, my speech impediment was completely healed. I could speak just as clear and precise as anyone. Yet this supernatural evidence of God moving in my life did not seem to touch him in the least.

For a brief period of time after I was discharged from the Navy I spent a short period of time back in Wisconsin. I could tell that he desperately wanted to play a game of chess with me, I am sure he wanted to play me just so that he could rub my nose in the fact that he was a chess champion, and I a dummy. He was convinced that he could easily beat me at this game like he had done so many times in the past. I truly perceived in my heart that God wanted me to play him, so I agreed to play him one game of chess. What I am about to tell you, is the absolute honest truth.

As I looked down at that board with all the chess pieces laid out before me, I felt in my heart that God was about to do something amazing and supernatural. I am telling you that the spirit of the Lord quickened me, taking over this chess game. I began to move pieces across the board by the leading of the Holy Ghost not even thinking about my moves. This chess champion literally began to laugh at the dumb moves that I was making. He literally began to mock me as I began to lose piece after piece to him. When it looked like the game was utterly lost to him and that he had one me easily, out of the blue, and unexpectedly I put his King in checkmate. Neither him or I could believe what just took place. He was so frustrated and upset because he knew that I had played the game in such an unconventional and foolish way that there's no way I could win.

During the time that I was playing I was speaking about Jesus as much as possible. He had no choice but to listen to me because of the game in front of us. He insisted that it was simply luck that I had won, and that I needed to play him again. Yes, I told him let's play another game. Once again we set all the pieces up, and I made the first move. It was almost an exact repeat of the first game in the seemingly stupid moves I was making. He laughed and mock me as I made stupid move after stupid move. Then to our utter and complete surprise, once again he found his King in checkmate. He could barely contain himself because of his total frustration and anger at me winning this game with making so many stupid moves.

At that moment He became like a gambler who could not stop gambling until he won his money back. What I am sharing with you is the absolute truth, with no exaggeration whatsoever. The spirit of the living God was directing my every move in this chess game. I was not leaning to the understanding of my mind. It was like I was watching God pick up these pieces with my right hand, and move them around the board. I won five games, eight games, 11 games, a total of 13 games straight in a row. After 13 games of winning this chess champion, I finally quit because I knew he was about to lose his mind. From that day to now, over 40 years have passed and he has never played me another game of chest. He declared that I had won these games because I was so stupid. That I did not know the normal way to play chess.

God had used this circumstance in order to reveal himself in a wonderful way to this man who was antagonistic towards the gospel. God was using this circumstance to touch his heart, to let him know that he was not playing mike Yeager!

1 Corinthians 1:27 But God hath chosen the foolish things of the world to confound the wise; and God hath chosen the weak things of the world to confound the things which are mighty;

We need to be careful that we do not find ourselves fighting against God. You can set your heart, and your mind upon something you want, and the next thing you know you are doing anything it takes to get what it is you desire. Instead of simply praying, asking the Lord if this is his will, we end up manipulating the situations to our advantage. Through the years I have watched people pursuing that which they want, getting it, and then wishing to God that they had never Got it. The very first prayer that Jesus taught his disciples to pray was:

Matthew 6:9 After this manner therefore pray ye: Our Father which art in heaven, Hallowed be thy name.10 Thy kingdom come, Thy will be done in earth, as it is in heaven.

Like Two Bulls in a China Closet

One day as I stepped out of my house, going towards the church, an older vehicle pulled into our parking lot. A tall burly man, probably in his late 30s, with a beard and mustache, got out of his car. As I was walking towards him, he literally began to run towards me. I had no idea what was going on. By the time he reached me, he was weeping and wailing like a baby. Out of his mouth he began to repent of his sins, declaring that he wanted to get right with God. He told me the Holy Spirit arrested him as he was driving past our facility. He was a back slid-den believer, who needed to get right with God. Immediately I took him into our sanctuary where other brothers were already waiting for me for. I had these brothers pray with this man.

The spirit of God moved on him in such a wonderful way that he wanted to get water baptized at that very moment, on the spot. We baptized him in the sanctuary's baptism pool that afternoon. I watched for the next couple months as God began to do a marvelous work in his life. He was faithful to every service, loud and boisterous for Jesus. At the same time we had another sister in Christ which we had led to the Lord who was also attending our services. She also was in her late 30s. Eventually this brother and sister began to talk together. Now, please do not misunderstand me, I'm not saying that this is wrong, yet I perceived by the spirit of God that things were about to happen that should not happen.

I very lovingly took this brother aside, encouraging him at this moment to not get involved with anyone. He actually had a divorce wife, with children. He had made her life, and their children a living hell because of his alcoholism and violence. I encouragied this brother to get strong in Christ, and to believe that God could restore his marriage. Amazingly his first wife was open for reconciliation.

I saw that the devil was trying to set him up. He assured me very strongly that he was not interested in anyone or anything but Jesus at this time in his life. In my heart of hearts though I knew he was not telling me the truth. There were times when I was doing different things on the campus of our property, when I would run into this couple whispering in a hallway, or the gymnasium, or outside behind a building. I did not want to believe what I knew in my heart was true. This dear brother and sister had fallen into the trap of the devil. Things were going on, that should not be happening. It came out at a later date that sure enough they were extremely involved sexually.

Now my wife and I were headed off to a Ministers conference in West Lafayette Indiana. I like to drive at night when there's hardly any traffic, as my wife sleeps. As I was headed out to Indiana praying for different situations, including this couple, the Lord began to speak to me, giving me specific directions and information about different situations. The Lord told me that this couple was sexually involved, and that they were like two bulls in a China closet. That they had made up their mind, and that they were not going to let anybody stop them from having this relationship. The Lord instructed me to be there for them even in the midst of their sin. He specifically told me to tell them, Okay, I'm here for you, and yet the Lord told me to tell them that as a result of this decision they made they were going to have many difficulties and troubles!

When my wife and I got back from this Ministers conference, I called the brother into my office. When I told him what the Lord had told me to tell him, he started crying and got extremely excited. He did not hear the part where the Lord said that they would have many difficulties and troubles because of this decision. So many times we set our heart against the will of God, wanting what we do not need, or what we should not have. Through the years I have seen many women and some men pursue someone they should not have had a relationship with. When they get what they wanted, they wish to God they had never gotten it. Yes the Lord will allow us to have what we want, but it's not his will. He sees and knows the future more than we could ever understand or comprehend.

I told them that I would perform the wedding whenever they were ready. To my shock and amazement, they came back to me and said that they wanted to get married next Saturday. Sure enough, the next Saturday I performed this ceremony. I wish I could tell you that they lived happily ever after, but I'm sorry to say that all hell broke loose. In a very short period of time the brother went back to alcohol. It got so bad that I had to forbid him from coming unto our church property. He became very physically and verbally abusive with his wife, and his mother-in-law. He eventually was pulled over by the police, receiving a DUI. I'm sorry to say that he ended up in prison. His wife then received some type of terrible affliction of the body. Sad to say this couple is no longer together.

You see it is so important that we keep our hearts right with God. The only thing we should truly desire and want is that which the Lord wants for us. If we set our heart upon that which we want, and attain it, we will wish to God that we never obtained it. May God help us, and have mercy on all of us.

I actually believe that God loves us so much that he will set up certain scenarios in our lives in order to rescue us. For instance God can put you behind a slowpoke on the highway to save your life from a major car accident. If you would've been able to get around that slowpoke, you would have been involved in that terrible car accident that happened just a couple miles ahead of you. I have read some amazing stories about people who should have been in the twin towers of the World Trade Center on 9/11. Some silly, or strange event transpired on that day that kept people from being there when the planes crashed into the building! It was God supernaturally protecting them from dying with the other 3000 people who died on that dreadful day.

One of the best examples of God using circumstances to our benefit is Joseph and his brothers. They sold this young man into slavery because of the dreams and visions he shared with them. There was also jealousy because of the fact that Jacob loved him more then all of his other children.

Genesis 37:3 Now Israel loved Joseph more than all his children, because he was the son of his old age: and he made him a coat of many colors.

Joseph experienced many hardships in Egypt after he was sold as a slave. He eventually ended up in prison being falsely accused of something he did not do. In all of these circumstances God was preparing him to make a way for his family to be saved from the coming terrible famine that was about the hit the earth. When Joseph and his family were finally reunited, he made an amazing statement to his brethren.

Genesis 45:7 And God sent me before you to preserve you a posterity in the earth, and to save your lives by a great deliverance.8 So now it was not you that sent me hither, but God: and he hath made me a father to Pharaoh, and lord of all his house, and a ruler throughout all the land of Egypt.

Now Joseph could have gave way to bitterness, grumbling, griping, and depression. He could have became hateful towards God because of the circumstances he found himself in, and yet, these circumstances did not destroy Joseph, but rather brought him to a place of amazing spiritual wisdom and maturity. It is not the circumstances that come to us that will make us or break us, but our response to them. Joseph told his brothers, you meant it for evil, but God meant it for good.

Too Many Believers Are Spiritual Pacifist

David made an amazing statement when it came to the afflictions he experienced.

Psalm 119:71 It is good for me that I have been afflicted; that I might learn thy statutes.

When the enemy comes in like a flood, if I will trust God, act upon the word, God will raise up a standard against the enemy. I'm amazed at how many believers are such pacifist when it comes to fighting the fight of faith. You have to rise up in the name of Jesus

Christ and speak against that circumstance which is contrary to God's will. If the circumstance does not seem to change, you do not let go of having a heart that is thankful, grateful and worshipful towards the Lord. Here is an illustration in my own personal life.

The other day I was laying in bed all night long with terrible pain racking my body, yet I am fighting the fight of faith, praying quietly as I'm laying in bed. I never allow a spirit of fear to control and dictate my actions. The next thing I know my left hand went completely numb with my fingers all curled up. The devil said to me: you're having a stroke. Immediately I jumped out of bed, and I took my numb left arm with its curled up fingers and began to beat it against my right hand commanding it to be healed. I knew that this circumstance was not of God because by his stripes we were healed! I had to rise up in the spirit of faith speaking to this circumstance.

After over 40 years of practice I know in most situations what is, and what is not the will of God. After I commanded my arm and my hand, my body to be healed, I began to thank the Lord that it was done. Now, in the natural my arm and my hand is still in the same condition it was before I spoke to it in the name of Jesus, but I know that God Cannot Lie. Praise the Lord, within a short period of time my left arm and hand was completely restored, and all the pain left my body. This took place back in about 2009. We should never give into the lie, or the symptoms that the enemy is trying to use against us. The minute the enemy sticks his ugly head up, we need to cut it off with the word of God.

When I was a kid we used to fish in a favorite fishing hole. It was filled with pan fish, crop-pies, and blue gills. The only problem is that it also had lots of nasty mud turtles. These nasty turtles would kill anything that was in their path. Whenever we went fishing we would always carry our 22 rifles, and when these mud turtles stuck their heads up, we popped them with our 22s. We were not going to allow them to devour the fish we were trying to catch. If we had not done this there would have been no fish left in this pond. It is the same way spiritually. You cannot allow the devil, and is demonic host to simply run you over. We must rise up, and overcome spiritual pacifism.

A Major Accident with Our Bus Prevented

It is amazing how God uses circumstances for our good. There are times that we really do not even know that God is directing our steps, but God is in the details. Here is one amazing illustration: we were getting ready to take our large 52 passenger (VanHool) bus out to a conference in West Lafayette Indiana.

Psalm 37:23 The steps of a good man are ordered by the Lord: and he delighteth in his way.

It came into my heart to check the bus out about a week before we were leaving for this conference. As far as I knew all of the mechanics of the bus, inspections and examinations were up-to-date. I simply began to check all the fluids, belts, tires and anything else that might go wrong. After I completed this task I decided to do one more walk around the bus again. As I was walking past the right middle duel wheel of the bus, I saw what looked like a small trace of oil coming from the main hub. Immediately the Spirit drew my attention to this bit of oil. Inside of my heart red lights began to go off. God used this circumstance to get my attention.

Immediately I was on the cell phone, calling up our mechanic. I told him what I was looking at, and what he thought about it? He assured me over the phone that he did not think that it was a big deal. It must have been the spirit of the Lord because I told him he needed to come over and pull this wheel. Unbeknownst to me at the time the Lord had given to me a word of knowledge that this axle had some major problems. Our mechanic agreed to come and look. About an hour later he showed up to examine the wheel. Once again he told me that he did not think it was a problem. I insisted that he Jack the bus up, and pull off the tires. This was no simple job because it was labor intense. We really did not have the equipment to do this job, especially out in the churches parking lot. He reluctantly agreed to do it. I walked away, as he got ready to do this job.

Later in the day the mechanic walked into my office, telling me he needed to show me something. We walked over to the buss where he had removed the outer tire. He told me: Pastor if you would have drove this bus out to Indiana, you would have had a major accident. He pointed to the wheel axle, informing me that the axle bearings were totally shot. That the steel rings that kept the axle in place had been broken and stripped off completely. He said that we could have been driving down the highway, and the axle with the tires would've simply pulled right out. He informed me that he had known of other people that this had happened to, and that the accidents were always major and tragic.

We could have easily been doing 60/70 miles an hour on the turnpike, or on a back road, and lost complete control of the bus. Not only could I have been killed with all of our passengers, but possibly oncoming traffic would also have been involved. God used the circumstance of a little trace of oil by the hub of the tires in order to give me a strong premonition of danger. How many believers have lost their lives because they did not take heed to that red light within their hearts.

Gideon is another example of how God can use circumstances to give us direction. If you really study this situation with Gideon, the wet and try lambskin was simply used to confirm something that God had already told Gideon. The Lord used this situation to help Gideon because he was so timid and uncertain in his walk with God.

Judges 6:36 And Gideon said unto God, If thou wilt save Israel by mine hand, as thou hast said,37 Behold, I will put a fleece of wool in the floor; and if the dew be on the fleece only, and it be dry upon all the earth beside, then shall I know that thou wilt save Israel by mine hand, as thou hast said.

Saving a Barracks Full of Sleeping Men

This happened before I was even born again. Back in the late summer of 1973 after I had completed my boot camp at great lakes Naval base, I was moved to a training center to become an electrician's mate at a nearby military base. One night as I was peaceably sleeping at about 3 AM in the morning I smell smoke. Now this in itself was amazing because my sense of smell was almost nonexistent. My nose had been broken at least three times if not four. The worst time was when I had been knocked to the ground, and a guy who was quite a bit bigger than me took his right foot and slammed it right down onto my face, crushing my nose.(God healed me of this condition in 1975). My sense of smell at this time was completely gone, and yet here I am smelling smoke. A sense of urgency hit my heart as I smelled the smoke, and I jumped up immediately out of my bunk. I slipped on my pants, and headed out to try to find out what was wrong. It was like my heart was possessed with an extreme urgency. I approached the man who was standing guard duty at the entrance to our barracks, asking him if he smelled any smoke? He informed me that he did not smell smoke whatsoever. I decided that I needed to walk around outside and see if I could find out what was going on.

This action was highly unusual for me because I was usually in my own little world, being a total slacker. The only thing I cared about was getting drunk and getting high. Now here I was with his sense of urgency to find out where this smokes was coming from. This had to be God moving upon my heart before I was even born again. I walked around to the back side of our barracks looking as I went to see where the smoke was coming from. Right behind our barracks was another barracks approximately five story high. Immediately I saw that smoke was pouring out of a window on the second floor. I ran towards the barracks, past the guard who had fallen asleep. I ran towards the nearest fire alarm, grabbing it and pulling it as I ran past.

The next 20 minutes or so were busy as other men joined me in evacuating all of the men from the barracks, and fighting the fire. God must have supernaturally enhanced my sense of smell, then gave me a great sense of urgency so that he could save those men in that barracks. I did receive a letter from the commanding officer, the Admiral of the base, thanking me for my quick thinking, response, and heroics of my action on that day saving the lives of of my fellow sailors.

Every circumstance whether of God or of the devil is an opportunity for us to walk by faith. It is extremely important in the day and hour that we are living in to be directed and led by the Holy Ghost every moment. What comes to us does not make us or break us, but it is how we respond. Those around us can be full of hate and bitterness, but we needed to be full of the divine love of Christ. The spiritual principle that we reap what we sow is in operation whether we believe it or not.

Luke 6:38 Give, and it shall be given unto you; good measure, pressed down, and shaken together, and running over, shall men give into your bosom. For with the same measure that ye mete withal it shall be measured to you again.

CHAPTER TEN

#19 Imaginations

I've been teaching about the **20 ways** that God speaks to us. When you picked up this book and you began to read it, that is God speaking to you. Many times I have heard believers say God never talks to me, but when you read your Bible that is God speaking to you! Before my wife and I were ever married, we would send each other wonderful letters. She still has my letters to this day, and she still reads them. Those letters were me, and is still me speaking to her! If you ever want God to speak to you, simply pickup your Bible and read it. What ever you do never say again: God doesn't speak to me. That is the devil and his demonic spirits lying to you.

The next to the last way that God speaks to us is by or through our imagination. The **imagination** is an amazing and wonderful creative part of your mind. Everything that man has ever built, developed or designed has come from his imagination. We recognize that there are many imaginations that are satanic, and yet on the other side, there are many that are wonderful and amazing. God himself has always been in existence way before the spiritual or the material world was created. According to the book of Genesis God spoke it all into existence. What exactly did he speak? He spoke that which he imagined in his mind and in his heart. The universe, galaxies, our solar system, the earth and all that is in it was created in his imagination before he ever spoke it into existence. The good and the bad comes forth out of our imagination. When Job said the things which he feared came to pass, he was talking about that which was dwelling in the arena of his imagination.

Job 3:25 For the thing which I greatly feared is come upon me, and that which I was afraid of is come unto me.

The Bible says that it is our enemy, the devil that messes with our imagination. He wants to fill our imagination with those things that are contrary to the divine nature, character and will of the heavenly Father. This is why God has given to us supernatural and divine weapons in order to to bring every thought into controle

2 Corinthians 10:3 For though we walk in the flesh, we do not war after the flesh:4 (For the weapons of our warfare are not carnal, but mighty through God to the pulling down of strong holds;)5 Casting down imaginations, and every high thing that exalteth itself against the knowledge of God, and bringing into captivity every thought to the obedience of Christ;

We must bring our **imaginations** into captivity. We dare not let our imaginations run wild. Every imagination that is not brought under the control of the authority of God will become a playground for the devil. Their is a brother who comes to our church in a spasmodic fashion, and yet he has been coming here for years. Now this particular brother is extremely paranoid. In his imagination he thinks that everybody is plotting against him., and that there is a spy behind every corner. He actually came to me a short time ago, asking me in a whisper exactly how many people have come to me to talk about him. I asked him if he was referring to all the years sense I have known him. (It has been probably seven years when he first showed up at our church). Yes, he told me, he wanted to know how many times people had come to me about him, and who exactly it was that had asked these questions? I asked him once again: are you sure you want to know? Yes, he excitedly said.

Okay, I told him that there had not been even one person in all of these years who had ever come to me, called me, or asked me about any information pertaining to him. He seemed in complete and total shock. He said: really? I said: absolutely, no one has ever said one word to me about you. You see, here is a born again, spirit filled man who was allowed the enemy to mess with his imagination. How many people's lives are destroyed because they have not brought their imaginations into captivity with the word of God.

The Bible says that God had to destroy all living creatures in the days of **Noah** because the imaginations of men were nothing but continually evil.

Genesis 6:5 And God saw that the wickedness of man was great in the earth, and that every imagination of the thoughts of his heart was only evil continually.

The imaginations of our mind are like a wood stove fire. The only way that the fire will keep burning is if you keep feeding it fuel. It's the exact same thing with our imaginations. The Scripture says: **as a man think of so is he**. We could also say that the imagination of the mind of a man will determines what kind of man he becomes. Nobody who is a murderer, rapist, adulterer, or any other type of evil person started out that way. They began with a twisted corrupt seed in the imagination of their minds. They kept on feeding that seed until it germinated and sank its roots deep into every part of their lives. That imagination took them over, bringing death and destruction where ever they went. In order for the fire of this twisted thought to go out you need to use the water of the word to douse it. The divine weapons of our warfare are more than sufficient to overcome these demonic imaginations. David gave to his son Solomon this solemn warning that God knows all of the imaginations and the intents of the heart.

1 Chronicles 28:9 And thou, Solomon my son, know thou the God of thy father, and serve him with a perfect heart and with a willing mind: for the Lord searcheth all hearts, and understandeth all the imaginations of the thoughts: if thou seek him, he will be found of thee; but if thou forsake him, he will cast thee off for ever.

God has given to us his word in order that we can paint upon the canvas of our imagination his perfect will. We literally need to imagine ourselves (see ourselves) exactly the way that God's word proclaims. In the book of James we are told to be doers of the word and not hearers only. We need to look at the mirror of Gods word, see what God says, agree with it, and act accordingly.

James 1:22 But be ye doers of the word, and not hearers only, deceiving your own selves. 23 For if any be a hearer of the word, and not a doer, he is like unto a man beholding his natural face in a glass: 24 For he beholdeth himself, and goeth his way, and straightway forgetteth what manner of man he was.

Let me share a story with you that I was told is a true story. There were two men laying in the hospital in the same room. Somehow one of the nurses or doctors put the wrong chart at the end of the beds. A doctor came into the room, standing at the end of each bed he picked up the charts and began to read them. The man who had a terminal disease was told by the doctor that his condition was minor. The doctor naturally was reading the wrong chart at the end of his bed which had been switched with the other patient. The story goes on to say that this man with a terminal disease was filled with great joy when he was given the good news. Based upon the wrong chart, he was sent home, and lived for many years.

Now, the man who had a minor problem, was told by the doctor of his impending death. That he had a very serious illness and that they could not do any thing for him. This particular gentleman was sent home to die, and he did die shortly there after. This mans imagination was filled with gloom and doom from the wrong and negative report. If this story is true, both of these men were drastically affected by the imaginations that were fed to them by the doctor. How much more serious is it when it comes to the word of God. Almost all mental and emotional illnesses began within the human mind. We must bring our imaginations into subjection, and in to the authority of Jesus Christ.

The devil loves us to take a molehill and make it into a mountain, and then there are mountains that need to be dealt with as mountains, and we treat them like molehills. Our imaginations need to be filled, crammed and packed with the truth of God's word. Our mind is like an incubator, whatever eggs you plant within it, will hatch. When God called Abraham out of the city of the Chaldean s, he fed the mind of Abraham with a wonderful image. He gave to him a graphic description of how many descendants he would have.

Genesis 22:17 That in blessing I will bless thee, and in multiplying I will multiply thy seed as the stars of the heaven, and as the sand which is upon the sea shore; and thy seed shall possess the gate of his enemies;

The Bible says that God has given his angels charge over us to keep us in all of our ways. We need to imagine our angels with you right now. Whether you be in the car, a house, in the shopping center, they are with you right now. There is nothing wrong with imagining this, because it is truth. With our imagination we need to see God the Father with us in every situation. Can you see that Jesus Christ himself by his spirit is living in you? The Bible says that God gives to us the desires of our hearts when we delight in him.

Psalm 37:3 Trust in the Lord, and do good; so shalt thou dwell in the land, and verily thou shalt be fed.4 Delight thyself also in the Lord: and he shall give thee the desires of thine heart.5 Commit thy way unto the Lord; trust also in him; and he shall bring it to pass.

The desires of your heart, could be understood as the imagination of your mind. It's the image you have created in your mind by that which you have been feeding and feasting upon. God can and does speak to us through our imaginations. Of course it is absolutely necessary that we make sure that which we are imagining is from God. We need to use this God-given imagination in order to see God that which he said he would perform. I believe the woman with the issue of blood in the gospel of Matthew, had with in her mind an image of being made whole when she presses through the crowd in order to touch the hem of the garment of Jesus.

If she had not created with in her mind the image of her being healed when she touched the hem of the garment of Jesus, she would have never pressed through and received her miracle. I strive to use my imagination in the way that I believe God would have me to use it. I can imagine people being healed, saved, delivered, and set free.

Our minds to some extent are like our bellies, which crave to be filled with food. Our belly really doesn't have much choice in what we are going to put in it. That is a matter of our own choosing. This is exactly the same way when it comes to that which fills our imaginations. We can fill our mind with the images of that which God's word promises and declares, or we can can put in them that which is against his will. There are well over 3,500 promises in the Bible, and God wants to fulfill every one of these promises in our lives. In order for this even to begin to happen, I believe that we must imagine it so.

2 Corinthians 1:20 For all the promises of God in him are yea, and in him Amen, unto the glory of God by us.

The womb of our imagination is extremely important, even more so than the stomach of our belly. If you plant the wrong kinds of seeds in your imagination, you will be giving birth to that which is a nightmare. God has given to us an imagination and we need to make sure that our imagination is being subject to the word of God. As we bring every thought subject to the authority of Christ, God will begin to flood our mind with the images, and the imagination he wants us to have.

Through the years God has used images in my mind in order to show me what was going on in certain situations. It could be a word of wisdom, or a word of knowledge. It could be the operation of the gift of the spirit of discernment. Every building that has ever been built, every car that has been manufactured, and all cloths that people have made has always first been in the imagination of the one who made it. We need to allow God to fill our imagination with the images that he desires us to live, walk and give birth to.

#20 DIVINE DOWNLOADS

The last and **20th Way** that God leads and guides us is by a Divine Download. Now a Divine Download is when God supernaturally, instantly puts within our mind and heart information that you have not learned in the natural. We use the terminology "download" with that of a computer. We hook up our computer to the Internet, connect it to a specific link or URL. Then we can download a program, a video file, audio file, or down load certain information. If you have a high-speed Internet connection your program can download very quickly.

God is the original author of giving people divine downloads. I will give you some examples of God giving people divine supernatural downloads in the Bible. When God led the children of Israel out of Egypt, all of those men and women had been slaves the whole life. In the natural they probably had very little education. Once they were in the wilderness, God went to Moses and told him that he was going to have the people of Israel build a very special and unique Tabernacle, a portable house, where the presence of God would abide. If you study this in the book Exodus you'll discover that it was quite exquisite and complicated. He told Moses that he was going to supernaturally downloaded this information to the people that he himself had chosen. The Bible then very explicitly tells us the name of every one of these people, and the divine abilities God gave them. These were people who were never trained or taught to work with wood, silver, gold, animal skins, or specialized cloth.

Personally I have experienced more downloads than I can share with you in this one book. Suffice it to say that I quit school at 15 years old. If you get an opportunity you can purchase my other books, and see the amazing things that the Lord has enabled me to accomplish by his spirit. My boasting and bragging is all found in Jesus Christ. Without Jesus Christ, his word, and his spirit I could do nothing. As you seek first the kingdom of God and his righteousness, crying out for the Lord, and hungering for nothing but him, you will begin to experience supernatural and divine downloads.

David the shepherd boy is another amazing example of God giving someone divine downloads and supernatural abilities. If you study the Scriptures you will actually discover that it was David that designed and gathered much of the needed building material, to build the temple of God in the heart of Jerusalem. Yes, Solomon was filled with wisdom to buy a Divine download, but it was David his father that came up with the design of the temple.

When David the father of Solomon went home to be with the Lord, Solomon cried out to God. God supernaturally visited him in a dream. In this dream God divinely downloaded wisdom beyond the comprehension of all-natural and mortal men in the world at that time. The results of this divine download is what we call the book of Proverbs. It is filled with wisdom that men have studied and been amazed by for thousands of years.

1 Kings 4:29 And God gave Solomon wisdom and understanding exceeding much, and largeness of heart, even as the sand that is on the sea shore.

1 Kings 4:30 And Solomon's wisdom excelled the wisdom of all the children of the east country, and all the wisdom of Egypt.

1 Kings 4:34 And there came of all people to hear the wisdom of Solomon, from all kings of the earth, which had heard of his wisdom.

Solomon did not go to school to learn these things, or sit at the feet of old wise man. He did not have a PhD or doctorate of divinity, or a bachelor's degree, Associates degree or any other degree. God gave Solomon a divine download on how to be the man of God that the Lord wanted him to be. This is exactly what he also did with Joseph in Egypt. We could talk about Daniel and the wisdom he demonstrated before King Nebuchadnezzar. God still imparts divine downloads to those who are hungry and thirsty for him.

Divine Down Load of Engine Schematic

We owned a 1979 Cadillac Seville with fuel injection. My engine had started giving me major problems, with loss of power. I went to a local mechanic to happen examine my engine. He informed me that it was a hydraulic lifter that had collapsed. At the time, I did not have the money for a mechanic, so I decided to fix this fuel injected complicated engine myself. I pulled the Cadillac into my little old garage, which had a dirt floor, and proceeded to tear the engine apart piece by piece. Valve covers, intake manifold, rocker arms, wires, electronic pieces all the other parts were scattered everywhere throughout my garage. What a mess!

Eventually, I was able to get to the hydraulic lifters and discovered the one that was collapsed. I went to pick up a new lifter at an automobile supply store where they had available. At the same time, I decided to replace all of the lifters at once. When I got back to my garage, I just stood there staring at my car, and all the parts scattered everywhere. Now I really was in a jam because I had no idea how to put the engine back together again, with all of its intricate parts. I did the only thing I knew to do. I cried out to God for mercy, I prayed: "Heavenly Father, please help me, in the name of Jesus, to get this car back together again."

This was the only vehicle we owned. Amazingly, knowledge entered into my brain at that very minute of how to do it step-by-step. It was like this divine download of the engine schematic flooded into my mind. If this had not happened to me, I would not believe it either. With this schematic in my mind it was as easy as one, two, and three. Through this whole process I followed what I saw on this schematic in my mind. The peace and the joy of the Lord was his flowing up out of my heart. There was absolutely no confusion or question what to do. It was like the Holy Ghost was telling me step by step along the way what needed to be done.

Now, I did not have an mechanics book next to me. It was a divine schematic in my brain.

To my amazement, when I was finished I had used every single part that was there in the garage. As I looked at the engine, everything seemed to be exactly where it needed to go. I closed the hood of my car, jumped behind the steering wheel, put the key into the ignition, turned the key, and it started right up and ran beautifully! Praise God for supernatural divine downloads.

Supernatural Download to Build a Million Dollar Complex

We had approximately thirty volunteer men who had come together to help us put the steel up for a new church facility. There was a good handful of men who were not even a part of our church who came to help us with this endeavor. The majority of these men were not construction workers in any fashion of the word. The Lord had put in to our hearts to use volunteers to get the job done. The man we had gone through to purchase the steel building was to oversee this very complicated part of the construction of the building. He had been consistent with us all of this time to help us do the footers and concrete piers, in which she had done excellent quality work. The large crane which we needed to begin to put all of this steel was on the property with its operator sitting in the cab, and the diesel engine running. I think the cost of this crane and the operator was over $150 an hour back in 1985. The big machine was idling and waiting to go to work. Everyone was standing there waiting to work. There was some kind of holdup with the gentleman who was overseeing the project.

We all began to bombard him with questions and asking for directions of what beams that we should begin to put in place. He had the blueprints in his hands, and every time he went to look at them someone would approach him. The pressure on him was overwhelming. It was easy to see that he was getting extremely frustrated, and even to some extent angry. In the midst of all of this we discovered that he had never put up a building this large before. This building was 100 feet wide by 150 feet long, 25 feet high in the middle. Not only had he not put up a building this large before, but it turned out that it had been many years ago since he had even put up a steel building. The next thing I knew one of the men from the church said, "Pastor Mike! There goes so and so!" I looked to see where he was pointing. Sure enough, there he was going down the road in his automobile. I did not hear from or see him again for quite a number of years later.

At the time of construction, it seemed as if this was a satanic attack. Now though I can now say what Joseph said, that although this situation seemed as if it was meant for evil, God meant it for good. The Lord was stretching my faith. Here I was, standing in front of all of these volunteer men who were waiting to go to work. The steel was lying on the ground. The crane was idling. I can still remember walking away from everybody, looking up to heaven, and crying out to God. I said, Lord, please show me how to put this building up. I had never even built a doghouse, let alone a large steel commercial building! The Bible says that if we lack wisdom, we can ask God. I absolutely was crying out, and asking God for divine wisdom.

At that very moment when I finished praying it was if an invisible blanket came down upon me. This is what I have discovered to be a divine download from heaven. Wisdom entered into my heart as I looked at the blueprints I knew instantly what to do. I I could actually understand the instructions of the blueprints. I walked toward the crane operator, and began to tell him what steel beams and purling as we were putting up first. I began to yell instructions to all of the men that were standing there. I would point to certain beams, and tell the men were it went. This was absolutely incredible because in the natural I should I had no way of knowing what to do. The building began to go up! Through the process we lost volunteers and gained volunteers. The Lord began to send us skilled labor. Not much of it, but just enough. Within approximately five months we held our first service in our new sanctuary.

James 1:5 If any of you lack wisdom, let him ask of God, that giveth to all men liberally, and upbraideth not; and it shall be given him.

Divine Download of 40 Major Dimensions on Faith!

I was up and at it early one morning in prayer, simply speaking to the Lord and praying in the spirit, when suddenly the heavens were opened to me. Within three minutes the Spirit of God downloaded into my mind 40 major dimensions and aspects of faith. My mind was filled with a Revelation of faith that I had never had before. For over 30 years I have studied the subject of faith, and yet within those three minutes I perceived things about faith I had never heard, or been taught. I had even sat underneath renowned men of faith, read many books, and I had attended a school that majored on the subject of faith.

Each of these 40 major dimensions of faith had many truths. Some of them were up to 28 points. Immediately I grabbed a pen and paper, as I sat at my dining room table writing page after page of amazing truths. I did not have to think what to write, I simply began to put down on paper what the Lord was quickening to me. What he gave me in three minutes, took over three days for me to write down.

Every dimension of faith that was quickened to me, I have gone to the Scriptures to make sure it is absolute truth. Even dealing with the 28 ways that faith comes, I wanted to see it in the word. Sure enough faith does come by at least 28 ways. Every dimension of faith he spoke to my heart is in perfect agreement with the Bible.

This event took place in 2008 and ever since then revelation knowledge keeps flowing to me on this subject. I have written a book on the 28 ways that faith comes. The other aspects of faith would have to be a library of books. Over 95% of what the Lord had quickened to my heart was downloaded into me within three minutes or less. Now, I can personally understand how the prophets of old penned the prophetic words of the Old Testament. It was by the Holy Ghost that downloaded into their hearts and our minds that which God wanted to speak to the human race. We still have the same Holy Ghost. God is not giving us any new revelation, he is simply causing the Revelation that is in his word to come forth. Oh Lord let it come forth!!!

2 Timothy 3:16 All scripture is given by inspiration of God, and is profitable for doctrine, for reproof, for correction, for instruction in righteousness:

Back in 1996 God downloading into me the ability to memorize Scriptures. I had simply been pressing in, and taking a hold of God and his word, when out of nowhere I had an open vision. With in that open vision God quickened my mind with the divine download of his ability. God chooses the foolish to confound the wise, and this is why I am convinced is one of the main reason why the Lord has done so much in and through my life. There is no way in the natural that I could ever accept any kind of recognition, praise, or adoration for that which I have accomplished. All of the praise and the glory and honor belongs to Jesus Christ.

As I finish with this book, I would strongly encourage you to begin to become obedient to the voice of God in every area of your life. This is not you leaning to the understanding of your natural mind, but it is a total surrendering of your heart, your will, and your mind to the purposes of heaven. This book is not meant to be in any form or fashion a complete and total revelation of all the ways in which God will lead us and guide us. I believe in my heart that the Lord wanted me to write this book in order to help people better understand the workings of God when it comes to divine guidance. I would like to leave you with to major Scripture about being led by God.

1 Peter 4:1 Forasmuch then as Christ hath suffered for us in the flesh, arm yourselves likewise with the same mind: for he that hath suffered in the flesh hath ceased from sin;

Romans 8:12 Therefore, brethren, we are debtors, not to the flesh, to live after the flesh.13 For if ye live after the flesh, ye shall die: but if ye through the Spirit do mortify the deeds of the body, ye shall live.14 For as many as are led by the Spirit of God, they are the sons of God.

ABOUT THE AUTHOR

Dr. Michael and Kathleen Yeager have served as pastors/apostles, missionaries, evangelists, broadcasters and authors for overt four decades. They flow in the gifts of the Holy Spirit, teaching the Word of God with wonderful signs and miracles following in confirmation of God's Word. In 1983, they began Jesus is Lord Ministries International, Biglerville, PA 17307.

Websites Connected to Doc Yeager

www.docyeager.com

www.jilmi.org

www.wbntv.org

Made in the USA
Middletown, DE
08 November 2015